S0-AAD-780

BULGARIA DURING
THE SECOND WORLD WAR

Bulgaria

DURING THE
SECOND WORLD WAR

MARSHALL LEE MILLER

Stanford University Press

STANFORD, CALIFORNIA

1975

Stanford University Press
Stanford, California
© 1975 by the Board of Trustees of the
Leland Stanford Junior University
Printed in the United States of America
ISBN 0-8047-0870-3
LC 74-82778

To my grandparents
Lee and Edith Rankin and Evelyn Miller

Preface

❦

THE POLITICAL history of modern Bulgaria has been greatly neglected by Western scholars, and the important period of the
Second World War has hardly been studied at all. The main reason
for this has no doubt been the difficulty of obtaining documentary
material on the wartime period. Although the Communist regime of
Bulgaria has published a large number of books and monographs
dealing with the country's role in the war, these works have been
concerned mostly with magnifying the importance of the Bulgarian
Communist Party (BKP) and the partisan struggle. Despite this
bias, useful information can be found in these works when other
sources are available to provide perspective and verification.

Within recent years, German, American, British, and other diplomatic and intelligence reports from the wartime years have become
available, and the easing of travel restrictions in Bulgaria has facilitated research there. As recently as 1958, when the doctoral thesis of
Marin V. Pundeff was presented ("Bulgaria's Place in Axis Policy,
1936–1944"), there was very little material on the period after June
1941. It is now possible to fill in many of the important gaps in our
knowledge of Bulgaria during the entire war.

The Bibliography lists the books and other published materials on
which I have based this work, but I have also relied on confidential
personal interviews in Bulgaria and elsewhere, and on archival materials located on three continents. The most helpful institutions include

the Bulgarian Academy of Sciences, the National Library, the Sofia Synagogue Archives, the Institute for Balkanistics, the Museum of the Revolutionary Movement, and the Central State Historical Archives, all in Sofia; the German Federal Archives in Koblenz; the Military Research Office in Freiburg; the Institute for Contemporary History, the South-East Institute, the East Europe Institute, and the Faculty of Economics and the Eastern Europe Seminar of the University of Munich, all in Munich; the American Memorial Library in Berlin; the British Museum, the Imperial War Museum, the Public Record Office, and the Wiener Institute, all in London; St. Antony's College, Oxford University; Yad Washem and the Hebrew University of Jerusalem; the U.S. Department of State Archives in the National Archives, the Library of Congress, and the Department of Defense Library, in Washington, D.C.; and Yale University Library, New Haven, Connecticut.

Part One, which covers the period from the outbreak of war in 1939 to May 1941, deals mostly with the diplomatic moves that brought Bulgaria onto the Axis side and relies on published and unpublished British, American, German, and Italian documents. Parts Two and Three, which are concerned with the interaction between foreign policy and domestic political struggles, make use of previously unavailable Bulgarian and German documents: Part Two, covering the period from June 1941 through the death of Tsar Boris in August 1943, deals with the efforts of the Tsar to maintain at least a partially independent policy despite pressure from Germany and from internal pro-Nazi factions; Part Three, from September 1943 to the Communist coup of September 9, 1944, examines the political crisis that arose after the Tsar's death, the effects of the Allied air raids, and the failure of Bulgaria's attempts to negotiate a withdrawal from the war.

This is primarily a political and diplomatic study. Because Bulgaria's participation in the war prior to the Communist takeover was limited mainly to occupation duty in Greece and Yugoslavia, military affairs do not figure prominently in this work. Some consideration, however, is given to the German Balkan campaign of 1941, the Allied bombings, the partisans, and the Soviet advance into the Balkans in the fall of 1944. The space devoted to the Bulgarian partisan campaign and the activities of the Communist Party—though insufficient to satisfy my Bulgarian colleagues—is somewhat greater than is warranted by their actual significance, but the subsequent importance of the Communists in Bulgaria justifies this slight expansion.

Economic affairs are also not discussed in any great detail. Bulgarian official historians have generally contended that there was a drastic economic decline during the war and that this led to widespread dissatisfaction with the regime. To determine whether there was enough validity in this theory to warrant a fuller discussion, I sifted through Bulgarian and German statistics on the marketing of various products, cost-of-living indexes, fluctuations in the average weight of marketed livestock, and even medical records (to compute the average weight loss of Bulgarian schoolgirls during the war—14 lbs.). The results indicated—not surprisingly—that Bulgaria experienced economic difficulties due to the war, particularly after the Allied bombings in late 1943 and early 1944, but that the country was far better off than its neighbors. Because the Bulgarians were well aware of this fact, inflation and wartime shortages were not major political issues.

In transliterating foreign languages, I have followed pronunciation as much as possible but have avoided encumbering the text with diacritical marks. Thus certain Bulgarian names are given in a somewhat simplified form: for example, Alexander, Peter, Dimiter, Stambolisky, and Kioseivanov. Place names generally follow the usage of the Columbia Lippincott Gazetteer of the World, but I have called the capital of Macedonia by its Bulgarian name, Skopie, rather than by the Macedonian Skopje or the Serbian Skoplje.

For convenience, the word "Allies," unless qualified, refers only to the Western Allies, not to the Soviet Union.

I particularly would like to thank for their assistance Harry Willetts, Nissan Oren, William Deakin, Fred Chary, Clifford Siskin,

George Cummins, Ann Abley, Basil Condos, June Roth, Catherine Schirmer, Peggy Diapoulis, William Maier, Landon Miller, Charles Moser, the late Georgi M. Dimitrov, J. G. Bell and Peter J. Kahn of Stanford University Press, those persons in Bulgaria who preferred anonymity, and my wife, Marlene.

M.L.M.

Contents

꙰

Historical Introduction   1

PART ONE: SEPTEMBER 1939–MAY 1941

1. The Outbreak of the War   13
2. The Dobruja Crisis   24
3. Competition for the Balkans   32
4. Bulgaria Joins the Axis   45
5. Operation Marita   52

PART TWO: JUNE 1941–AUGUST 1943

6. From Barbarossa to Pearl Harbor   59
7. Parries and Parleys   71
8. No Friends, Just Foes   81
9. The Jewish Question   93
10. The Allied Threat   107
11. The Bulgarian Occupation of Macedonia   122
12. The Death of Tsar Boris   135

PART THREE: SEPTEMBER 1943–SEPTEMBER 1944

13. The Regency and Bozhilov   151

14. Bombs and Peace Feelers   165

15. The Bagryanov Government   174

16. The Partisans   195

17. The Last Phase   204

    Epilogue   217

        Notes 223   *Bibliography* 256   *Index* 279

BULGARIA DURING
THE SECOND WORLD WAR

Historical Introduction

And those that have been able to imitate the fox have succeeded
best. But it is necessary to be able to disguise this character well,
and to be a great feigner and dissembler.
—MACHIAVELLI, *The Prince*, chapter xviii

TSAR BORIS of Bulgaria frequently complained, "My army is pro-
German, my wife is Italian, my people are pro-Russian. I'm the
only pro-Bulgarian in this country."[1] As a Bulgarian, Boris's wartime
goals included both the satisfaction of his country's irredentist aspirations against its Balkan neighbors and noninvolvement in the fighting.
Achieving these apparently irreconcilable aims necessitated a cunning
aptly described by Hitler: "Boris is by temperament a fox rather than
a wolf, and would expose himself to great danger only with the ut-
most reluctance."[2]

Boris's dealings with the Germans seemed to confirm Hitler's assess-
ment. While resisting Nazi demands to sever diplomatic relations
with the Soviet Union, to deport Bulgarian Jews to Germany, and to
join the war on the Eastern Front, he managed to gain their support
for the Bulgarian occupations of the Southern Dobruja, Macedonia,
and Aegean Thrace. Even as Boris was persuading the Germans that
Bulgaria was their staunchest friend, he succeeded in convincing
many British and Americans that his country's real sympathies lay
with the Allies.

In the early part of the war, therefore, Bulgaria was a small state
pursuing its self-interest with a high degree of diplomatic skill and
a fair amount of success. And yet, as the war neared its end, Bulgaria
achieved the dubious distinction of being simultaneously at war with
Great Britain, Germany, Russia, and the United States.

The Bitter Heritage

The seeds of Bulgaria's involvement in the Second World War were sown over sixty years earlier, in 1878, when Russian troops under Alexander II helped liberate Bulgaria from five centuries of Turkish subjugation. By the Treaty of San Stefano in March 1878, Bulgaria was granted its independence and more territory than it was ever again to have. This victory was short-lived, however. Great Britain and Austria-Hungary were alarmed by the creation of a large, pro-Russian Slavic state within striking distance of the Turkish Straits; and on the invitation of German Chancellor Bismarck, a second peace conference was convened that summer in Berlin, which resulted in a drastic reduction of Bulgarian territory. The year 1878 thus produced three forces that were to be constants of Bulgarian politics for the next six decades: gratitude to the Russians as liberators, frustration at being despoiled of territory the Bulgarians considered rightfully theirs, and recognition that Bulgaria was a mere pawn in the diplomatic maneuvering of the Great Powers.

Turkey's weakening grip on its European possessions prompted Bulgaria in 1912 to join with Greece, Serbia, and Montenegro in the First Balkan War. The allies were victorious but soon quarreled over the division of spoils. In the ensuing Second Balkan War the following year, Bulgaria confronted its former allies, who were aided by Rumania, while Turkey seized the opportunity to recover Edirne (Adrianople) and part of Thrace. The Bulgarians were overwhelmed and lost most of their previous gains.

The outbreak of the First World War a year later offered Bulgaria a chance to recoup its losses. Because of its strategic geographical position, Bulgaria was ardently wooed by both opposing parties, but the Central Powers (Germany and Austria-Hungary) had several advantages: first, they were more likely than the Allies to satisfy Bulgaria's territorial demands; second, Tsar Ferdinand of Bulgaria was himself of German origin; and third, in the autumn of 1915, when Bulgaria decided to enter the war, the Central Powers seemed the probable victors. The Bulgarian army fought well, and with some German assistance managed to halt the large expeditionary force of British, French, Serbian, and Russian troops that attempted to advance north from Salonika. But Bulgarian resistance finally crumbled in October 1918, and Tsar Ferdinand was forced to abdicate in favor of his twenty-four-year-old son, who ascended the throne as Boris III.

Once again Bulgaria was on the losing side. By the Treaty of Neuilly in 1919, Bulgaria lost its outlet on the Aegean to Greece, the Southern Dobruja (the area between the Danube and the Black Sea) to Rumania, and additional portions of Macedonia to Serbia (Yugoslavia). Limitations were imposed on the size of the Bulgarian army, and a large indemnity was demanded. This bitter heritage ruled out any cooperation between Bulgaria and its Balkan neighbors, prevented the formation of a unified and effective Balkan alliance against outside aggression, and was a principal reason for Bulgaria's joining the Axis in the Second World War.

Politics and Parties During the Interwar Period

The Agrarian Party under Alexander Stambolisky assumed power amidst the disillusionment following the war. Stambolisky realized that the peasantry, although comprising eighty percent of the population, had long been neglected by the government, but his Agrarian regime overcompensated. Public officials were dismissed in favor of office seekers whose only qualifications were peasant origin, education was derided and curtailed, and Agrarian politicians became as entangled in graft and election-rigging as their predecessors had been. Every decision taken by the Agrarians seemed to antagonize powerful opponents. Nationalists resented the trials of their wartime leaders, Macedonians were angered by Stambolisky's conciliatory policy toward Yugoslavia, the opposition political parties objected to the harassment of their activities, and monarchists were alarmed by rumors that Stambolisky planned to proclaim a republic.

On June 9, 1923, Stambolisky was overthrown and tortured to death in a bloody right-wing coup. The leader of the new government coalition, Professor Alexander Tsankov, had previously played little part in politics but was to become a key figure during the Second World

War. The Bulgarian Communists were initially undecided whether to support the scattered Agrarian armed resistance to the new regime, for they had bitter memories of Agrarian persecution. In September 1923, however, on orders from Moscow, the Party attempted a general insurrection. The revolt was ill-timed, poorly managed, and quickly suppressed. This revolt, and the later abortive bomb attempt on the Tsar, resulted in the official suppression of the Communist Party in 1925. Although it continued thinly disguised as the Bulgarian Workers' Party (BRP), the second largest party in the country after the Agrarians, it ceased to be a significant political force during the remainder of the 1920's and most of the 1930's.

In addition to the Agrarians, the democratic parties (commonly called the "legal opposition") included the Radicals, the Democrats, and the Social Democrats. Size often had little to do with a party's importance. One of the most influential parties, for example, was sometimes called the "*kamion*" ("truck") party, because all of its members supposedly could have ridden in a single truck. The boundaries between the parties were rather vague, based as they were along class lines in a society where classes were difficult to distinguish. The parties also tended to splinter easily into "wings, winglets, and feathers." The Agrarians, for example, were deeply split between two main factions—*Vrabcha* ("sparrow"), led by Dimiter Gichev, and *Pladne* ("zenith"), headed by such men as G. M. "Gemeto" Dimitrov, Kosta Todorov, and Nikola Petkov. The latter group was somewhat more willing to cooperate with the Communists than the former, but the differences between the two were more historical and personal than ideological.

Along with the democratic parties and the Communists, a third major political bloc existed in interwar Bulgaria—the heterogeneous nationalist parties and right-wing organizations. These ranged from the patriotic society *Otets Paisii* ("Father Paisi") to the fascist *Ratnitsi* ("warriors") and Legionnaires supporting General Hristo Lukov. The most prominent nationalist was Alexander Tsankov (Premier from 1923 to 1926), who headed a mass movement during the 1930's modeled on Mussolini's, but his pedantic orations soon cooled the enthusiasm of his followers.

One nationalist party deserves special mention. *Zveno* ("link"), with its companion organization the Military League, was a small group of idealistic military officers and politicians that had an influence on Bulgarian politics far out of proportion to its size. Under Kimon Georgiev and Damian Velchev, it participated in the right-wing 1923 coup, led the elitist coup of 1934 that made Georgiev the prime minister, and played a leading role in the Communist coup of 1944. It was not given a fourth chance.

In 1931, the Agrarians returned to power following an upset victory in an inadequately rigged national election. The ensuing coalition of Democrats, right-wing Agrarians, and liberals brought together older political leaders with younger men such as Dimiter Gichev and Konstantin Muraviev, who would later lead the opposition during the war. Instead of rekindling the democratic spirit in Bulgaria, however, the coalition soon degenerated into factions of greedy, squabbling politicians.

On May 19, 1934, the coalition was overthrown by Zveno, which established diplomatic relations with the Soviet Union (while maintaining the ban on local Communists) and launched ambitious plans for economic development. However, the anti-monarchist tendencies of the Zveno government alarmed Tsar Boris, who quietly began exploiting dissension among the government leaders. Within eight months Prime Minister Georgiev resigned, and Boris assumed personal rule of Bulgaria until his death in 1943.

Although Bulgarian internal politics had always revolved around the Tsar, his authority was neither absolute nor unvarying. During the disorders of the 1920's and early 1930's, his power waxed and waned several times, but after each crisis he emerged stronger than before. The relative weakness and disunity of the Bulgarian political parties and their poor record when in office contributed to his increasing influence. At last in 1935 the Tsar asserted his authority and appointed the pliable Georgi Kioseivanov prime minister. Kioseivanov had first held office under Stambolisky and had acquired a reputation for being stupid but honest. He survived Stambolisky's fall in 1923 and held a number of cabinet and diplomatic posts, including that of foreign minister early in 1935; but in the process he lost his reputation for honesty.

New rigged elections in 1938 produced a tractable *Narodno Subranie* (National Assembly), and the Tsar was able to turn his attention to the external situation, which in the late 1930's was growing increasingly threatening.

Foreign Policy

As a small country, Bulgaria since 1878 had been dependent upon the favor of one or more of the Great Powers. Until the First World War, the two competing powers in Bulgaria were Russia and Austria, with Germany in the background. After the war, German influence replaced Austrian, and Italy also became involved in Balkan politics. Soviet Russia, after a revolutionary hiatus, resumed the traditional foreign policy of Tsarist Russia aimed at control of the Straits and access to the Mediterranean.

Foreign policy preferences played a major role in Bulgarian domestic politics, much as attitudes toward Britain and France did in American politics during the Jeffersonian era. During the interwar period, the Bulgarian nationalist groups generally looked to fascist Italy and Germany; the democratic parties preferred France and Great Britain, although they also professed friendship toward the Soviet Union; and the Communists were devoted to Moscow. For the nation as a whole, a simplistic but useful rule of thumb was that it had affection for Russia and admiration for Germany.

Although there was limited sympathy for the Soviet system, except of course among the Communists, years of official anti-Russian propaganda had also been largely ineffective. The ideological question was secondary to most Bulgarians; their affection for the Russians remained strong despite political and economic changes. The feeling was too complex to be attributed solely to Tsarist Russia's role as Bulgaria's liberator, but its existence was undeniable, even among many pro-Western, anti-Communist Bulgarians.

Admiration for Germany was especially marked among the leaders of Bulgarian public life. The Bulgarian military respected German prowess and efficiency, notwithstanding the final bitter days of the First World War. The rise of the Third Reich and the rebuilding of the German army were generally welcomed in Bulgaria, as was Germany's disregard of the Treaty of Versailles. Bulgaria was proud of its reputation as "the Prussia of the Balkans" and was receptive to appeals to the wartime comradeship in arms (*Waffenbrüderschaft*). Germany's intellectual and cultural achievements also appealed to many Bulgarians. About half of the Bulgarian professors had studied in Germany, and German books in the Sofia University library almost outnumbered the total of those in Russian, French, and English. Bogdan Filov, the wartime premier and a former professor of archeology, was known for his almost blind admiration of Germany; yet even he once complained that Bulgarian professors attending a conference in Leipzig had embarrassed their hosts by being more Nazi than the Nazis.

Like every other Balkan country, Bulgaria traded extensively with Germany; but Bulgaria depended on German trade more than any other country in southeastern Europe. Almost 70 percent of Bulgaria's exports in 1939 went to Germany, compared with 6 percent to Italy, 3 percent to England, and 1 percent to France. By comparison, Hungary and Yugoslavia sent only about 50 percent of their exports to Germany, and Greece and Rumania sent considerably less. At that time Germany may have been more interested in the trade than in its political consequences, but the two became increasingly intertwined.

Italian influence was appreciable during the 1920's and 1930's, owing to an initial regard for Mussolini, extensive Italian diplomatic machinations, and the marriage of King Victor Emmanuel's daughter to Tsar Boris in 1930. Italy's boasts, however, rang increasingly hollow, and by the outbreak of the Second World War they counted for little; eventually, whatever influence Italy possessed was essentially negative.

Great Britain and France had but slight political influence in Bulgaria, although they had some importance elsewhere in the Balkans. Nevertheless, they were not without their attractions. Paris was a mecca for Bulgarian students, including a number of future political leaders, and the British system of government was a model for those seeking an alternative to totalitarianism. But neither country displayed much interest in Bulgaria, and this attitude was reciprocated.

Least influential of all the Great Powers was the United States, which during the interwar years seemed all but oblivious to the very existence of Bulgaria. Even the two exceptions to this pattern were unofficial and indirect: the American colleges at Sofia and in northern Bulgaria, which steeped young Bulgarians in Western democratic ideals; and the Bulgarian-Americans in the Midwest, many of whom sent money back to their families in the "Old Country."

As noted earlier, Bulgaria's relations with its Balkan neighbors were less than cordial, and this was especially the case with Yugoslavia. This was the result of Bulgarian irredentism and particularly the activities of the Internal Macedonian Revolutionary Organization (IMRO), a terrorist group that had originally formed to fight against Turkish rule but that raided into Yugoslav Macedonia during the 1920's and the early 1930's. Relations with Greece also deteriorated; in 1925 the League of Nations had to intervene to halt a retaliatory foray by the Greek army into southern Bulgaria. Premier Stambolisky's attempt to reduce Balkan tensions in 1923 only succeeded in winning him an early grave at the hands of IMRO and its right-wing allies. Nevertheless, during the 1930's Tsar Boris made overtures to archenemy Yugoslavia. Although his discussions with King Alexander ended tragically with the latter's assassination by Croatian (and IMRO) terrorists in 1934, the suppression of IMRO that same year removed a major obstacle to further negotiations. Yugoslavia was a member of the Balkan Entente, an alliance including Rumania, Greece, and Turkey that was hostile to Bulgaria. Thus, the signing of a pact of perpetual friendship between Bulgaria and Yugoslavia in January 1937 signaled the end of Bulgaria's long diplomatic isolation. Finally, in July 1938 the members of the Balkan Entente agreed to remove the

1919 restrictions on Bulgarian rearmament in the hope that this would facilitate a common Balkan front against German and Italian penetration. The all-important territorial issue, however, remained unresolved.

Six decades of independence had produced a truncated, bitter Bulgaria, surrounded by hostile states and menaced by contending Great Powers. Tsar Boris—no reckless adventurer—supported Bulgarian irredentism but was personally more concerned with preserving his throne. He therefore favored a policy of accommodation with all the Great Powers; but, if a choice had to be made, he regarded Germany as less a threat to Bulgaria's internal order than Soviet Russia. Furthermore, Germany seemed increasingly the dominant power in southeast Europe. The perfect solution for Bulgaria, it seemed, would be an alliance between Germany and Russia, so that no choice between the two would be necessary. Yet such an alliance between the apparently implacable ideological foes seemed impossible. Then came the astounding news of the signing of the Nazi-Soviet Pact in late August 1939. For Bulgaria it seemed an ideal solution, and the Pact was widely acclaimed throughout the country.

A week later, Europe was once again plunged into war.

PART ONE

September 1939-May 1941

CHAPTER I

The Outbreak of the War

※Ω※

WITH THE outbreak of World War II on September 1, 1939, new pressures were brought to bear on Bulgaria. The French government believed that Bulgaria was already a silent partner of the Axis because of its strong economic links to the Reich and its irredentist aspirations, which could be satisfied only at the expense of France's allies Rumania and Yugoslavia. Consequently, France proposed to Britain that they give Bulgaria an ultimatum: issue a formal statement of neutrality or face invasion.[1] The British, however, adopted a more moderate and realistic position. Heeding the repeated admonitions of their Ambassador in Sofia, George Rendel, not to assume prematurely that Bulgaria had joined the enemy camp, they favored discreetly urging Bulgaria to declare its neutrality. Rendel reasoned that although there was little chance that Bulgaria would join the Allies, the country might be able to remain neutral.[2]

The British view prevailed. Although the request elicited criticism from some Bulgarian officials, who observed that Britain had made no such request to any other state, the Tsar announced Bulgaria's neutrality on September 16, 1939.[3] Once the declaration was issued, though, Britain failed to acknowledge it publicly. King George VI had sent Tsar Boris a personal letter, dated September 15, 1939, promising that Britain would respect Bulgaria's neutrality if "it is not violated by others," but the Bulgarians kept this letter secret at British insistence.[4] Underlying this British behavior were secret Allied plans to invade the Balkans; since they might later have to violate Bulgaria's neutrality by using the country as a corridor to the Rumanian oil fields or a back door to Germany, the Allies were loath to recognize it publicly.[5] Winston Churchill, then First Lord of the Admiralty, wrote to the Foreign Secretary, Lord Halifax, "A declaration at this stage about respecting Bulgarian neutrality, would seal the death warrant of the Balkans."[6]

The Allied plan assumed the support of the Balkan Entente, which included Bulgaria's traditional foes—Yugoslavia, Rumania, Greece, and Turkey.[7] Allied optimism about the effectiveness of the Entente was hardly warranted by their past record of cooperation, and Bulgaria did not take the threat too seriously. Nikola Momchilov, the Bulgarian Ambassador to Great Britain, remarked that the "mutual dislike and distrust" among the Balkan states "[was] so great that they never could unite against a common foe."[8]

Rather than oppose Bulgaria at the risk of bringing war to the Balkans, the Entente sought to draw Bulgaria into an alliance. The first steps in this direction had been taken with the Yugoslav-Bulgarian friendship pact of 1937 and the Treaty of Salonika the following year, but it was unlikely that Bulgaria would actually join the Entente without receiving substantial territorial concessions. Accordingly, Rumania proposed on September 19 that "each member of the Entente must contribute territory to the Balkan community with which to satisfy Bulgaria's demands."[9] The suggestion failed because no member proved willing to relinquish territory to a state whose appetite was considered insatiable.

The Germans regarded the Entente as naive for inviting Bulgaria to join without offering territory. Fritz von Papen, the German Ambassador to Turkey, acidly remarked, "No wonder this rump Bulgaria showed little enthusiasm for an alliance with her despoilers."[10] It is doubtful, however, that Bulgaria would have joined on any terms. Such an action, as Prime Minister Georgi Kioseivanov pointed out, would have seemed unfriendly to Germany and could have dragged Bulgaria into the war. The Bulgarian government therefore declined any invitation to enter the Balkan Entente.[11]

Soviet Overtures to Bulgaria

During the first week of October 1939, the USSR offered Bulgaria a friendship and mutual assistance pact, which was subsequently rejected. Purvan Draganov, the Bulgarian Ambassador in Berlin, explained afterwards to the Germans, "Up to now, Bulgaria has never concluded any treaty of alliance of this kind, not even with Germany, with which it has close and long-standing ties." The Bulgarian government did not wish to change this policy now, he continued, "nor, above all, conclude a mutual assistance pact with Russia first."[12] But the Soviets did not accept the refusal as final; for the next year and a half Soviet diplomats and their Bulgarian Communist supporters repeatedly urged the Bulgarian government to accept the proposed pact.[13]

The Soviet Union's interest in the Balkans, although not welcomed, offered Bulgaria an opportunity to exploit differences between Germany and the USSR. Since much of Germany's influence in Bulgaria was the result of its expected support for Bulgarian irredentism, the Bulgarians hoped that the Russian overtures would stimulate a renewed German interest in their expansionist desires. Thus, on September 16, Bulgaria confronted Germany with a hypothetical question that later proved prophetic: What should be done if the USSR took Bessarabia from Rumania and offered the Southern Dobruja to Bulgaria? Ernst Woermann, the *Unterstaatssekretär* of the German Foreign Ministry, cautiously replied that such a move did not seem imminent, but that if the USSR should do this, "the only right course for Bulgaria would be to trust us and get in touch with us."[14]

Bulgaria feared, however, that Hitler might be willing to sacrifice it to secure better relations with the Soviet Union. Rumors of a secret protocol between the Reich and the Soviet Union giving Russia a free hand in the Balkans so concerned Tsar Boris that on December 4 he consulted Herbert von Richthofen, the Reich's Ambassador to Bulgaria. Richthofen denied that Russia had been granted any Balkan concessions except Bessarabia, which had once been a Russian province, but this assurance was skeptically received in Sofia.[15] Ten days later Bulgaria again asked Germany's attitude toward Soviet penetration into the Balkans. More revealing than the vague German reply was the original draft, which contained the following brusque admonition: "We expect that Bulgarian foreign policy will be conducted in such a way that Bulgaria does not come into conflict with the Soviet Union, in which despite all our friendship for Bulgaria and all our willingness to help her in difficult situations, we could not, in view of the present situation, support Bulgaria."[16]

Even without the German warning, Bulgaria recognized and uneasily adjusted to the new power structure in the Balkans following the Nazi-Soviet Pact.[17] In fact, Bulgarian relations with the Soviet Union improved to such a degree that in January 1940 Yugoslavia expressed the fear that Bulgaria was drifting into the Soviet orbit. Bulgarian officials privately denied this: nothing more was involved than "prudence in the face of a strong neighbor."[18] Boris told the British press attaché that his father, Tsar Ferdinand, had shown himself a Russophobe in a Russophile country; his son would not repeat that mistake.[19]

Then the Russian reverses in the Finnish "Winter War" (1939–40) suggested to Bulgaria and the world that the Soviet Union was not such a "strong neighbor" after all. Although eventually victorious, Russian forces suffered humiliating reverses in the early part of the campaign. The lesson was drawn that "the calculations of Berlin had been wrong on two counts—wrong in regarding Russia as a first-rate military factor, wrong in supposing that she carried influence with the laboring masses of other countries."[20]

The BKP After the Nazi-Soviet Pact

Two dramatic events—the Nazi-Soviet Pact of August 23, 1939, and the USSR's invasion of Poland on September 17—temporarily stunned the Bulgarian Communist Party.* Although the Party newspaper *Rabotnichesko delo* attempted to explain that the Soviet Union had to

---

* The official title of the Bulgarian Communist Party during most of this period was the Bulgarian Workers' Party (BRP); in this work, however, the term "Communist" or the initials BKP will be used throughout to avoid confusion.

resist being dragged into the war by England and France,[21] staunch Party members felt betrayed by the Soviet alliance with the Nazis. An influential pamphlet by Todor Pavlov* tried to justify the Soviet invasion of Poland by claiming that the USSR had only intervened to protect fellow Slavs after the disintegration of the Polish state. Since no state existed, he argued, the intervention could not really be an invasion.[22]

The Nazi-Soviet Pact may have bewildered many Party members, but ironically it put the BKP itself in a strong position. After years of persecution, the Party discovered that its new stance toward Germany coincided with official government policy. And in one important respect the Party line was even more favorable to Germany than the government position: the government refrained from caustic attacks on the Western Powers in an attempt to maintain correct if not friendly relations, but the BKP was under no such restraints.[23] It did advocate the signing of a mutual assistance pact with the USSR, but as the government's reluctance to do so was supposedly based only on technicalities, there was no open conflict on this issue.

The Communists were therefore allowed a measure of relative freedom at a time when right-wing activity was being officially restricted because of events in Rumania. On September 22, 1939, the Rumanian Prime Minister, Armand Calinescu, was assassinated by members of the Iron Guard (a mystical and violent Rumanian nationalist organization), and it was feared that fascist groups in Bulgaria might attempt some similar action. As a result, the activities of the local right-wing groups, especially the Ratnitsi and Legionnaires, were curtailed and their members warned that they risked dismissal from government positions, universities, and the armed forces.[24] Emboldened by its new prominence, the Communist Party launched a vocal attack on the Western Allies and their Bulgarian supporters. Members of the democratic opposition were accused of advocating Bulgaria's entry into the war on the Allied side instead of supporting the official policy of neutrality.[25] The campaign inten-

---

* Pavlov, a Communist of Macedonian origin, became one of the three Regents of Bulgaria after the Communist coup of September 1944.

sified in mid-1940 after the Allied defeat in Norway; Britain and France were denounced as warmongers for trying to widen the war, and ridiculed as incompetents for mishandling the operation. The BKP's *Rabotnichesko delo* demanded that the government take action against such opposition leaders as Nikola Mushanov, Dimiter Gichev, and Hristu Pastuhov: "Rejected by the Bulgarian people, they see that their only hope of coming to power is to get the support of Great Britain and France.... And what is ... [the] government doing about all this? While saying Bulgaria will defend its neutrality [it] allows these Anglo-French agents to operate freely in the country."[26]

One of the clearest indications of the Party's improved relations with the government can be seen in the decline of Communist militancy in the May Day celebrations. In May 1939, before the conclusion of the Nazi-Soviet Pact, there had been a demonstration involving between ten and twenty thousand people, speeches criticizing German and Italian fascism, and charges that the Kioseivanov government was working with those "paid German agents"—the Ratnitsi and the Legionnaires. In 1940, however, May Day was rather quiet: only one minor clash with the police at Sofia and a few brief demonstrations elsewhere.[27]

Although a few Communist operatives and one underground press were seized during this period, the Party was able to operate with little government interference. The government even pardoned and restored the citizenship of 500 Bulgarian leftists who had fought in the Spanish Civil War. And for the first time in years, large numbers of Russian books, films, and newspapers were allowed into the country.[28]

The decline of this "era of good feeling" began with a labor dispute in Plovdiv.[29] On June 19, 1940, the tobacco workers there went on strike for a 30 percent wage increase and were quickly joined by workers in Sofia and Sliven. It is not known to what extent the strike was the result of Communist agitation, but the BKP assumed control of the movement. Although the issues were mainly economic, among the slogans were appeals for neutrality and for a friendship pact with the Soviet Union.[30] The strike was broken within a couple of days by a combination of repression and concession: the workers were given a 15 percent raise, but all the strike leaders—including three members of the BKP Central Committee—were arrested. Despite its short duration, the strike had considerable political significance. First, it became clear that the relatively tolerant relationship between the government and the Communist Party was merely a transitory arrangement thinly veiling basically irreconcilable differences. Second, the strike revealed that the government would not tolerate any disturbances, whether political or economic in nature. Significantly, there was not another important strike until the eve of the Communist coup d'état in September 1944. Third, the regime was warned that substantial (although often exaggerated) economic unrest did exist and had to be controlled.[31]

The continuing popular sympathy for Russia was dramatically demonstrated in early 1940 when the Soviet soccer team "Spartak" arrived in Sofia. The reception at Bozhurishte airfield was so enthusiastic that the crowd reportedly tried to pick up the planes and carry them on their shoulders. The team was joyously hailed everywhere it went, and on the field it was cheered louder than the Bulgarian teams it opposed.[32]

The Elections of 1939–40

Despite occasional unrest, the political situation within Bulgaria was generally quiet during the early months of the war. But the Tsar was not satisfied. The Narodno Subranie elected in 1938 seemed outdated by subsequent international and domestic events and was now an embarrassment to the regime. Although the opposition included only a third of the deputies, it had managed to elect Stoicho Moshanov, the forty-six-year-old nephew of the distinguished opposition politician Nikola Mushanov,* president of the assembly, and he was well known for his pro-Allied views.[33] Tsar Boris's dissatisfaction

---

* Moshanov had changed the spelling of his name to differentiate it from that of his more famous uncle, the head of the small Democratic Party and prime minister from 1931–34.

extended even to Prime Minister Kioseivanov. Once described as "a soft pillow on which King Boris finds it convenient to sleep,"[34] Kioseivanov in 1939 no longer seemed satisfied with this role and was trying to build up his own power.[35] It was also rumored that he was involved in many "murky" personal matters, did not attend to the affairs of state, and was not in good health. The Nazis considered him sufficiently pro-German, but had recommended as early as January 1939 that the Tsar "appoint a personality stronger than the constantly ailing, easy-going prime minister, who, because of these traits and his regime of favoritism, is slowly but surely growing to be the best-hated and most derided man in Bulgaria."[36]

The Tsar, however, did not wish to dismiss Kioseivanov before new elections could be held. On October 23, 1939, Boris directed Kioseivanov to reorganize the cabinet and then to dissolve the Narodno Subranie and call new elections for the end of the year.[37] The opposition parties faced the electoral campaign in a state of disarray. The Communists' recent bitter attacks on the democratic opposition rendered impossible a repetition of their effective coalition of 1938. Instead, the BKP organized a narrower coalition composed only of leftist groups favoring closer ties with the Soviet Union. The Tsar, meanwhile, was determined to prevent the opposition groups from again capturing a substantial minority of the seats. Election districts were gerrymandered to an absurd degree, campaign regulations were designed to hamper opposition candidates, and, as in 1938, different voting dates were set for various electoral districts to enable the police to concentrate on a few localities each week.[38] It was therefore no surprise that the government-supported candidates won all but twenty seats in the Narodno Subranie.* Such outstanding opposition leaders as Stoicho Moshanov and former Prime Minister Kimon Georgiev were defeated; but among the survivors were Nikola Mushanov, Petko Stainov, and the fascist leaders Alexander Tsankov and Todor Kozhuharov.

Prime Minister Kioseivanov considered the victory a personal one.

---

* Despite the political blandness of the government slate, twenty to thirty of these deputies occasionally voted with the opposition.

He was thus doubly surprised when the Tsar accepted his perfunctory offer of resignation following the elections. In addition to having lost all confidence in Kioseivanov's ability and integrity, Tsar Boris had also been irritated by the flattery heaped upon the prime minister by his followers, who "forgot that the Bulgarian language has only three degrees of comparison—positive, comparative, and superlative—and when they applied the superlative to Kioseivanov, there was nothing higher for Boris."[39] Kioseivanov was replaced on February 15, 1940, by Professor Bogdan Filov, who had only been in the cabinet since October. Filov—former rector of Sofia University, president of the Bulgarian Academy of Sciences, and member of several foreign academies—was one of Bulgaria's most distinguished scholars. His prestige was expected to improve somewhat the tarnished image of the premiership, and his lack of political experience was considered by the Tsar to be an asset rather than a liability because he was thus less likely to challenge Boris's personal control of governmental affairs. Filov also had another essential qualification—he was an ardent Germanophile.* Another Germanophile, Peter Gabrovsky, was promoted to the key post of minister of the interior, although he had been in public affairs only since his admission to the cabinet four months before.† A statesman with a reputation as a moderate, Ivan Popov, was named foreign minister.

The Waning of Neutrality

Despite the increased pro-German orientation of the new government, the Tsar stated in his speech from the throne at the opening of the Narodno Subranie on February 24, 1940, that there was to be no change in Bulgaria's policy of neutrality. Unofficially, however, there was little sympathy for the Allies, as illustrated by the cartoon in the humor magazine *Papagal*: Russia was depicted as the strong, friendly older brother; Germany was an admired and respected fig-

---

* Ironically, Filov's father, a Russophile military officer, was killed in the 1887 uprising against the anti-Russian government of Stefan Stambolov.

† Gabrovsky was associated with the fascist organization Ratnitsi, which the Tsar feared and usually excluded from positions of influence.

ure; France was a shameless prostitute; and England was first a pompous, and later a deflated, John Bull.[40]

The Tsar himself attempted to maintain a semblance of impartiality, and on several occasions went out of his way to be friendly toward British diplomats. Although this irritated the Germans, Boris was reluctant to isolate his country by severing all ties to the West. Haunted by memories of the 1918 upheaval that had forced his father to abdicate, he gave the impression that "his first thought was how to save his country's skin and with it his own."[41] Sir Hughe Knatchbull-Hugessen, the British Ambassador to Turkey, had a long discussion with Boris in the spring of 1940 and afterward concluded that the Tsar "was in the position of a man who knew he had no control over events and realized that whichever way the tide flowed he and his country would be swept along by it."[42]

The turning point in Bulgaria's relations with the Allies came in May 1940 with the German invasion of France and the Low Countries. Allied prestige, which had been seriously damaged by the failure of the Norwegian campaign earlier in the year, was virtually destroyed by the swift collapse of France. Belgium's fate was particularly disturbing because of its strenuous efforts to remain neutral with the aid of an army about the size of Bulgaria's and even better equipped.[43] Furthermore, Mussolini's belated entry into the war against Britain and France deprived Bulgaria of its best example of a pro-German but neutral country.[44]

Although Prime Minister Filov reaffirmed the policy of neutrality on June 15, 1940, Bulgaria had already begun to strengthen its ties with Germany: the Gestapo, for example, was allowed to operate more freely within Bulgaria. Private contact with Western embassies was discouraged, and a rise in anti-Semitism caused many frightened Jews to request visas to Palestine.[45] The Germans were deluged with congratulations and praise from all over Bulgaria, and in turn they invited the World War I Bulgarian Commander, General Nikola Zhekov, for a tour of the battlefields of France.[46] When a performance in the National Theater in Sofia was interrupted to announce that German troops had penetrated the French defenses, the audience spontaneously cheered and applauded for several minutes.[47] The Allied defeat in France may have resolved one problem for Bulgaria, but it revived a more serious one: Should Bulgaria move closer to Germany or to the USSR? This problem became more acute during the summer of 1940 with the development of the Dobruja crisis.

CHAPTER 2

The Dobruja Crisis

❧

O N JUNE 23, 1940, only one day after the surrender of France, Soviet Foreign Minister Molotov* informed Schulenburg, the German Ambassador in Moscow, that "the solution of the Bessarabian question brooked no further delay."[1] The solution to which Molotov referred could only have meant that the Soviet Union wanted the return of this Danubian province, a part of Russia from 1812 to 1918. At ten o'clock in the evening three days after Molotov's warning, the Soviets presented Rumanian Ambassador Davidescu with an ultimatum to be answered no later than the next day demanding the cession not only of Bessarabia but also of northern Bukovina, which had never been a part of Tsarist Russia.† Both territories were to be evacuated within four days, and all equipment and installations left behind in good condition. Rumania, unable to obtain support from either the Balkan Entente or the Axis, was forced to yield.[2]

Despite Molotov's assertion that "the Soviet Government had no intention of encouraging other states to make demands on Rumania,"[3] during the same period the USSR tacitly endorsed both the

---

* Technically, the Soviet Foreign Ministry (the Narkomindel) was still called a "Komissariat," not a Ministry.

† Bessarabia had been ceded to Russia by Turkey in 1812 by the Treaty of Bucharest; the southern part reverted to Rumania after the Crimean War but was reoccupied by Russia from 1877 to 1918. Bukovina was ceded by Turkey to Austria in 1775 and remained part of the Austro-Hungarian Empire until it was united with Rumania in 1918. Seton-Watson, *History of the Roumanians*, pp. 555–64. The Nazi-Soviet pact of August 1939 had specifically excluded Bessarabia from Germany's sphere of influence.

Bulgarian and the Hungarian claims against Rumania and hinted that Hungary should occupy Transylvania by force while the Rumanian armies were deployed along the Russian border.[4] Hungary's Foreign Minister Csaky had earlier warned that Hungary would also insist on concessions if Rumania yielded to Russian demands. While Rumania was still considering the Russian ultimatum, Bulgarian Ambassador Draganov in Berlin suggested to Unterstaatssekretär Woermann that this was an opportune moment for Germany to settle the Southern Dobruja question for Bulgaria once and for all.[5]

The Dobruja was the area along the Black Sea between the Bulgarian seaport of Varna and the mouth of the Danube.* In 1878 Russia had awarded the northern portion to Rumania to compensate for Russia's seizure of Bessarabia. After the Second Balkan War (1913), Rumania took the Southern Dobruja from Bulgaria by the Treaty of Bucharest, although then only two percent of the population was Rumanian. Bulgaria temporarily regained the Southern Dobruja during World War I, but the Treaty of Neuilly in 1919 restored Rumanian control. Despite Rumanian attempts to colonize the area, the census of 1930 revealed that Bulgarians still outnumbered Rumanians by two to one.[6]

In contrast to the Yugoslavs and the Greeks, who bitterly disputed Bulgarian claims to Macedonia and Thrace, "few Rumanians had ever cared very deeply" about the Southern Dobruja.[7] Rumanians were, of course, not eager to surrender any of their territory without good reason, but their main objection to a transfer of the Southern Dobruja to Bulgaria was the fear that it would encourage Hungary to demand Transylvania.†

* The area of the entire Dobruja is approximately 9,300 square miles, of which 2,900 were claimed by Bulgaria. Rumanians were 19 percent of the population in the Southern Dobruja, Bulgarians 38 percent; in the north the comparable figures were 65 percent and 10 percent. (The remainder were Turks and a variety of other ethnic groups.) The total population of the Dobruja in 1930 was 815,000, of which about half lived in the south. Spector, p. 219; Seton-Watson, *History of the Roumanians*, p. 534.

† Hungary had threatened in January 1940 to seize Transylvania if Rumania ceded land to Bulgaria (and Russia) without fighting. Ciano-Csaky discussions, 6.i.40 and 7.i.40, *Ciano's Diary*, p. 331.

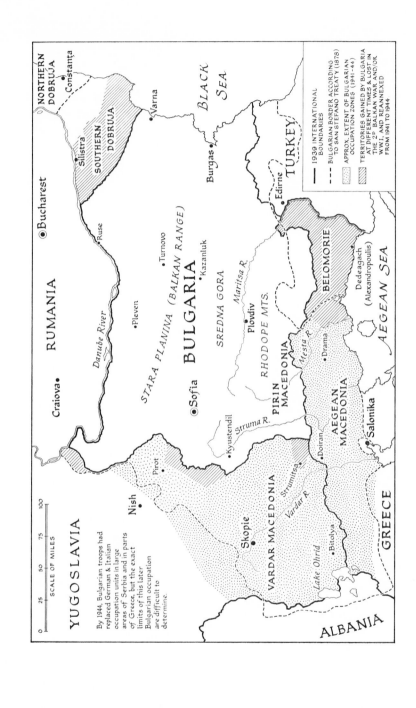

SCALE OF MILES

0   25   50   75   100

YUGOSLAVIA

By 1944, Bulgarian troops had
replaced German & Italian
occupation units in large
areas of Serbia and in parts
of Greece, but the exact
limits of this later
Bulgarian occupation
are difficult to
determine.

Nish

Skopie

VARDAR MACEDONIA

Bitolya

Lake Ohrid

Strumitsa

Vardar R.

Doiran

AEGEAN
MACEDONIA

Salonika

GREECE

ALBANIA

Prizren

RUMANIA

Craiova

Danube River

Pleven

STARA PLANINA (BALKAN RANGE)

BULGARIA

Sofia

Kyustendil

Struma R.

PIRIN
MACEDONIA

Kazanluk

Turnovo

SREDNA GORA

Plovdiv

RHODOPE MTS.

Maritsa R.

Mesta R.

Drama

Bucharest

Ruse

NORTHERN
DOBRUJA

Constanţa

SOUTHERN
DOBRUJA

Silistra

Varna

BLACK
SEA

Burgas

Edirne

TURKEY

BELOMORIE

Dedeagach
(Alexandropoulis)

AEGEAN SEA

1939 INTERNATIONAL
BOUNDARIES

BULGARIAN BORDER ACCORDING
TO SAN STEFANO TREATY (1878)

APPROX. EXTENT OF BULGARIAN
OCCUPATION ZONES (1941–44)

TERRITORIES GAINED BY BULGARIA
AT DIFFERENT TIMES & LOST IN
THE 2ᵈ BALKAN WAR AND/OR
IN WWI, AND REANNEXED
FROM 1941 TO 1944

The Problems of Territorial Revision

Germany and Italy, although sympathetic to Bulgaria's claims, were concerned lest such a drastic redrawing of Balkan frontiers set the whole peninsula aflame with war. This would have disrupted the shipment of vital raw materials such as oil and chrome and could have necessitated the deployment of German troops in the Balkans. Both countries, therefore, urged that territorial revisions regarding Rumania should be postponed until after the war. Ciano wrote in his diary on June 28, 1940: "We must at any cost avoid a conflict in the Balkans which would deprive us of their economic resources. For our part we shall keep Hungary and Bulgaria from joining the conflict."[8] The German attitude, as expressed by their Ambassador in Bucharest to his Bulgarian counterpart, was, "Germany is interested in managing an obedient Rumania, and at present tranquillity is needed in Southeast Europe."[9]

Hungary, however, had no intention of waiting. Rumors that Magyars in Rumania were being evicted to make room for Bessarabian refugees had aroused the Hungarian government, which was further inflamed by the reports of armed clashes on the Hungarian-Rumanian border. The Hungarians also feared that if they did not move swiftly, the Russian troops occupying Bessarabia might resume their advance and occupy Transylvania.[10] Bulgaria was also impatient. On June 29, 1940, Tsar Boris told German Ambassador Richthofen that Bulgarians, although still stunned by the Soviet takeover of Bessarabia, would soon come to their senses and clamor for the return of the Dobruja. Citing the recent Communist-led tobacco-workers' strike in Bulgaria, the Tsar said, "The situation would be intolerable if Bulgaria did not at least receive a promissory note. If not, there would be the danger of a violent revolution, followed by a very close association with Moscow."[11]

Boris sought to avert German procrastination by warning that although the Bulgarian government preferred to receive the Southern Dobruja from Germany, it would accept it from the USSR if necessary.[12] The threat's credibility stemmed from Russia's being, for several reasons, a more logical supporter of Balkan border revision than Germany. First, because the Soviet Union was not yet involved in the war and not dependent on the Balkans for raw materials, its intervention would have less serious economic consequences. Second, since Russia had already deprived Rumania of Bessarabia and Bukovina, only one additional push would have been necessary to include the Southern Dobruja in a general territorial settlement. Third, the closer the Bulgarian border moved toward Soviet territory, the greater the pressure the USSR could eventually exert on Bulgaria. And fourth, the Slavic bond between the two states could not be entirely dismissed. The Tsar realized, however, that if Russia, long-esteemed as the liberator of Bulgaria from Turkish domination, should also become the unifier, pro-Russian feeling would increase with incalculable political effects.* For this reason, Tsar Boris privately determined that a Dobruja settlement, when it came, would be with German assistance rather than Soviet. His threat to deal with Moscow, however, was taken quite seriously by the Germans, who remained sensitive lest any other country, even Italy, receive the credit for returning the Dobruja to Bulgaria.†

The Rumanian government, concerned by its inability to fight a full-scale war‡ (the premier confided to the American minister that the army had only enough ammunition for one and a half months), favored making concessions while its army was still intact, rather than suffering defeat and facing dictated terms.[13] The longer a confrontation was delayed, however, the more time Rumania had to convert from a British to a German ally, thereby increasing Germany's reluctance to force territorial concessions. On June 1, 1940,

---

* Alexander II, the "Tsar Liberator" of Russia's serfs, was honored with the same title (*osvoboditel*) by the Bulgarians in 1878. In imitation, Tsar Boris assumed the title "Tsar Unifier" (*obedinitel*) in 1941, and one of the main streets of Sofia was renamed in his honor.

† Draganov told Woermann, "What disturbed him especially was the danger that Bulgaria might now receive the Dobruja as a gift from the hands of the Soviet Union rather than from Germany, although he readily conceded that the entire present situation was a result of the German victories." Woermann memo, Berlin, 27.vi.40, DGFP, 10: 37–38.

‡ However, in the only modern war between the two states, the Bela Kun campaign of 1919, Rumania had decisively defeated Hungary and occupied Budapest.

the Western-oriented Rumanian Foreign Minister, Grigore Gafencu, was replaced by Ion Gigurtu, who was more sympathetic to the Reich. Eighteen days later, as French armies staggered and collapsed under Hitler's blitzkrieg in the West, Rumania's King Carol gave an audience to Horia Sima, the leader of the fascist Iron Guard, and Rumanian newspapers shifted to a sharply critical attitude toward the Allies and the Jews. Rumania renounced the Anglo-French guarantees, and three days later Gigurtu formed a cabinet that included Sima and two other Iron Guardists.[14] Nevertheless, German special envoy Hermann Neubacher and German Ambassador Wilhelm Fabricius reportedly warned King Carol that these last-minute efforts to jump on the Nazi bandwagon would be futile.[15]

King Carol appealed to Hitler, only to be told on July 15 that in the event of a Balkan war Germany would "disinterest itself entirely from further developments in Southeastern Europe." Germany was powerful enough, Hitler claimed, to defend itself without any help from this region and could even do without Rumanian oil, if need be; he had no desire to get involved in a Balkan war just because other countries "could not find it in themselves to permit just reason to prevail over passions and emotions."[16] Rumania was advised to come to terms with Bulgaria and Hungary, and in return Germany and Italy would guarantee the borders of all three states.

The cession of territory was understandably an unpopular idea in Rumania. Peasants began digging trenches in Transylvania, troops were sent into the Dobruja, and resolutions were passed urging war rather than dismemberment. Feeling against Germany ran high, and an unmistakable atmosphere of defiance surrounded Rumania's celebration on August 6 of its 1917 victory over German troops at Marasesti. But all of this was hopeless. Rumania had no outside support: even its ally, Yugoslavia, declared in favor of Bulgaria's claim.

The Craiova Agreement and the Bulgarian Reaction

On August 21, 1940, agreement between Rumania and Bulgaria was reached at Craiova. According to the treaty signed on September 7, Bulgaria received all of the Southern Dobruja, including the towns of Silistra and Balchik; the 110,000 Rumanians in this area were exchanged for 65,000 Bulgarians from the Northern Dobruja.[17] Bulgarians greeted the treaty with jubilation. Since Germany's reluctance to assume the role of "unifier" was not known outside government circles, the popular celebrations accorded full credit for the settlement to the Axis. Tsar Boris, in his address to the Narodno Subranie on September 20, 1940, thanked Hitler, Mussolini, King Victor Emmanuel, Ribbentrop, Ciano, and the Hungarian government for their support.[18] Streets were renamed in honor of the Axis leaders, and on October 30 the German and Italian Foreign Ministers were awarded Bulgaria's Order of St. Alexander. No official mention, however, was made of the Soviet Union or its leaders.[19]

Both pro- and anti-Soviet opposition leaders in the Narodno Subranie expressed regret that the Soviet Union's support for the Bulgarian claims was not acknowledged in the public message of appreciation. The Russophile Petko Stainov and the fascist leader Professor Alexander Tsankov asserted that the USSR deserved equal credit with Germany, and one prominent member of the government majority, Peter Dumanov, reminded the deputies that the Soviet newspaper *Izvestiya* had supported Bulgaria's position.[20] The Bulgarian Communists naturally took an active part in this effort to secure credit for the Soviet Union. At the celebration in Sofia, for example, where various orators were praising the Axis, several Communists mounted the platform and praised Stalin.* One speaker, Asen Panev, even claimed that "the Bulgarian people should thank not Hitler but the Soviet Union" for the Dobruja award.[21]

The Bulgarian government surprisingly did thank Great Britain for its support—prompting a German protest—but this was little noticed in the swirl of exuberance following the Craiova agreement.[22] Great Britain had decided to support Bulgaria with the hope that it might steal some of Germany's thunder, but this belated gesture, coming at a time when British power and prestige were at their

---

* Bulgaria did express appreciation privately to the Soviet Union for its moral support (see Dallin, *Soviet Russia's Foreign Policy*, p. 279), but this fact never became well known, even within the Bulgarian government.

nadir, accomplished little.* A secret British intelligence study concluded: "Britain expressed its approval of the change, but the fact that it was made under the aegis of Germany naturally increased Axis prestige enormously, and British approval at that date had little significance."[23] It is important to note that the significance of the Dobruja crisis lay not in the effect it had on the Bulgarian government, which already was pro-German, but in the pro-Axis feeling it strengthened among the people. The British Ambassador in Sofia summarized this result of the settlement: "The jubilation with which this was received took the form of enthusiastic gratitude to our two principal enemies, and did our case an infinity of harm.... Many waverers who had not yet committed themselves to the German side were swept into the vortex of pro-German enthusiasm."[24] As a result of the Dobruja offer, Bulgaria, which had long looked to Russia as the liberator, now turned to Germany as the benefactor.

* In a speech on September 5, 1940, Churchill said, "Personally I have always thought that the Southern part of the Dobrudja ought to be restored to Bulgaria, and I have never been happy about the way Hungary was treated after the last war." Churchill, *Speeches*, 1: 246; D. E. Sargent and P. Nichols, London, 12.vii.40, FO R6416.38.9; Lukacs, p. 314.

CHAPTER 3

Competition for the Balkans

꽃

FOLLOWING THE Dobruja settlement, the strained relations between Germany and the USSR continued to worsen, resulting in a period of intense diplomatic activity. An early indication of a schism was the exclusion of the Soviet Union from the Craiova and the Vienna settlements; and the ink had hardly dried on those treaties before two other German moves—the appointment of Italy rather than the USSR to Britain's place on the Danube international commission, and the formation of the Tripartite Pact with Italy and Japan on September 27, 1940—further alarmed the Soviets. The Tripartite Pact, which the Russians regarded as a dangerous revival of the 1938 Anti-Comintern Pact, was particularly disturbing despite German assurances that the alliance did not concern the Soviet Union but was "directed exclusively against American warmongers."[1]

The growing rivalry between Germany and the USSR focused attention on the Balkans, where each of the powers vied for dominance in Bulgaria. Although Hitler professed no interest in the region aside from Rumania's oil fields, Germany urged Bulgaria's adherence to the Tripartite Pact. The USSR pressed for acceptance of the proposed Soviet-Bulgarian mutual assistance pact. But the Tsar had learned from the Dobruja settlement that neutrality was not incompatible with the satisfaction of Bulgaria's irredentist aspirations. On October 22, 1940, Boris wrote to Hitler that Bulgaria's policy of neutrality not only had "met with the deepest approval in the hearts of the Bulgarian people" but had "accomplished another important task of our common policy, namely, the preservation of peace in the

Balkans." Pointing out that Bulgaria's neighbors would feel threatened by an alliance between Berlin and Sofia, the Tsar concluded: "I would be deeply grateful to Your Excellency if you would reconsider the question whether it is absolutely necessary to subject the present unequivocal and imperturbable policy of Bulgaria, which has heretofore kept our and your enemies in check, to a change which might result in immediately exhausting our modest forces, aside from the fact that full mobilization would bring to a standstill our entire economic life and the country's production."[2]

But Germany's plans to intervene militarily in Greece led to intensified pressure on Bulgaria. On November 17, 1940, the Tsar and Foreign Minister Popov traveled to Germany for a meeting with Hitler, who had just concluded important discussions with Soviet Foreign Minister Molotov, and were told that all the nations of Europe, including the USSR and France, would be invited to join the Tripartite Pact. Little risk was involved for Bulgaria, Hitler said, since Germany had no designs on any Balkan country. Boris declined the offer for the usual reasons, ranging from fear of Turkey and the USSR to Bulgaria's military unpreparedness, but he expressed willingness to cooperate unofficially.[3] When Hermann Neubacher, Germany's special envoy for economic affairs, was asked after the war what date Bulgaria became firmly committed to the Axis cause, he replied, "All these matters had been settled by Tsar Boris's visit to the Führer on November 17, 1940."[4] This conference seems less conclusive than Neubacher believed, however, for six days later Ambassador Draganov informed Hitler that the Bulgarian government was prepared in principle to join the Pact but wished to defer the act for the time being. Hitler listened to a long exposition of the many reasons for delay, then stated unhappily: "The decision not to sign the Pact as yet was Bulgaria's concern. There were arguments pro and con. It was up to Bulgaria, who was best able to assess her own situation, to make the decision."[5]

The Sobolev Offer

An important reason for Bulgaria's hesitation was the attitude of the Soviet Union. The Soviets were concerned about Bulgaria's negotiations with Germany; within hours of the announcement of the Tsar's visit in November, Molotov summoned Stamenov, the Bulgarian Ambassador in Moscow, and quizzed him on its significance. The Soviet Union, Molotov declared, favored Bulgaria's territorial claims and was prepared to provide whatever economic assistance (food, oil, loans) the country might require, but would not tolerate Bulgaria's becoming a "Legionnaire state" like Rumania. If Bulgaria accepted a guarantee from Germany and Italy, the Soviet Union would insist on a similar agreement.[6] Several days later, on November 25, 1940, Arkadi A. Sobolev, the Secretary-General of the Soviet Foreign Ministry, arrived in Sofia to make a high-level appeal for the mutual assistance pact first proposed in October 1939.[7] If Bulgaria accepted the Soviet pact, Sobolev told Prime Minister Filov, Moscow would have no objection to Bulgaria's joining the Tripartite Pact as well; in fact, the Soviet Union itself would probably join soon.[8] A tempting prize was reportedly dangled before Filov's eyes— Soviet support for Bulgarian claims not only to Greek Thrace but to all of European Turkey except the Straits.[9]

While Sobolov's proposal was being discussed, the Bulgarian Communist Party distributed handwritten leaflets on November 28 that gave the more desirable features of the Soviet plan. The Bulgarian government had made no public mention of the proposed pact and was angry at the Soviets for trying to influence negotiations by leaking the contents of the note—a charge the Soviets denied.[10] Disclosure of the Soviet proposal resulted in a flood of letters, telegrams, and petitions from Bulgarians who demanded that their government agree to the Soviet terms. Within two months, a total of 340,000 such messages with a claimed one and a half million signatures were received by government offices, and the postal service complained of the burden.[11] Since Bulgaria's population was only six million, the one and a half million signatures—if authentic—would have meant that almost every literate, politically conscious adult had written to the government. The London *Times* reported that "Bulgaria had been profoundly shaken by what may be considered as the greatest subversive activity organized from abroad in the country's recent history."[12] The

BKP, describing this as a real plebiscite representing the will of the people, considered the campaign highly successful. Indeed, one Western scholar has suggested that the Soviets did not expect the Bulgarian government to accept their proposals but had only made the offer to arouse public opinion and to deprive Germany of a monopoly on the territorial issue.[13]

The ultimate effect of the Communists' public appeal, however, was to swing the Bulgarian government further from the course desired by the Soviet Union. First, the government bitterly resented both the attempt to influence Bulgaria by "street politics" and the indiscretion concerning the Sobolev-Filov discussions.[14] Second, the heavy Soviet pressure allowed the Germans to argue, as Hitler did on December 3, 1940, that "as long as the Russians knew that Bulgaria was not a member of the Tripartite Pact, Russia would try to blackmail Bulgaria in every conceivable way."[15]

The Italian Invasion of Greece

Another reason for Bulgaria's reluctance to commit itself openly to the Axis was the Italian debacle in Greece. Before the Italian invasion on October 28, 1940, Mussolini had realized that his attack would be considerably facilitated if Greece were simultaneously attacked by Bulgaria. Knowing that Bulgaria had strong claims on Greek Thrace and that irredentist feeling was running high, he believed that Tsar Boris would be eager to join the campaign.[16]

On October 15, Mussolini wrote to Boris, requesting his assistance and arguing that if Bulgaria ever hoped to regain an outlet to the Aegean, now was the time to act.[17] The Tsar replied that he saw the advantages of the proposal but that public opinion and fear of the Turks prevented him from doing anything at present. Mussolini, angered by the rejection, exclaimed: "Those chicken-livered kings [*regnanti senza fegato*] never succeed in taking any action! We'll do without him. Prasca's march will be so rapid that it will draw off Greek forces in the north, even if they don't disintegrate by every man going home."[18]

But within a week of the invasion, initiative passed to the Greeks.

As their defense stiffened, the vaunted legions of Mussolini became objects of ridicule. The landing of British troops in Greece on November 3 and the damaging British air attack on the Italian fleet at Taranto on November 11 added to the seriousness of the Italian situation. The Bulgarian government, noting the decline in Italian prestige, hesitated to ally itself with a coalition containing such an inept partner. Indeed, Hitler wrote to Mussolini on November 20, just after the Tsar's visit, that "Bulgaria, which showed little willingness to join the Tripartite Pact, is now completely disinclined to consider such a step."[19] As the military situation deteriorated, Mussolini sought help from Hitler. The contempt with which these requests were first received was described later by General Jodl: "Italy was beaten, as usual, and sent the Chief of the Operations Staff of the Supreme Command to me, crying for help. But in spite of this emergency, the Führer did not intervene."[20]

For a while the Germans were content to let the Italians suffer the consequences of their folly and their rudeness in not informing Hitler in advance of their invasion plans,* but Germany could not permit Italy to be defeated, nor could British intervention in Greece go unchallenged. In early November 1940 the Germans received reports—later proved false—that the RAF was preparing an air base on the island of Lemnos, near Salonika, from which planes would be within striking distance of Bulgaria and the Rumanian oil fields. On November 6, five squadrons of British planes from Greek bases began attacks on Italian shipping.[21] Reacting to this threat, Hitler ordered his generals on November 12 to make preparations "in case of necessity" for the invasion of Greece from Bulgaria.[22]

Leaning Toward the Axis

During Boris's visit to the Führer he had declined to commit Bulgarian troops to such an operation, but he had privately consented on November 18 to Germany's use of his country as a base against

---

*The Italians were not eager for German assistance. As one Italian diplomat noted, German involvement in Balkan affairs "will have most unfavorable repercussions for us in a zone of vital interest to us." Simoni, p. 196.

Greece. A small advance team of German officers under Colonel Zeitzler was sent to Bulgaria to establish fuel depots, strengthen bridges, arrange the billeting of troops, and study the terrain. Several hundred Luftwaffe personnel in mufti arrived to construct air observation stations, and by December 1940 German troops in Bulgaria numbered several thousand. The Bulgarian government nevertheless publicly maintained that there were no German troops in the country.[23]

Prime Minister Filov traveled to Vienna on January 2, 1941, ostensibly for medical reasons but actually to discuss Bulgarian policy with Hitler and Ribbentrop at Obersalzberg. Filov explained that the government still harbored misgivings about joining the Axis and listed the usual excuses: Turkey, armament deficiencies, the USSR, and Yugoslavia. Hitler completely dismissed all these objections except Russia. But even the USSR, he argued, was an unconvincing threat because Stalin was too much the realist to risk war with Germany. Any delay in joining the Tripartite Pact, Hitler warned, could doom Bulgaria to the same fate as the Baltic states, which had already been absorbed by the Soviets. Hitler added that the conflict with Greece was deplorable, but it provided Bulgaria an opportunity to satisfy its Aegean aspirations without even having to participate directly. Germany requested only that the Bulgarian army concentrate along the Turkish border to discourage a threat to the flank of the invading force. Although Filov was unable to extract a promise to receive Salonika or Yugoslav Macedonia, he assured Hitler that Bulgaria would eventually join the Tripartite Pact: "The only misgivings he had were that accession at this particular moment might create complications which could cause inconvenience to Germany as well as Bulgaria."[24]

Foreign opinion was divided about whether Bulgaria would ever actually join. In Italy, for example, Mussolini was convinced that Bulgaria would sign the Pact, "If only to reconcile itself more easily to the passage of German troops through the country"; but Count Magistrati, Ciano's brother-in-law and Secretary of the Italian Embassy in Berlin, believed that "Bulgaria will not openly array itself with the Axis but will allow itself to be invaded without even per-

functory opposition."[25] To the Bulgarians, however, there seemed to
be no realistic alternatives to an alliance with the Axis. In the words
of the Ambassador to Sweden, N. P. Nikolaev, "The German invasion was inevitable, but if they came as enemies it would be worse
for our country; it would be better to have them as friends provided
that they spared us from participation in the war."[26]

The shift in Bulgaria's foreign policy was paralleled by a marked
shift on the domestic political scene. As early as October 28, 1940,
the day Italy invaded Greece, observers noted that Tsar Boris's address to the Narodno Subranie lacked the usual phrase "peace and
neutrality." A government spokesman, Nikolai Nikolaev, explained
that since there was no longer any hope of Bulgaria's remaining un-
involved, the old phrase had become "defeatist propaganda and dangerous pacifism."[27] By December 1940, the word "neutrality" had become so unacceptable that when an opposition leader, Petko Stainov,
used it in an article in the respected newspaper *Mir*, the censor replaced it with the word "peace."[28]

Although the Assembly on December 26 rejected Alexander Tsankov's resolution urging Bulgaria's immediate entry into the Tripartite Pact, the pro-Axis trend in Bulgarian policy was unmistakable.[29]
A Bulgarian version of the German labor organization *Kraft durch
Freude* had been founded in September 1940, and a Bulgarian equivalent of *Hitler Jugend* named *Brannik* ("defender") was organized
two months later.[30] In December, the Assembly enacted legislation
against the Jews and groups with international affiliations such as
the Masons, Rotary, and the Pen Club. Ironically, Prime Minister
Filov found himself obligated to resign as president of the Bulgarian
Pen Club.*

Accompanying these measures were a series of official and semi-
official acts of friendship toward Germany. Bulgarians began con-
tributing to the German *Winterhilfwerk* soon after the Craiova
settlement in August, and by November significant deliveries were
reported. Tsar Boris awarded the Grand Cross for Civil Merit to the

---

* These laws will be discussed in detail in Chapter 9.

German Ambassador, while Bulgarian holders of Germany's Iron Cross were invited to the Reich as guests of the German army. In addition, the politically powerful Bulgarian League of Reserve Officers pointedly sent a large quantity of fine cigars to the German troops occupying Neuilly, where the hated peace treaty had been signed after World War I.[31]

The leaders of the democratic parties opposed this trend on January 18, 1941, by publicly advocating a continuation of neutrality. Two weeks later fifteen Communist and Pladne Agrarian opposition deputies demanded that the Narodno Subranie condemn any plans for the entry of German troops into the country and acknowledge the rumors that the Soviet Union had offered Bulgaria a friendship pact.[32] Prime Minister Filov did meet with two opposition representatives, Atanas Burov and Vladimir Karakashev, on February 8, 1941, but Tsar Boris declined their request to meet with him.[33] Public opinion also remained unsettled. According to a German intelligence report, much would depend upon the reaction to the arrival of German troops in Bulgaria. The entry of Soviet troops, the report admitted, would probably be accepted more easily.[34] The Slovak chargé d'affaires estimated that supporters of Russia outnumbered those of Germany by two to one and predicted that "a mass change of opinion by the general population against Germany could occur suddenly if Germany should suffer setbacks."[35]

Communist Reaction to the New Policy

The Bulgarian Communists attempted to enlist this latent pro-Russian feeling in their campaign for a treaty with the USSR. They had become disillusioned with the policy of collaboration and, unlike Communist organizations in other countries, were now sharply critical of the Germans.[36] Moreover, the Party cadres resented the way the Bulgarian government's Dobruja victory had won over many potential Party supporters who found nationalism more appealing than internationalism. It is unlikely that the BKP, traditionally so subservient to the Soviet Union, was acting solely on its own initiative in criticizing Germany. This exception may have been allowed because of German moves into what the Soviet Union regarded as its own security zone.

In September 1940 the BKP issued a polemical "Appeal to the Bulgarian People," which blamed Germany for creating anti-Russian feeling in the Balkans and attacked the Bulgarian government for allowing a flood of German "fifth columnists" into the country. The following month the clandestine Party newspaper indicted Germany as the Soviet Union's "enemy number one."[37] In late 1940 the "Sobolev campaign" focused Party efforts on gathering support for the pact with Russia. The Seventh Plenum of the BKP Central Committee, meeting in Sofia in January 1941, listed its basic tasks as (1) waging a determined struggle against the entry of Bulgaria into the war; (2) securing the acceptance of the pact of friendship and mutual assistance with the Soviet Union; and (3) achieving the union of all the Bulgarian people in a truly broad national front around the Bulgarian-Soviet pact.[38]

On January 13, 1941, Soviet displeasure with Bulgaria and Germany was revealed by a TASS communiqué denying foreign press reports that German troops were being sent to Bulgaria with Soviet approval:

1. If German troops really are present in Bulgaria and if further dispatch of German troops is taking place, then all this occurred and is occurring without the knowledge or consent of the USSR, since the German side never raised with the USSR the question of the presence of German troops in, or their dispatch to, Bulgaria.

2. In particular, the Bulgarian Government never approached the USSR with an inquiry regarding the passage of German troops to Bulgaria and consequently never could have received any reply from the USSR.[39]

The response to this protest was disappointing to the Soviets. Newspapers in Germany merely printed the message without comment, and diplomatic circles remarked on the unusual mildness of the communiqué. Even those diplomats generally inclined to find divergences in German and Soviet policy believed on this occasion that the Soviet Union had disinterested itself in Bulgarian affairs.[40]

Seeing that this protest had little effect, the Soviets delivered another that was more specific. Directed ostensibly at British and Turkish moves that could have transformed Bulgaria into a theater of military operations, the note declared:

> The Soviet Government has stated repeatedly to the German Government that it considers the territory of Bulgaria and of the Straits as the security zone of the USSR and that it cannot be indifferent to events which threaten the security interests of the USSR. In view of this, the Soviet Government regards it as its duty to give warning that it will consider the appearance of any foreign armed forces on the territory of Bulgaria and of the Straits as a violation of the security interests of the USSR.[41]

Ribbentrop replied on January 21 that the Reich had no intention of violating any Soviet security interests, "nor would this by any means be the case if German troops march through Bulgaria."[42]

A stronger Russian attitude was revealed to certain diplomats. The Soviet Ambassador in London, Ivan Maisky, told Nikola Momchilov, the Bulgarian Ambassador, that the Soviet Union was willing to assist Bulgaria and Turkey "if German troops should enter or march through either country against its will."[43] The Soviet military attaché in Sofia went even further and told the Bulgarian Minister of War that "if Bulgaria let German troops pass through its territory it would mean war between Russia and Bulgaria."[44]

Allied Diplomatic Efforts

Great Britain also attempted to discourage Bulgaria from slipping completely into the Axis camp. Hoping to provide an alternative, Britain had earlier offered Bulgaria a guarantee of its independence and territorial integrity if it did not aid Britain's enemies or become one itself. On October 12, 1940, King George VI had reaffirmed this commitment in a letter to Tsar Boris, adding that the British government "has never supported a policy based on rigid adherence to the *status quo*." The Bulgarians only poked fun at the British guarantees: Sotir Yanev said sarcastically in the Narodno Subranie that Britain was offering to guarantee the independence Bulgaria already possessed.[45] On a more clandestine level, Britain decided that the secret

Special Operations Executive (SOE) should step up its activities in the Balkans, especially in Bulgaria, where there was virtually no Allied intelligence network. A young agent, Julian Amery,* was sent from Belgrade to examine the possibilities in Bulgaria, but he only managed to arouse the ire of the British Ambassador, who thought the SOE was preparing a coup behind his back.

Britain's influence was so slight because, in the words of the Foreign Office, it was not "in a position either to bribe or to threaten."[46] Seeking to lend a hand, President Roosevelt sent a personal representative, the legendary Colonel William J. ("Wild Bill") Donovan, to visit various Balkan leaders in January 1941. Donovan went first to Athens, then to Sofia amidst speculation that he would announce the U.S. entry into the war in a few weeks.[47]

Nothing so momentous occurred. After an inconclusive interview with the Bulgarian foreign minister, Donovan met Filov. Since the Bulgarians had "neglected" to provide an interpreter for this meeting, the session was understandably brief; but Filov did get the impression that the American emissary "was very belligerent and was not interested in hearing about peace until the Germans were finally crushed."[48] The meeting with the Tsar went much more smoothly, although Donovan had difficulty in eliciting a firm statement from Boris about anything. Donovan told him that America intended to support Great Britain and warned him of the consequences of collaboration with the Nazis. Boris gave the impression that he was still trying to avoid trouble with Germany, whereupon Donovan asked him if the following summary represented the Bulgarian attitude: "That Germany is still uncertain as to what you will do in the event that she demands passage through your country; but that if a decision is forced and you are no longer able to delay, you will then permit Germany to come through, although you will not participate with her." Boris just looked Donovan in the eye and smiled.[49]

---

* Amery later was a liaison officer with the Albanian guerrillas and then Churchill's personal representative in the 1945 meeting with Chiang Kai-shek. In 1950 he became a Conservative M.P. and in 1962 the Minister of Aviation in the government of his father-in-law, Harold Macmillan. Sweet-Escott, *Baker Street Irregular*, pp. 53, 60.

Donovan was favorably impressed with the Tsar as "honest, idealistic, and devoted to peace," but he noted in his diary "I fear he has been so successful in maneuver that he places too great reliance on it."[50] After Donovan had left, American Minister Earle informed Washington that the visit had impressed the Bulgarian government: "it may not prevent the unmolested passage of German troops through Bulgaria but it very possibly may prevent the cooperation between the Bulgarian and German troops."[51] Uncertain threats from a faraway country, however, could not compensate for overbearing pressure from a Great Power with troops on the Bulgarian border.

The Bulgarian-Turkish Pact

Attempting to balance German pressure, Britain from the outset of the war encouraged Bulgaria's neighbors to threaten war if Bulgaria entered the Axis alliance. Strong and concerted action from the Balkan Entente was unlikely from the first, and out of the question after the Italian invasion of Greece and the entry of Nazi troops into Rumania and Hungary, but Britain did hope that Turkey would cooperate. The Turks were nominally allied to Britain, had a large if outmoded army, and still inspired fear among the Bulgarians.[52] The goal of British policy, as Churchill told Lord Halifax on November 26, 1940, was to get Turkey to declare that "any move by Germany through Bulgaria to attack Greece or any hostile movement by Bulgaria against Greece will be followed by an immediate Turkish declaration of war."[53]

Turkey's attitude was ambiguous. In late November 1940, Turkey hinted to Bulgaria that a nonaggression guarantee might be given "provided Bulgaria did not engage in any hostile acts."[54] The Germans favored such an arrangement because it would safeguard their flank in the event they went to the aid of the Italians in Greece—as they were to do in Operation Marita in March 1941. But the Turkish Minister to Sofia, Ali Berker, indicated that the entry of German troops into Bulgaria might itself be a *causus belli*. Having just declined a Russian pact, the Bulgarian government felt unable to accept a Turkish one.[55] The negotiations were further disturbed by

Turkish maneuvers along the Bulgarian border ("purely for defensive purposes") in early December, and by a Bulgarian decree changing all place names of Turkish origin.[56] As late as February 5, 1941, the Turkish newspaper *Yeni Sabah* challenged German propaganda claims that Turkey would not intervene if German troops entered Bulgaria: "Any power which penetrates into the Turkish zone of security is giving notice of her intention not to respect Turkey's frontier."[57] Such statements were becoming less credible as German strength in Rumania and Hungary grew to several hundred thousand men.[58]

Rather than risk national suicide, the Turks decided that "if they could do nothing to ensure the continued neutrality of Bulgaria, at least they could concentrate on remaining neutral themselves."[59] Turkey therefore proposed an agreement based on the 1925 Bulgarian-Turkish friendship treaty, subject to the reservation that previous commitments by the two countries would not be affected. Bulgaria accepted, and a nonaggression pact was signed on February 17, 1941. The British Ambassador in Sofia lamented the effect the pact would have on Bulgaria: "This let us down badly, and it was no longer possible for King Boris or anyone else in Bulgaria to plead the danger of possible Turkish or Yugoslav reactions as a reason for not letting the Germans in."[60] The American reaction from Ankara was that "an agreement not bad in itself has in the end taken a form that lends itself so readily to misrepresentation. The local Axis representatives are jubilant."[61]

CHAPTER 4

Bulgaria Joins the Axis

※¤※

O N MARCH 1, 1941, Bulgaria yielded to German pressure and finally signed the Tripartite Pact in Vienna. Prime Minister Filov explained that Bulgaria was joining the Axis Powers not only because of their assistance in obtaining the Southern Dobruja, but also because the Pact would "secure for the nation the possibility of developing in peace, strengthen its welfare, and safeguard a just and permanent peace."[1] Friendly relations with the Soviet Union and Turkey, he emphasized, would not be affected. That same day, Ribbentrop officially informed Filov that Bulgaria would receive an outlet to the Aegean between the Struma and Maritsa rivers.[2]

Upon his return from Vienna, Filov was applauded by the Narodno Subranie. No debate was allowed on the vote to ratify the treaty, and an interpellation by seventeen opposition deputies was blocked. Only one man, a little-known representative from Yablanitsa named Ivan V. Petrov, managed to ask why the Assembly had not been consulted beforehand and whether the Pact would involve Bulgaria in the war. Filov replied that Article 17 of the Constitution required only ratification by the Assembly, not consultation; as for the danger of war, he said, "There is a small risk, but those who will not run risks are the ones who never do anything." The Pact was ratified 140 to 20.[3]

Even Hitler recognized the superficiality of Bulgarian enthusiasm for the Pact: "I was struck to learn after the conclusion of the Tripartite Pact that the President of the Bulgarian Ministerial Council was scarcely acclaimed by the population of Sofia, despite the major importance of the Pact to Bulgaria. The fact is that Bulgaria is strongly affected by Panslavism both on the political and on the sentimental level. It is attracted by Russia, even if sovietized."[4] Yet German troops entering Bulgaria received a genuinely warm welcome. Inhabitants of many villages met the advance elements of the Twelfth Army with the traditional bread and salt and were hospitable in every way.[5] Officials in Berlin were delighted that the march was without incident.[6] Even the Bulgarian government, according to a German report, "was surprised by the great sympathy which the people showed to the German troops."[7] Filov subsequently claimed that this reception served as a "true plebiscite on the policy of the government,"[8] but many of the villagers were under the impression that, since Germany and Russia were allies, the incoming German soldiers would march alongside the Russians in a joint operation.[9]

The Soviet Protest

Although Filov believed the Russians would "reconcile themselves to the situation and do nothing,"[10] his first request on the morning after the signing was for news of the Soviet reaction. Ribbentrop claimed nothing was yet known, but in fact the Soviet government had already delivered a protest to the Germans. In this note, Molotov

expressed his deep concern that the German Government had in a matter of such importance to the Soviet Government, made decisions contrary to the Soviet Government's conception of the security interests of the Soviet Union. The Soviet Government had repeatedly stressed its special interest in Bulgaria to the German Government, both during the Berlin conferences and later. Consequently, it could not remain indifferent in the face of Germany's last measures in Bulgaria and would have to define its attitude with regard thereto. It hoped that the German Reich Government would attach the proper significance to this attitude.[11]

On March 3, 1941, *Pravda* published a brief announcement, not prominently headlined and without comment, revealing only that German troops had entered Bulgaria;[12] but the following day *Izvestiya* sharply criticized Bulgaria's new policy "inasmuch as this position results, regardless of the desire of the Bulgarian Government, not in the strengthening of peace but in the expansion of the sphere of war and in the involvement of Bulgaria in the war. Secondly, the Soviet Government, true to its policy of peace, cannot therefore render any support whatever to the Bulgarian Government in the conduct of the latter's present policy."[13] This message was broadcast by Radio Moscow on the Bulgarian language program for the next three days, and the leading Bulgarian Communists were informed privately of the USSR's disapproval.[14] On March 6, the BKP belatedly distributed leaflets declaring "The Bulgarian nation retains no confidence in the present government and refuses to support its anti-popular policy."[15]

The Bulgarian censor issued no instructions to the newspapers concerning the Soviet protests and made no attempt to prevent their publication.[16] Some observers were surprised at the relatively mild protests, as a Soviet ultimatum was expected and direct military intervention was considered a possibility. Speculation from Belgrade, according to German Ambassador Ulrich von Hassell, centered upon the "heavy blow" dealt the Pan-Slavic movement by Russian inaction.[17]

The British Break Diplomatic Relations

The signing of the Tripartite Pact signaled the beginning of a full-scale campaign against British interests. As early as February 1941 police harassments had reached ominous proportions. On February 24 a British consular official named Greenwich disappeared without a trace. On the 26th, about fifty persons described by Radio Berlin as in the employ of British intelligence were arrested in Sofia. Two days later a number of journalists, including the correspondents of the London *Times* and the Chicago *Daily Mail*, were arrested, as were about thirty opposition leaders. Dr. Georgi M. Dimitrov ("Gemeto"), one of the leading Pladne Agrarians, was smuggled out of the country in a packing case with the help of the British intelligence representative in Sofia, Norman Davis.[18] The British Embassy was ordered closed on March 1, the same day that Sofia police claimed to have found a bomb of British origin near the city waterworks. Bulgaria also broke diplomatic relations with the British-based governments-in-exile of Belgium, Holland, and Poland, but did refuse to hand over their representatives in Sofia to the Germans.[19] The Bulgarian Ambassador in London, Nikola Momchilov, resigned in protest against his government's actions.[20]

In response to these provocations, Great Britain officially severed relations with Bulgaria on March 5, 1941. Ambassador Rendel, in rejecting Filov's allegations that Britain had endangered peace in the Balkans, maintained that the British government was "not aware that such peace and tranquillity had ever been threatened or disturbed by any power which was not a member of the Tripartite Pact."[21] When Rendel warned Filov of the implications of an alliance with Germany, Filov haughtily replied that the Bulgarian government needed no advice on how to preserve its independence. Rendel angrily retorted that this remark would be remembered "and it might prove to be important to have it on record for a future peace conference that the Bulgarian Prime Minister had assumed full responsibility for the consequences of his policy."[22] Tsar Boris, after listening to a similar warning from Rendel, merely replied that Bulgaria suffered from its geographical position; he expressed no regrets at the rupture of relations with Britain.[23]

On March 11 the British Embassy staff arrived in Istanbul and proceeded to the Pera Palace Hotel. While they were waiting with their luggage in the lobby, two of the suitcases exploded, killing two diplomats and wounding seven. Two Turkish policemen were also killed and a score of Turks injured. The two suitcases, plus an unexploded third, were thought to have been placed among the other luggage by German or Bulgarian agents at the Sofia railroad station. However, some officials in London believed that the explosives in the suitcases belonged to the SOE. One SOE official, Bickham Sweet-Escott, recounts that he had a very difficult time trying to explain that his secret organization was not involved: "it would be an understatement to say that suspicion was cast on us."[24]

Boris had little reason to be grateful to Britain. Until British intervention in Greece aroused Germany's attention, Bulgaria had been able to avoid an alliance with anyone; and yet the British effort to aid Greece never had more than the slightest chance of success.[25] In retrospect, if Bulgaria had remained uncommitted until June 1941 when Germany invaded the Soviet Union, it is possible that Bulgaria could have avoided joining the Axis despite the government's sympathy for Germany.[26]

Developments in Yugoslavia

Since Bulgaria's territorial claim on Macedonia conflicted directly with Yugoslavia's, most Bulgarians naturally hoped that Yugoslavia would not seek Germany's favor by joining the Pact. The cooperation of Yugoslavia, however, seemed essential to the success of Operation Marita, for Hitler wanted to use Yugoslav lines of communication and protect the flank of his armies passing through Bulgaria. The Yugoslav government initially rejected Germany's demands, but the neutralization of its ally Turkey by the Bulgarian-Turkish agreement and the adherence of Bulgaria to the Axis on March 1 complicated its position. On March 4, 1941, the Yugoslav Regent, Prince Paul, told Hitler at Berchtesgaden that his cabinet might accept the Tripartite Pact if four generous conditions were met: first, a territorial guarantee; second, no transit for German troops; third, no active participation in the war; and fourth, access to the Aegean at Salonika.[27]

Tsar Boris, unlike most of his people, wanted Yugoslavia to sign the Pact, for he feared that Yugoslav stubbornness might upset the precarious stability of the Balkans and precipitate a war that could endanger his country and his throne.[28] For this reason, in mid-March 1941, the Bulgarian Foreign Minister, Ivan Popov, and War Minister Teodor Daskalov conveyed to Yugoslav Ambassador Milanovich the "friendly advice" that Yugoslavia should sign the Tripartite Pact. "Milanovich was very surprised by this advice," General Daskalov later wrote, "and asked whether we knew that Yugoslavia in this case would receive Salonika and that we must forego Macedonia. Popov replied that we realized this; it was now not a question of territorial gains but of saving our countries."[29]

Under pressure from Germany, on March 25, 1941, the Yugoslav government signed the Tripartite Pact in Vienna. Germany promised to respect Yugoslavia's territorial integrity, not to send troops through that country, and to permit the eventual cession of Salonika.[30] Although the Yugoslav leaders promised very little in return, Hitler observed that their behavior at the signing ceremony reminded him of a funeral.[31] Bulgarian reaction was mixed. Prime Minister Filov wrote in his diary that "everyone was very pleased,"[32] and Ulrich von Hassell, who was in Sofia at the time, wrote: "Here in Bulgaria a feeling of relief seems to prevail at the moment. How the atmosphere will be when one realizes that Yugoslavia has made demands is an open question. . . . The Bulgarians follow the affair with mixed emotions."[33]

Von Hassell was correct in predicting Bulgarian dissatisfaction upon learning the details of the agreement. Many Bulgarians felt the opportunity of obtaining Macedonia was worth the risk of war. A leading Bulgarian industrialist, Ivan Balabanov, related to von Hassell the general reaction after Bulgarians learned of the German concessions to Yugoslavia: "The Axis lost twenty percent of its followers here in the last twelve hours. Reserve officers who associate freely with Germans have received threatening letters."[34] Hitler, however, was delighted at Yugoslavia's adherence because, as he told Ciano, action against Greece would otherwise have been "militarily an extremely foolhardy venture."[35]

The Yugoslavs, instead of being relieved, reacted with anger. Riots and demonstrations against the Pact broke out in many cities, especially in Serbia, and several army units mutinied. On March 27, 1941, the commander of the Yugoslav air force, General Dushan Simovich, and General Bora Mirkovich staged a successful coup d'état against the government of Prince Paul. The Prince was deposed and forced into exile, and seventeen-year-old King Peter was proclaimed monarch in his own right.[36] Churchill declared, "Yugoslavia has found its soul."[37] The coup was acclaimed throughout Yugoslavia by crowds of demonstrators who displayed Allied flags and chanted anti-Nazi slogans.[38] Although General Simovich refrained from renouncing the Tripartite Pact, Hitler was enraged by the coup and decided "to destroy Yugoslavia militarily and as a national unit."[39] The Macedonian question, Hitler told von Ribbentrop, could now be settled in Bulgaria's favor.[40]

CHAPTER 5

Operation Marita

⁂

O N APRIL 6, 1941, German troops stormed into Greece and Yugo-slavia. The Greek defenses along the Bulgarian border were quickly outflanked, and the secondary defenses at the Aliakmon line south of Salonika were breeched. The Greek army and the hundred thousand men of the British expeditionary force in Greece were forced to retreat toward Athens.[1] German forces also entered Yugoslavia and pushed deep into the country without encountering substantial resistance. The Luftwaffe razed Belgrade, bombed the port of Athens, and ranged at will over the battlefields.

Although Bulgaria had declined to participate directly in the invasions, its role as a German staging area made it a target for British air attacks. On the first day of the campaign, six RAF Wellington bombers attacked the marshaling yards at Sofia, and a group of Blenheim bombers hit the railroad line leading from Sofia into Greece. The bombing, according to American Minister Earle, was "accurate and effective."[2] On April 13, British bombers staged a three-hour night raid on Sofia, setting ablaze a number of buildings around the main railroad station and blowing up an ammunition train.[3]

These bombings had an effect on Bulgaria far out of proportion to the actual damage inflicted.[4] After the second attack on Sofia, there was widespread panic and a mass exodus from the city. The authorities hoped to still the alarm by mentioning the raids only briefly on the radio and in the press; instead, they only fueled the rumor that Sofia had been completely destroyed.[5] In addition, since the British raids had coincided with the presence of vulnerable ammunition trains in the marshaling yards, both the Bulgarians and the Germans assumed that Britain had agents in Sofia who were furnishing accurate intelligence on troop and supply movements. The Bulgarian police proceeded to arrest scores of people on the slightest suspicion of espionage, sabotage, or contact with a hostile foreign government.[6] Leaders of the political opposition with Western sympathies were placed under close watch and their homes searched.[7] The newspaper *Mir*, the most objective and respected in the country, was temporarily forced by the censors to suspend publication.[8]

The Communists, however, were not included in this roundup of political dissidents. In fact, those leaders who had been arrested in February 1941 or who had not been included in the October 1940 amnesty were now released.[9] They emerged from prison into a confusing new situation. Many of their former sympathizers had been won over by the government's nationalist policy; even some of the leaders were wavering. According to German intelligence, only the old dyed-in-the-wool (*eingefleischte*) BKP labor leaders continued in active opposition to the government.[10]

The Bulgarian Entry into Macedonia

Although Bulgaria had refused to participate in the campaign, Yugoslavia claimed that Bulgarian troops were fighting alongside the Germans and asked Turkey to fulfill its obligations under the Balkan Entente. Numan Menemenchoglu, the General Secretary of the Turkish Foreign Ministry, replied that his government had been assured that Bulgarian troops were not participating in the German operation but promised to take action if the situation changed.[11] Despite the fact that Bulgaria was not participating militarily in the campaign against Yugoslavia, it did encourage the pro-Bulgarian Macedonians to undermine the vanishing authority of the Yugoslav government. A committee had formed in Skopie espousing the union of Macedonia with Bulgaria, and the Tsar decided on April 11 to send Danial Krapchev, the editor of the influential pro-government newspaper *Zora*, to meet with the committee to coordinate propaganda for Macedonia. At the same time, he sent Professor Yaranov to German-occupied Salonika on a similar mission.[12] What the Bulgarian leaders apparently feared most were the autonomist tendencies among some of the Macedonian groups; therefore they made every effort to encourage those favoring union with Bulgaria.[13]

On April 15, Bulgaria officially broke diplomatic relations with the Yugoslav government on the grounds that Yugoslav soldiers had made a number of unprovoked attacks on Bulgarian border posts since the first of the month, that air raids had been made on Bulgarian towns despite Bulgaria's neutrality, and that members of the Yugoslav Embassy in Sofia were in contact with subversive elements.[14] On the same day, Germany recognized the independence of Croatia and declared the state of Yugoslavia dissolved. Bulgaria could thus enter Macedonia without technically violating the Balkan Entente. On April 19, Bulgarian troops occupied Skopie.[15] Only then did the Greek government sever relations with Bulgaria.[16]

Once again, Bulgaria received part of its national patrimony from the hands of the Germans. The alliance with the Axis had quickly borne fruit and pro-German feeling increased. The few people who had retained trust in the Western powers were disillusioned by Britain's defeat in Greece and were reluctantly forced to agree with Filov's statement that the Marita campaign had "once again proven the almost criminal folly of a small country opposing a great mechanized nation."[17]

Bulgarian-American relations deteriorated rapidly after the launching of Operation Marita. President Roosevelt announced that the United States rejected the argument that the Yugoslav state was dissolved, and thus he considered Bulgaria's occupation to be an invasion.[18] The Bulgarian government complained to the U.S. about this attitude, claiming it would "create a painful effect" in Bulgaria. Under Secretary of State Sumner Welles replied that this was precisely the desired intention: Bulgaria's recent actions "could only be interpreted here as an indication that Bulgaria was committed heart and soul to the Axis policies."[19] Minister Earle in Sofia was even more pessimistic about the new course of Bulgarian foreign policy:

The Bulgarians are an intensely practical people. German propaganda has magnified in their eyes the new territory given them until they are now wholeheartedly with Germany. They now think of the Bulgaria a thousand years ago reborn. I am forming the impression, and every day it is stronger, that Germany will take this hard-bitten and grateful Bulgarian people and use them as a nucleus to build a powerful nation, strongly equipped with the most modern and mechanized weapons, whom Germany can depend upon to guard for her southeastern Europe.[20]

The Bulgarian government remained relatively unconcerned about relations with other countries because of the increased intimacy with Germany. Hitler and the Tsar met in Vienna on April 18, 1941, to determine the boundaries of the Bulgarian occupation zone in Macedonia before the Italian delegation arrived the next day. During this cordial meeting, Boris thanked Hitler for the "mighty assistance of allied Germany," and Ribbentrop praised their "common destiny" and the "renewed Waffenbrüderschaft" from the First World War.[21]

The Bulgarians expressed their gratitude to the Reich in other ways. For example, they solicited donations for the German soldiers wounded in the Marita campaign. Although described as gifts from the Bulgarian people, most of the money was contributed by banks and organizations doing business with the Germans.[22] Even so, the feeling in Bulgaria was one of euphoria. The anti-German opposition leader Nikola Mushanov expressed delight at the attainment of Bulgaria's national goals and declared, "The Bulgarian nation is happy, and rightly so."[23] Another anti-German Bulgarian politician gave an excellent description of the attitude prevailing in Bulgaria in the period following the Nazi Balkan campaign:

We were all intoxicated by the idea that for the first time in history we would get our just due, which we had demanded in vain for so long. To be sure, we had somewhat of a bad conscience because we had not fought for and conquered but rather received it as a gift.

Also, we had the strange feeling that it was a lovely dream from which we would have a horrible awakening one of these days. But in general, all of us, from the most extreme nationalist to the Communists, were satisfied over the successes which Hitler's New Order in the Balkans had brought.[24]

PART TWO

June 1941-August 1943

CHAPTER 6

From Barbarossa to Pearl Harbor

⚜

Two dramatic events initiated by Bulgaria's allies in June and December of 1941 completely altered the international situation and greatly affected Bulgaria's foreign policy. The first was the German invasion of the USSR, Operation Barbarossa; the second was Japan's attack on American and British installations in the Pacific. During the second half of 1941, it began to look as though the Tripartite Pact, which Bulgaria had regarded in March as a concession to Operation Marita, might ultimately drag the country into war.

Barbarossa and the Bulgarian Reaction

The German attack on the Soviet Union on June 22 came as an unwelcome surprise to most Bulgarians. Even Prime Minister Filov admitted that the nation heard the news with despondency. The American Minister in Sofia cabled the following observation to Washington:

First reactions of Bulgarians to Russo-German war are confusion and shock, mainly on account of distinct division of sympathy for the two countries. Some Bulgarians recall with apprehension Hitler's words in *Mein Kampf* that slavs were only good to be slaves, while others who hitherto looked upon Hitler's frequent breach of word with equanimity have been struck pretty hard by Hitler's complete lack of good faith as exemplified by his latest aggression. Others fear involvement of Bulgaria in war.[1]

The cabinet accepted the news calmly, however, and determined that no special measures were needed other than the placing of the Com-

munist deputies under house arrest.[2] Germany initially neither requested nor expected Bulgarian participation in the invasion of the
USSR; the war was expected to last only a few months and Germany preferred not to create complications by involving Bulgaria in
it. As the only German ally that still had diplomatic representation
in the Soviet Union, Bulgaria took charge of German interests there
on June 24, after the withdrawal of Germany's diplomatic staff.[3]

Bulgaria's recent territorial gains had brought the country closer
to Germany, but they had also made Bulgaria more difficult for
Germany to control. Most of Bulgaria's irredentist goals had been
achieved before the Russo-German war, thereby greatly reducing the
extent to which Germany could manipulate Bulgarian policy.* Germany approached this problem in two ways. First, it tried to make
the Bulgarians feel that their territorial gains were only tentative:
exact boundaries would be fixed only after peace was restored, and
presumably they would be influenced by the amount of support Bulgaria had given to Germany.[4] Second, "in German propaganda regarding Bulgaria's role in the New Order, the emphasis had to be
placed less upon German-Bulgarian economic and cultural cooperation and more upon the role which pro-German figures were playing
in Bulgarian political life."[5] Another factor probably had greater influence on the Bulgarian government, although it seems not to have
been the result of a conscious Nazi policy: this was the Tsar's obses-
sive fear that Germany would replace his regime with a puppet one
headed by General Lukov, Professor Tsankov, or some other Bulgarian fascist. The Bulgarian government seemed almost paranoid
on this issue, which will be discussed in more detail in later chapters.†

Hitler and his General Staff believed that most of the objectives of
Operation Barbarossa would be attained within a month of the invasion and that the campaign against Russia would be over by the

---

* There was no other country in the Balkans, with the possible exception of Turkey,
that Germany could play off against Bulgaria as Hitler was to do with Hungary and
Rumania over Transylvania.

† Perhaps Boris was influenced by the memory of the Byzantine practice of keeping
at Constantinople a pretender to the Bulgarian throne in order to influence the Bulgarian Tsars.

autumn. At the end of the second week in July, the Germans had already taken over half a million Russian prisoners, a large percentage defectors.[6] The pro-German Bulgarian newspapers fully reported accounts of the campaign and suggested that the country participate in the war in order to share the spoils of victory. As late as October 1941, a headline in *Slovo* predicted that within three weeks Moscow would be taken and the Soviet Union would collapse.[7]

This optimism never really penetrated Bulgarian official circles. Even in early August 1941, when the situation on the Eastern Front was quite favorable, Filov wrote that a difficult period was expected during the coming winter and that "there was great anxiety and fear because of the great losses and hardships."[8] Ulrich von Hassell reported a conversation with Bulgaria's Ambassador Draganov in mid-September in which Draganov said he no longer saw any prospect of a German victory.[9] It would be a mistake, however, to attach too much significance to these accounts of Bulgarian pessimism; the leading Bulgarian officials, including the Tsar, were habitually pessimistic. By and large, there was little real doubt of an Axis victory until Stalingrad in January 1943.

The members of the Narodno Subranie had no hesitation in expressing their support for Germany in the most effusive terms. Nikolai Nikolaev reminded the Assembly that "there on the battlefields of Murmansk, across the broad steppes, the frozen villages of Russia and the deserts of Africa, our brave allies are fighting, and though Bulgaria is not taking a direct part in this action, it stands at its post like a true ally."[10] Young Nikola Minkov dramatically proclaimed that Bulgaria had a great mission in the Balkans and described the ideological battle against Bolshevism, whose biggest supporters were now the capitalist-plutocratic countries. The two systems would perish together, he said; "Socialism in its new national form waits at the door of Europe."[11] Sotir Yanev, one of the more prominent government supporters, made the most effective of the speeches. During an official visit to Moscow in 1941, he and another deputy had seen a map of the Balkans marked with desired Soviet bases. On this map, Yanev said, Bulgaria was not even shown as large as it had become in 1941, and in the case of Macedonia the Russians had contemplated no change from the old boundaries. Yet Moscow believed that Bulgaria was a ripe field for sovietization and stood on the threshold of revolution. What would have happened, he asked, if Bulgaria had followed the disastrous advice of some and allied with the USSR back in 1940?[12]

The Failure of Clandestine Communist Activities

On the night of July 23, 1941, three Bulgarian cities were bombed by unidentified planes that were believed to be Russian. Bulgaria sent a strong protest to the Soviet government, but the Russians replied that the charges "did not correspond to reality" and denied that Soviet planes had been anywhere in the area. They suggested that perhaps the attacks had been arranged by Germany.[13] When the incident was repeated on the night of August 11, 1941, Bulgaria delivered another strong protest to the USSR but politely suggested that perhaps the Soviet planes had been piloted by Serbs or Greeks. The Soviets refused to accept this charge either, claiming that the attacks were German provocations (which they may have been), and on September 10 they issued a general denial to all allegations of interference in Bulgarian affairs.[14]

Relations between the two countries had also grown worse because Communist agents were landing from submarines and were being dropped by parachute onto Bulgarian territory. These agents were generally Bulgarian Communists who had been in exile in the Soviet Union and were returning to help organize the resistance movement. Landings were made in Bulgaria on August 11 and 28 and on September 13 and 21, 1941, but all were unsuccessful because the agents were apprehended on arrival or were quickly betrayed. The failure of peasants and villagers to assist the Communist agents came as a surprise to Moscow, which had also underestimated the alertness of Bulgarian army patrols. Only an estimated twenty of the 58 men landed were able to make contact with the resistance movement, and of these twenty most were soon arrested.[15]

The Bulgarian Communist Party, which had taken advantage of

the favorable conditions after September 1939 to rebuild its battered organization, was once again repressed.* Several hundred important Communists were arrested in the period between the signing of the Tripartite Pact and Barbarossa, and most of the other leaders were arrested by the first week of July 1941. Of the 291 most-wanted Communists, the police managed to locate 244 in the first two weeks after Barbarossa. Of the five members of the BKP Politburo, one was jailed in July, two others were apprehended in September, and the last two were caught within a year. The Central Military Commission of the Bulgarian Communist Party, which was the directorate for the resistance, had a complete change of membership by the spring of 1942.

One of the reasons for the BKP's swift collapse may have been the size of the "cells" that were uncovered: the average number of people in each was 23, which was far too large for clandestine activity.[16] Another reason may have been that the Party was surprised by Barbarossa and was unprepared to go "underground." A third reason was the effectiveness of the Bulgarian police, as Minister Earle reported on July 4, 1941: "So thorough, however, are the military and police precautions taken by the Government that, while it's possible there may be minor demonstrations, 'which if they occur will be ruthlessly dealt with,' I see no possibility of a major Communist uprising unless there are serious German reverses."[17] Police repression was so severe that a man in Kyustendil who had remarked that Russia would never be conquered was sentenced to eight months in jail and fined an impossibly large 175,000 leva. A student who had written anonymous letters to high government officials accusing them of leading the country to disaster received a ten-year sentence and an equally large fine. Thus it was not long before the Gonda Voda, Enikyoi, and St. Nikola (for women) concentration camps were filled, and other camps had to be built.[18]

---

* By the spring of 1941, Party membership had risen to slightly over 10,000, compared with 30,000 before the May 1934 coup; the youth organization RMS (*Rabotnicheski mladezhki suyuz*) numbered 19,000. See Oren, *Bulgarian Communism*, pp. 167–68.

New German Pressures

The domestic situation might have changed for the worse if Bulgaria had been forced to break relations with the USSR or, more importantly, to participate in the war on the Eastern Front. Despite alleged Soviet air attacks, parachuted Communist agents, and open Russian support of the partisan struggle, however, the Bulgarian government continued to maintain diplomatic relations with the Soviet Union. The Germans were less than pleased with the unusual situation of a Soviet legation functioning in an Axis country during wartime, for the legation and its consulate were undeniably centers of espionage and propaganda. According to von Papen, they were "a thorn in Hitler's side." The Führer wanted them closed, but he was persuaded that this would cause too much difficulty for Tsar Boris.[19] Ribbentrop instructed Ambassador Adolf-Heinz Beckerle (who had replaced Richthofen) in late September 1941, "In the question whether Bulgaria should maintain or break off diplomatic relations with the Soviet Union, please take a noncommital attitude and do not take a position in one sense or the other."[20] Five days later Beckerle reported that he had met Filov, who had told him that Bulgaria would welcome a break in relations with the USSR but "would not do the Russians the favor of breaking off relations of its own accord."[21]

Whenever the Germans complained about the presence of the Soviet legation, as they did throughout the war, Boris would reply that he had the building under very close observation and had complete confidence in his police and guards. The Russians, in turn, complained of this surveillance and charged that the Bulgarians were "doing everything possible to annoy and isolate the Legation. Every member of the delegation is openly followed by police and every visitor, except diplomats, leaving the Legation is questioned by police and sometimes arrested."[22] Government surveillance was constantly increased until not only Soviet diplomats but also many of the White Russian immigrants in the country were followed.[23]

Germany was not fully satisfied, though, and believed that Bulgaria could at least close the Soviet consulate in Varna, even if the legation in Sofia had to remain open. If it could not be closed—and in fact it was not for over a year—then German military authorities requested that at least the radio antenna should be removed from the roof of the consulate. Even though such installations were forbidden in Bulgaria, this limited German request met with no success.[24]

All traditions of diplomatic conduct were violated when the Soviet counselor of the legation was physically assaulted and an attempt made on the life of the assistant military attaché on September 7, 1941.[25] Although conceivably these acts of violence were not instigated by the Bulgarian government, Molotov was prompted to send a note on September 10, 1941, condemning Bulgarian behavior: "the conduct of Bulgarian affairs was not in conformity with normal intercourse between nonbelligerent countries and has deteriorated to such an extent as to be impossible." The note also charged that "facts in the possession of the Soviet Government prove undeniably that Bulgaria has been transformed into a *place d'armes* for the military attack by Germany and her allies on the Soviet Union," and seven specific examples were provided.[26] The Bulgarian Minister in Moscow denied the charges and refused to make any apology. Bulgarian-Soviet relations worsened to such an extent that the Russians would probably not have maintained their diplomatic mission if Bulgaria had not become such an important intelligence center.

One of the major questions involving Bulgarian relations with the USSR and Germany was whether Bulgaria should take direct military action against the Soviet Union. Germany had agreed at the outset of Operation Barbarossa that there would be no pressure on Bulgaria to declare war on the USSR, but as the invasion progressed, Hitler began to desire some form of Bulgarian participation. A volunteer Bulgarian Legion was proposed, to be either modeled on the Spanish Blue Division or formed as a national unit of the Waffen-SS, but the idea was rejected by the Bulgarian government. The refusal was motivated by a double fear: first, that such a legion could bring full-scale war with the USSR; and second, that the Bulgarian fascists and extreme nationalist elements would come to dominate it (thereby gaining additional favor with Germany) and then use it for purposes other than fighting Russia. As a concession, the Bulgarian government agreed to send a medical train under Bulgarian command to the Eastern Front, where it would help the Axis troops and, supposedly, any Russian prisoners requiring medical attention.[27] Bulgaria's strategy at this time, according to the Tsar's secretary, was to "conciliate Germany by making many comparatively unimportant concessions."[28]

Uncertainty About Turkey

Turkey was a genuine problem for Bulgaria, but it was also an excuse for not sending Bulgarian troops to fight in Russia. The Bulgarian-Turkish nonaggression pact of February 1941 had officially removed the danger of Turkish intervention, but there remained a substantial amount of uneasiness and suspicion between the two countries. Among high Bulgarian staff officers there was strong support for a preemptive attack on Turkey. General Nikola Mihov, the commander of the First Army and later one of the three Regents of Bulgaria, was "strongly convinced that Turkey was completely on the side of our enemies and would not honor its neutrality."[29] Other high-ranking officers eagerly discussed the possibility of a military operation against Turkey in the spring of 1942.[30]

Turkey had signed a friendship treaty with Germany on June 18, 1941, only four days before the beginning of Operation Barbarossa. This fortuitous timing suggested to some that Turkey knew of Barbarossa in advance and was hoping to make some territorial gains at the expense of the Soviet Union.[31] In early August 1941, the Turkish government informed Ambassador von Papen that in view of the German success in Russia, the Turks were interested in the future of the Turkic peoples living on the Soviet borderlands, especially those in Azerbaijan.[32] Turkey, however, had no desire to involve itself in the war. Turkey had declared its neutrality immediately after Barbarossa began, and Hitler said approvingly, "It was better for us if Turkey was indifferent than if she pursued a wavering policy."[33]

Despite Germany's desire to see Turkish neutrality preserved, the geographical position of that country made this difficult. As the gateway to the Middle East from German-occupied territory, Turkey was a key factor in any plan for threatening the Suez Canal from the rear or for extending German hegemony to the Arab world. This had been shown in May 1941, when Rashid Ali seized power in Iraq and requested immediate German assistance, which would have required the transit through Turkey of men and materials. Germany promptly began negotiations for a secret treaty with Turkey granting right of passage. The Germans interpreted international law as allowing a neutral state to permit the shipment of matériel, and they expected that Turkey would not object to a certain number of German soldiers "accompanying" the trains. As an inducement for the plan, Ambassador von Papen promised Turkey several of the Aegean islands and the rectification of the Turkish border near Edirne (Adrianople), although the latter would have been at the expense of Bulgaria.[34]

The collapse of the pro-Axis Iraqi regime in late May 1941 and the defeat of Vichy forces in Syria removed the need for mere German assistance; the German plans were changed to include outright military intervention. Hitler's war directive number 32, "Preparations for the period after 'Barbarossa,'" stated that "a German attack from Bulgaria through Turkey will be planned, with the aim of attacking the British position on the Suez Canal from the East also. To this end plans must be made as soon as possible to assemble in Bulgaria sufficient forces to render Turkey politically amenable or to over-power her resistance."[35] This directive fueled the rumors of an impending invasion of Turkey in the spring of 1942, but events on the Eastern Front caused the operation to be postponed indefinitely. The idea of Turkey as a gateway was not abandoned, but the subsequent plans envisaged not an advance into the Middle East but an attack through the Caucasus to catch the Russians in the rear and to link up with German forces advancing across the plains of Russia.[36]

Pearl Harbor and Its Significance

Although a member of the Axis, Bulgaria sought to maintain friendly relations with the United States. Bulgarian Foreign Min-

ister Popov reassured American Minister Earle—in Earle's words—
of the "strong desire of the King and Government to maintain cordial relations with our country no matter what happens."[37] Bulgarian
newspapers, however, did not reflect this attitude and were once
again printing bitter articles against the United States. The Bulgarians ignored American protests against these articles but complained
when American newspapers spoke of Bulgaria's preparations for
aggressive action against Russia. On November 22, 1941, the Tripartite Pact was secretly amended to provide for German-Bulgarian
cooperation in matters concerning the press and propaganda.[38]

The Japanese attack on the American fleet at Pearl Harbor on December 7, 1941, aroused surprisingly little concern in Bulgaria. Nevertheless, when Germany and Italy, viewing the United States as the
aggressor, declared war in support of their Axis ally Japan, the Bulgarian government assumed that a decision had to be made to follow
suit. America seemed far away and Great Britain was thought to be
facing certain defeat. A declaration of war on these countries was
therefore regarded as an easy way of pleasing Germany rather than
a step toward disaster. Prime Minister Filov appeared before the
Narodno Subranie on December 13 and stated that Bulgaria must
satisfy its obligations under the Tripartite Pact by declaring war.[39]
When asked a year and a half later why he had favored this declaration, Filov replied that Germany had been so insistent that there
had been no possibility of avoiding it. The architect Yordan Sevov,
the Tsar's closest friend and adviser, said that the decision had been
made only after the German Ambassador had had three meetings
with the Tsar in one day.[40] Rumania and Hungary had already declared war, and Bulgaria was told that it must show solidarity with
the other nations of the Axis.[41]

Public reaction to the declaration of war was mixed. There were
many who believed it was of little importance and foresaw no danger,
but a common feeling was, "Why, and in the name of what, had
Bulgaria to be involved in the world war without being attacked? ...
What have we to divide with the Americans; what wrong have they
done us?"[42] The youth organization Brannik reacted more violently

to the news of war—its members attacked the American and Russian legations and threw stones through the windows. Foreign Minister Popov later confessed that each of the attackers had been given three cobblestones and the generous fee of 200 leva.[43] The Tsar expressed outrage at these attacks and ordered that the damage be repaired that very night in order not to bring disgrace upon Bulgaria. The Bulgarian newspapers, however, intensified their attacks on the West and praised Japan, which they claimed was seeking only "to free Asia from Anglo-Saxon influence which harms its interest and hinders its development."[44]

The United States treated the Bulgarian declaration of war with contempt. President Roosevelt wrote a memorandum to Secretary of State Cordell Hull stating, "It is my present thought that the United States should pay no attention to any of these declarations of war against us by puppet governments."[45] In addition, he asked that congressional leaders be informed of this policy so that they would not advocate a declaration of war. According to Hull, "We realized that their Governments were puppets of Hitler and had merely jumped when the strings were pulled."[46]

The year 1941 marked a distinct change in Bulgarian relations with Germany. Prior to 1941, Bulgaria had been under German influence and generally pro-Axis, but there had been no major issues on which Germany had compelled Bulgaria to make a definite decision against its will. On the questions of rearmament and the Dobruja, for example, Germany had provided support to Bulgaria but had required no immediate concessions in return. During 1941, however, Germany had put considerable pressure on the Bulgarian government—first to sign the Tripartite Pact, and later to declare war on the United States and Great Britain. Although the Bulgarian government may not have fully realized the risks involved in either case, considerable German persuasion was necessary before the decisions were taken. Significantly, though, Bulgaria's adherence to the Tripartite Pact and declaration of war on Great Britain and the United States were not only the first major decisions taken under

German pressure, but also the last. Bulgaria managed to avoid breaking off relations with the USSR, participating in the war on the Eastern Front, or expelling the Bulgarian Jews to German extermination camps. As we shall see in the following chapters, the Germans were sufficiently convinced of Bulgaria's friendship and loyalty that they accepted the Tsar's excuses with a surprising lack of skepticism.

CHAPTER 7

Parries and Parleys

❧❦❧

As THE NEW year of 1942 began, Bulgaria was officially at war, despite the government's efforts to avoid it; but few then thought that the declaration of war against the United States and Great Britain would be of more than symbolic importance. At least it temporarily staved off German demands for military action against the Soviet Union. One writer has said that "neither King Boris of Bulgaria nor his Government dared (or probably wished) to declare war on Russia, and this was the one move that might have stirred the Bulgarian people to revolt."[1] However, the Tsar himself was so discouraged about prospects for success that on January 9, 1942, he reportedly considered abdicating his throne, and on March 6 he mentioned a desire to commit suicide.[2] He was also under pressure from his influential sister Evdokiya, who feared that the alliance with Germany would lead to a repetition of the events of the First World War, when Tsar Ferdinand was forced into exile. She told Boris, "How long will these Germans stay here! I know how this war will end; I will never live through a second exile."[3]

Continuing Bulgarian-Soviet Ties

Meanwhile, the Germans were urging Bulgaria to join the war against the Soviet Union or at least to break off diplomatic relations. Tsar Boris insisted that this would not be to Germany's advantage and produced five arguments to prove his point. First, he said that it was necessary to have a strong army in the Balkans to guard against Turkish intervention. Second, troops were needed to protect the Black Sea coast from a Russian invasion. Third, waves of unrest and sabotage in the occupied countries of the Balkans could be expected in the spring, and a force had to be held in readiness to deal with this threat, especially in view of the Greek rebellion in Bulgarian-occupied Thrace in late September 1941.* Fourth, the arms and equipment necessary for participation in a modern war had still not been delivered to Bulgaria. The Bulgarian army would be much more useful when not forced to oppose a more advanced army; as Filov recorded in his diary, "In general, our troops 'carry weight' only in the Balkans." And fifth, the Bulgarian army was "not suitable for distant campaigns, because of the attachment of the rural masses to their land"; they would be disinclined to fight for any cause not related directly to its protection.[4]

The Germans accepted these arguments for a short time, but in mid-March 1942 a German-inspired statement published by Agence Anatolia informed the Bulgarians that "they cannot expect to keep their territorial acquisitions or to receive additional awards unless they make a more effective contribution to the war against Russia."[5] The Bulgarian government's reaction, however, was merely surprise that the Germans had put so little pressure on Bulgaria. "The general feeling," said the prime minister, "was that we would not be made to participate in the war against Russia."[6]

Bulgaria's fear of a Soviet invasion may seem unwarranted when we remember how desperate Russia's plight was in early 1942, but this fear was real, and even the Germans took it somewhat seriously. In February 1942, the Germans suspected that the USSR had become disgusted with the Bulgarians and was negotiating with the Turks, promising them Bulgarian territory as far north as Burgas.[7] Manfred von Killinger, the German Ambassador to Rumania, took seriously the predictions of a Soviet landing between Varna and Burgas sometime in the spring—a landing designed not only to create a second front but also to provoke a Communist uprising in Bulgaria.[8] The Bulgarian Minister of War, General Daskalov, sensibly told Filov that the Soviets did not have sufficient troops for such a landing, but

---

* For details of the uprising in Drama, Greece, see Chapter 11.

he promised to treat the reports seriously and to take the necessary precautions.[9] In the unlikely event of a landing, German military experts saw little chance of the poorly equipped Bulgarian army's coping with the situation and warned that this weakness could nullify any gain from Bulgaria's entering the war against Russia.[10]

These German reports made it easier for Boris—on a visit to Germany in late March—to avoid Ribbentrop's formal request on the 25th that Bulgaria sever diplomatic relations with the Soviet Union, although Ribbentrop again complained that the Soviet legation in Sofia was an espionage center not only for Bulgaria but also for the rest of Axis-occupied Europe.[11] Tsar Boris met Hitler shortly afterward during his visit and explained to him that Bulgaria felt compelled to continue its present policy for a while longer to reduce the threats from the Soviet Union and Turkey. Boris later told von Hassell that Hitler had shown "complete understanding for his present attitude" and had agreed that Bulgaria would have to keep its army intact and up to maximum strength in order to restrain the Turks.[12]

The Nationalist Opposition

The nationalist opposition (i.e. the Bulgarian fascist groups) made every effort to convince Germany that the Tsarist government was not sufficiently favorable toward the Axis and should be replaced by a fascist regime. The most important of these groups was the Legionnaires under General Hristo Lukov, who was thought by the Bulgarian government to be in close contact with certain German agents. The government tried to repress Legionnaire activities as much as possible without antagonizing the Germans. When the Legionnaire newspaper, which had been advocating Bulgaria's intervention on the side of Germany, was suppressed in January 1942, the German Ambassador demanded that the ban be lifted and that action be taken instead against the "Anglophile" newspaper *Mir*.[13]

In February, Lukov scheduled a large public rally, but this, too, was banned by the government on the grounds that undesired demonstrations and disorder might break out. Actually, Interior Minister Gabrovsky and Prime Minister Filov had agreed beforehand that neither Lukov nor Alexander Tsankov would be allowed to hold meetings.[14] The Tsar was convinced that German Ambassador Beckerle was completely sympathetic to the Legion and would increasingly intervene on its behalf.[15]

Professor Alexander Tsankov, who had been prime minister from 1923 to 1926, was the other prominent nationalist opposition leader, and he too attempted to persuade the Germans that the current Bulgarian regime was unsatisfactory. Tsankov admitted that the Tsar was following a pro-German course but said that Boris did not truly believe in a German victory and was following this course only because "at present he had no alternative." According to Tsankov, Germany would never be able to rely on Boris to be a true friend or a loyal ally.[16] Germany would have liked a cabinet headed by Tsankov but recognized that the Tsar would never willingly select such a strong personality as Tsankov to become prime minister.[17] Lukov also enjoyed strong German support, but he was not as clever a politician as Tsankov, and his failure to gain broad popular support raised doubts that he was the right man to lead the country— except perhaps during a revolutionary crisis.[18] Nevertheless, until his mysterious assassination in early 1943, many of the German political reports sent to Berlin from Sofia pleaded the urgency of a government headed by Lukov.[19]

The Tsar was very concerned about being replaced by his "Byzantine rivals," Lukov and Tsankov, if he did not cooperate with Hitler. Since his relations with the Germans were based on the confidence they had in him, it might be instructive to investigate the seriousness of the threat posed by the nationalist opposition, particularly General Lukov. In late March 1942, the Tsar became so convinced of a widespread conspiracy against him led by Lukov that he demanded that Ribbentrop clarify the German position. The Tsar's fears were prompted by reports from his personal intelligence service that liaison between Lukov and the Germans was conducted by a man named Volchev, a representative of *Welt-Presse* in Sofia who, like Lukov, had connections with several Bulgarian youth organizations. Beckerle, in Sofia, promised Boris that he would look into these allegations and that he would put a stop to any clandestine dealings.[20]

The resulting German investigation left an abundance of material in the German archives on this matter. An intensive check was made by the Germans in April 1942, and many persons who had suspicious contacts were questioned. Volchev's connections with the German Embassy were confirmed, and it was learned that an engineer named Hristov had once taken a letter from Lukov to Hermann Göring. Significantly, however, no other contacts were uncovered. Schellenberg, the head of Section VI of the *Sicherheitsdienst* (SD) claimed at first that the German air attaché in Sofia, Colonel (later General) Schönebeck, was engaged in undercover activities with the Bulgarian fascist groups, but Schönebeck angrily refuted this accusation. This long and involved investigation indicated that the Germans were sincere when they said that they had no official connections with the nationalist opposition behind the Tsar's back. Schellenberg's official summary of the findings stated flatly, "I do not believe that General Lukov has any nonprivate connections with Germany and German circles."[21]

Two things should be noted about this affair. First, the Tsar had no way of knowing for certain that the official denial actually corresponded to the facts; for all he knew, the Germans had only claimed to make an investigation when in fact they did have secret contacts with Lukov. He was therefore not long satisfied with the denial. Second, it is still difficult to believe that someone as pro-German as Lukov would be so pathetically isolated from them for over a year and a half. The various German agencies often had private policies of their own and attempted to increase their influence by secret maneuverings. There can thus be no absolute certainty that some German agency was not in clandestine contact with Lukov, despite Schellenberg's investigation, although available evidence does not support this suspicion.

Hitler and Tsar Boris

Hitler had a very favorable opinion of the Tsar. After Boris's March 1942 visit to Germany, he was for a time a favorite topic of conversation at Hitler's headquarters. Boris's ability and cleverness were acknowledged by everyone in these discussions. At the same time, however, Hitler accepted at face value the Tsar's plea that he was powerless to take the measures Germany had requested. Hitler told his entourage one evening: "I recognize that the King of Bulgaria is a very intelligent, even cunning man, but he does not seem to be capable of guaranteeing the stability of his regime. He himself said that he could not change a single minister or relieve a general of his command without endangering his crown."[22] This is a surprising statement. Not only was it an inaccurate appraisal of the Tsar's position, it was also contrary to the many German intelligence reports that Boris was the unchallenged leader of Bulgaria. One such report about him, although highly critical, had concluded: "All this shows such talents of statesmanship and energy that objections, which are always raised that he is a liberally inclined and, in the final analysis, a weak ruler who knows only how to help himself through intrigues, are contradicted by the facts."[23] And indeed, a few days after his first remark Hitler said, "If there had been [in 1918] a single German prince of the stamp of Boris of Bulgaria, who remained at the head of his division, declaring that he did not dream of withdrawing a single step, we would have been spared a lamentable collapse."[24]

German Propaganda Minister Joseph Goebbels initially had an ambivalent attitude toward Tsar Boris. On January 25, 1942, Goebbels wrote in his diary that the Tsar "is said to be playing a somewhat double-faced game. He is a sly, crafty fellow, who, obviously impressed by the severity of the defensive battles on the Eastern Front, is looking for some back door by which he might eventually escape."[25] Two months later, however, after Boris's meeting with Hitler, Goebbels had a lengthy conversation with the Tsar and concluded: "The King is extraordinarily charming and has returned from the Führer full of new ideas and suggestions.... Boris is an impassioned devotee of Hitler's genius as a leader; he really looks upon him as a sort of emissary of God."[26]

Although Boris had made a good personal impression, Hitler came away from the March 1942 conference convinced that Bulgaria was not a country on which Germany could completely rely. This was owing not to lack of confidence in the country's leadership but to the pro-Russian sympathies of the Bulgarian people, which the Tsar had described in great detail. German propaganda had tried for a decade to undermine this sympathy for Russia, and on the eve of Operation Barbarossa Hitler had even suggested that Bulgaria should change from the Cyrillic to the Latin alphabet in order to lessen Russian influence.[27] The Germans had also launched a minor propaganda campaign to convince the Bulgarians that they were not really Slavs and thus were not ethnically connected to the Russians.[28] This theory was not without basis. The traditional view that a small group of Turkic warriors, the Bulgars, had been quickly submerged in a Slavic majority in the seventh century was not fully satisfactory.[29] Moreover, since that date, the Slavic stock had been repeatedly diluted by mixing with other Balkan ethnic groups. Whatever may be the truth in this complex area, the Germans and pro-German writers went much too far in claiming that the invading Bulgars had destroyed almost all the Slavs inhabiting what is now Bulgaria. Although the propaganda campaign gained a limited acceptance among a few army officers, in general it did little more than irritate the Soviet Union and the Bulgarian Communists.[30]

Turkey and the German Plans

Turkey played a vital role in German-Bulgarian relations during the war. The Bulgarian government considered Turkey both a threat and a handy excuse; the German government minimized the risks of a Turkish attack on Bulgaria but never quite dismissed them. As a result of the March 1942 conference with Boris, Hitler had concluded that Germany could place only limited reliance on Bulgaria, saying "As allies I prefer the Turks to the Bulgarians."[31] This was at a time when Bulgaria was loyally, if unenthusiastically, following a pro-German policy, whereas Turkey was officially still an ally of Great Britain and was cooperating with Germany only to the extent of allowing chrome ore to be sent to the Reich.[32] Bulgaria's religion, Hitler believed, bound that country to Russia, but Islam presented no such difficulties. The Turks appeared confident of a German victory and had expressed interest in the Soviet territories of Armenia and the Turkic border states. As Ambassador von Papen put it, "To sum up, as regards Bulgaria and Turkey, it is certain that conditions have scarcely changed since the First World War. From our point of view, Bulgaria can be regarded as reliable only in so far as we are allies of Turkey."[33]

Hitler was not concerned with finding a way to remove Bulgaria's fear of Turkey. It is difficult to understand why he did not regard the proposed German-Turkish alliance in terms of removing the Turkish threat from Bulgaria, thus facilitating the employment of Bulgarian troops elsewhere, especially since at the recent conference the threat of Turkey had been one of Boris's main excuses for not sending troops to the Eastern Front.

Bulgaria was engaged in a minor border dispute with Turkey over a small but strategic area near Edirne that had been Greek before Operation Marita. The important railroad line from Central Europe to Istanbul ran through this area, and since the land had been Bulgarian before 1919, the Bulgarians naturally expected that it would be returned to them. However, Germany wanted to use this land to pacify Turkey and reward it for remaining neutral during Marita. Boris justifiably complained that "Bulgaria, as an active ally, was entitled to more consideration than a country allied to the enemy."[34]

In accordance with Hitler's desire to improve the Turkish defenses against Allied intervention, Germany negotiated an agreement with Turkey in June 1942 giving Turkey a credit of one hundred million Reichsmarks for the purchase of military materials.[35] This only increased Bulgaria's fear of Turkey, despite German assurances to Bulgaria that there was no danger of a Turkish attack. Even if one were planned, the Germans pointed out, only a few roads led to the border; the troop concentrations would thus be discovered well before an attack could be launched.[36] Germany quickly realized, however, that it could not as confidently rely on Turkey as on Bulgaria; by August 1942, Hitler had reverted to his original position, commenting, "In the Bulgarians we have an ally on whom we can rely against the Turks."[37]

The Zaimov Affair

At the end of March 1942, shortly after the Tsar's return from Germany, Reserve-General Vladimir Zaimov was arrested in Sofia for treason. Zaimov was well known as a leading figure in the 1934 coup and the attempted coup of 1935, and he had held the post of Inspector-General of Artillery before being forced into retirement. The official reasons for his arrest were an alleged remark he had made that the Soviet Union would never be defeated and his close association with the Soviet military attaché, but the real reason was that he was involved in a conspiracy against the government. Forty other people were arrested at the same time for preparing a campaign of sabotage and terror.[38]

The arrest of a general, even one so noted for conspiratorial activity, created a sensation in Sofia. The discovery of opposition groups and Communist cells in the army was not unusual, but they had been small and generally ineffective; rarely was even a low-ranking officer connected with them. Zaimov was tried and executed in June 1942, and the Bulgarian Communist Party proclaimed him a hero and added him to the list of resistance martyrs.* The police investigators did not believe the conspiracy had ever posed a very serious threat, and they minimized the role of foreign personalities, but the Tsar felt that the affair had politically embarrassed him. Far more embarrassed was War Minister Teodor Daskalov, who had continually assured everyone that morale in the army was high; now he acted "like a man who had lost his nerve."[39]

A heated controversy erupted between General Daskalov and Minister of the Interior Gabrovsky, which was one reason why the Tsar decided a week later to name a new cabinet.[40] Daskalov was replaced as minister of war by General Nikola Mihov, the commander of the First Army. Foreign Minister Popov, who had long been accused of pro-Allied tendencies, was replaced by Filov, who remained prime minister as well; two "difficult" ministers, Slavcho Zagorov and the

---

* In 1965 a Bulgarian film of this incident was released entitled *The Tsar and the General.*

incompetent Dimiter Kushev, were removed from office. Only four of the ten cabinet posts remained unchanged. Except for Mihov, the new ministers were even more obscure than their predecessors. Germany was satisfied with the changes. Beckerle reported that Filov continued to be the best guarantee of a pro-German policy. The German military attaché said tersely, "Filov is safe."[41]

CHAPTER 8

No Friends, Just Foes

WHEN BULGARIA declared war on the United States in December 1941, President Roosevelt declined to dignify the "satellite states" with a declaration in reply. On March 24, 1942, however, the American representative in Bern was instructed to inform the Bulgarian, Rumanian, and Hungarian governments that the United States had refrained earlier from declaring war because "they were vassals of Germany, but now that they were engaged in military activities directed against us and were planning to extend them, we intend to declare war unless they give prompt evidence of a definite character that they would not assist the Axis forces."[1] This note brought no response. A draft was prepared of the message the President would send to Congress, if and when he decided that war should be declared, but it was held back for some time in the hope that the March 24th note would have some effect. Instead, it was learned that the Bulgarian government planned to close the two American colleges in the country on the pretext that the school officials were hostile to Germany. Since Bulgaria continued to ignore the American note, on June 5, 1942, the United States declared war.*

Bulgarian relations with its Axis ally Italy were not much better. Italy's prestige had risen during the first few months of 1940, when its neutrality gave hope to the Balkan states that they too might remain out of the war. Italian defeats since then had made Italy a

* In the First World War, Bulgaria and the United States had avoided declaring war on each other.

standing joke, and audiences in Sofia movie theaters would laugh
when Mussolini appeared in the newsreels.[2] Germany, however, was
suspicious of Italian moves in the Balkans and believed that Bulgaria
was trying to reduce German influence by establishing ties with
Italy.* In February 1942, Beckerle complained that the head of the
official youth organization Brannik was trying to model it after the
Italian *Balilla* instead of the Hitler Jugend.

During that same month, when representatives of the Bulgarian
handicraft and peasant unions visited Italy, the Tsar's friend and adviser, Yordan Sevov, was quoted as saying "For us the Italian corpo-
rate system is the most suitable."[3] The visiting Bulgarian delegations,
according to questionable German sources, were enthusiastic about the
system and suggested that Bulgaria adopt a similar one. When the
representative of the peasant union was asked why the Italian model
was being favored rather than the German one, he supposedly replied
that it was the Tsar who wanted it this way.[4] There is no confirma-
tion of these allegations from the Bulgarian side, either by documents
or by events. Italian agents had been active in Bulgaria between the
wars, particularly with the Macedonian terrorist organization IMRO,
and there had been a few informal ties between Bulgaria and Italy,
but the thought that Bulgaria in 1942 was interested in copying the
Italian system seems a bad joke.†

Moreover, since Operation Marita, the two countries had been engaged in a bitter dispute over the boundaries of their respective occupation zones in Macedonia, especially around the mines in the Jesserina area. The Tsar was worried that the Italians intended to remain
permanently in this area to form a Greater Albania under their control.
Feelings had been so inflamed that when an outbreak of partisan activity occurred in the Italian zone in July 1942, the Bulgarian government was delighted. Filov wrote that these events "could be of use to
us since they will be a brake on Italian pretensions for expansion."[5]

---

* The King of Italy, Victor Emmanuel III, was the Tsar's father-in-law. Boris himself was half-Italian: his mother was Marie Louise of Parma.

† The question of Bulgarian contacts with Italy arose again in the summer of 1943,
around the time of Mussolini's fall, but then the context was completely different.

In early August 1942, Italian troops began moving into disputed parts of the Bulgarian occupation zone, forcing Bulgaria to dispatch troops to the area. Germany—naturally concerned that fighting not break out between two of its allies—tried to mediate the dispute by persuading the Italians to withdraw to the line of the original Vienna settlement of 1940. When a Bulgarian noncommissioned officer was killed by an Albanian irregular, the Bulgarian government hurried further reinforcements to its army in the area.[6] Mussolini became quite angry over the border dispute and wanted to order that any Bulgarian soldiers found over the Italian demarcation line be shot. His advisers persuaded him to refrain from such an order, but he did send more troops into the disputed area and ordered that any further Bulgarian moves should be dealt with by bullets.[7]

A clash finally came on August 13, 1942, when 200 Albanian troops, supported by an Italian battalion, attacked two outposts of the Bulgarian Fourteenth Division. This skirmish alarmed everyone and intensified the German attempts at mediation. Germany supported the Bulgarian position and emphasized the importance of resolving the matter as soon as possible to restore unity in the common war. Boris expressed regret that the Italians had now begun to play *Komitadzhii* (guerrillas) and thought they would only hurt themselves in the long run.[8] The Tsar claimed that he had staked his personal reputation and that of his government on the border issue, and he urged the Germans not to let him down when the Bulgarian position was so clearly in the right. He added that it was much better to have Bulgaria rather than Italy occupy any given territory, for the Italians had no experience in dealing with Balkan peoples and with revolts in the Balkans. "Where there are Bulgarian troops, there is tranquillity and transportation is undisturbed; where the Italians are, revolts are brewing."[9]

The most serious clashes between Italy and Bulgaria came on October 16 and 30, when Bulgarian outposts rejected Italian demands to withdraw from territory claimed by both sides. In the resulting fights, each side suffered several killed and wounded. This alarmed everyone, and the military confrontation was replaced by protracted negotiations. The border question remained unresolved, however, until Mussolini's government collapsed in 1943 and Bulgaria occupied the disputed region.[10]

This dispute was important for three reasons. First, it made unlikely any attempt by Bulgaria to play off Italy against Germany to gain more freedom of action—as Bulgaria had done earlier with Germany and Russia. Second, Bulgaria was forced to rely more on German support than would otherwise have been the case. But, third, Germany surprisingly did not take advantage of Bulgaria's plight to extract more concessions from Tsar Boris, and this restraint —or error—is in itself significant.

Germany had not abandoned its efforts to make Bulgaria break relations with the Soviet Union, although the pressure for Bulgaria to send troops to the Eastern Front had temporarily diminished. German Ambassador Beckerle raised again in June 1942 the old complaint that the Soviet legation was a center of espionage. Filov countered with the original reply that the Bulgarian Ambassador to Japan was scheduled to leave soon for Tokyo, via Moscow, and Bulgaria wanted to avoid provocations until he reached his destination. This concern had delayed the Bulgarian plan to close the Varna consulate, the prime minister claimed, but afterward there would be no hesitation. At the same time, Germany requested permission to open consulates in Ruse and Kavalla and to be given a duty-free zone in Dedeagach. Bulgaria immediately agreed.[11]

No action was in fact taken against the Soviet diplomatic posts, but there was a growing feeling in Bulgarian government circles that the time might be ripe for more direct assistance to Germany's war effort. Two factors were responsible for this sentiment. First, the Germans had hinted broadly that unless Bulgaria quit playing the role of a bystander there could be no guarantee that a postwar peace conference would permit Bulgaria to retain its territorial gains. The prime minister, who had previously been in favor of a cautious approach, now urged the Tsar to take some action: " I told him continually and persistently that we had to participate in the battle against Bolsheviks, although only symbolically with a volunteer unit. We are almost the only ones in Europe who are not taking part in the fight. Our conduct would make things very difficult for us at a conference. Italy would be able to take advantage of our position. Occupation of part of Serbia is not enough."[12] Second, the war was believed to be going very strongly in Germany's favor because of recent victories in North Africa and at Sevastopol; now would be a good time to intervene, for Russia no longer was a serious threat to Bulgaria.[13]

The Tsar was impressed by these arguments but had misgivings. A German victory did not seem inevitable to him, particularly in view of recent Soviet successes around Rzhev. Furthermore, as he told Filov, "Hitler is a bad strategist; he is burdened by lackeys who around men like him [are] more dangerous than around crowned heads with tradition, for they are always putting matters to him in the most favorable light."[14] Interestingly, Hitler also became somewhat critical of the Tsar at this time: "The Bulgarians are now behaving as if the developments in the Balkans were all the result of their own decisive action. In reality, Boris, caught between his cupidity on the one side and his cowardice on the other, was so hesitant that the strongest intervention on our part was necessary to make him do anything at all. Old Ferdinand wrote some very forthright letters, too, pointing out that the hour of Bulgaria's destiny had struck."[15]

The Continuing Deterioration of Bulgarian-Soviet Relations

Relations with the USSR suddenly became worse on September 13, 1942, when once again several Bulgarian towns were bombed. The planes, which had come from the direction of Russia, were believed to be of American or British manufacture; the bomb fragments had Cyrillic lettering and the hammer and sickle emblem. The Soviet Minister, Lavrishchev, denied that the planes were Russian and pointed out that Germany had many Russian-made bombs available. This reply only angered Filov, who exclaimed, "These people will call black white."[16] Lavrishchev also refused to discuss Bulgaria's request for fifteen million leva in damages. Consequently, relations between the two countries became very cool.[17]

Probably it was no coincidence that on September 15 an organized mob attacked the Soviet consulate in Varna. The police then searched the premises in the hope of finding incriminating evidence that an informer had said was there. The results were disappointing: three kilograms of thermite and a radio transmitter were found, but no trace of the rifles or other military equipment that had been reported. One reason for this disappointing outcome may have been that the police were kept waiting at the door of the consulate for two hours, thereby giving the Russians time to destroy or remove any compromising evidence. The affair did no credit to Bulgaria, but at least some concessions had been made to German wishes, even if an air attack had been necessary to provoke them.[18]

On September 27, 1942, the Anti-Comintern Exhibition opened in Sofia. This exhibition had been planned long before, but its coincidence with the two incidents just mentioned brought Bulgarian-Soviet relations to a low point. Had the Soviets not considered their legation in Bulgaria so valuable as a window into German-occupied Europe, it is probable that they would have broken off relations that month.

Boris had not been in favor of the exhibition and had postponed it as long as possible, but he had angrily criticized Minister of the Interior Gabrovsky for trying to escape any responsibility for the plans.[19] Nevertheless, the exhibition was considered a success. The displays of Communist brutality—mostly photographs from the Spanish Civil War—were well arranged and forceful, and it was claimed that 250,-000 people visited the exhibition. The Soviet Union protested, but the Bulgarian government innocently denied that the exhibition was directed against either the people or the government of the USSR. As the deputy Sotir Yanev pointed out, since the USSR had long insisted that the Comintern was not the Soviet government, there were no grounds for Russian complaint.[20]

Although Bulgaria was less careful about the sensibilities of the USSR now that Soviet military power did not seem so awesome, the Tsar as always was worried about possible Soviet reprisals. He told a German official in September 1942 that the Soviet Black Sea Fleet might launch one last attack before its final defeat, and the harbor of Burgas seemed a likely target. There the Germans had assembled all the equipment they would need for oil-drilling in the Caucasus, and this equipment's destruction would be a serious blow to German plans to utilize the Russian oil fields.[21] The Tsar was closely following the progress of the German advance on Stalingrad. He did not believe that Germany would be able to reach its objective in 1942, and he wanted to take no action until it did.[22] Nevertheless, during November 1942 the rumor spread in Bulgaria that a break with the USSR was imminent. The army was delighted. As a result of this rumor the Tsar felt compelled to declare emphatically: "the break of Bulgarian-Soviet relations is out of the question under any circumstances; at the moment I do not want to hear any more about it."[23]

Fear of an Allied Invasion

In late 1942, for the first time in the war, Bulgarians began to worry seriously about an Allied invasion of the Balkans. General Mihov, Minister of War since April, stated in December 1942 that he did not exclude the possibility of an Anglo-American landing in the Balkans during the coming months. It was expected that the Allies might land near Salonika, or even on the Black Sea coast— perhaps with the help of the Soviet fleet—to occupy the Rumanian oil fields. Turkey's attitude was obviously crucial, and Bulgaria never doubted that the Turkish government would yield in the face of Allied pressure.[24]

The idea of a preemptive attack on Turkey had been popular in Bulgaria for over a year. The Tsar revived the question by suggesting that vigorous action toward Turkey—at the least a large-scale Bulgarian deployment on the border—was the best course of action, but he stopped short of recommending an attack.[25] The ranking army generals were not so hesitant. When a war council of twelve senior generals considered this question, ten were in favor of a proposed joint Bulgarian-German attack; the other two only objected because Germany would command the operation. The generals asserted, despite clear evidence to the contrary, that the Bulgarian army was both materially and morally ready for a campaign.[26] In reality, the Bulgarian army was still poorly equipped and unsuited for modern warfare. The best divisions were tied down in occupation duties, and the coastal defenses were admittedly inadequate. The growing expectation was that an Allied invasion, if and when it came, would resemble the Salonika campaign of World War I. The government therefore shifted the defense emphasis from the Black Sea to the Aegean coast, but little was actually implemented beyond the formation of a new infantry division.[27]

It was essential that Bulgaria should be able to depend upon a substantial amount of German military support in the event of an Allied invasion of the Balkan peninsula. Unfortunately for the Bulgarians, however, the Germans had to confess that they could spare no troops at present and could not promise any direct help in the event of an invasion.[28] Rather than being able to help Bulgaria, the Germans were themselves hard-pressed at Stalingrad and wanted to withdraw some of their occupation forces from the Balkans. Because of increasing partisan activity in Greece and Serbia and growing unrest, the Germans requested that their forces be replaced by Bulgarian units, thereby increasing the Bulgarian occupation area considerably. As recently as October 1942, the Bulgarian government had requested an extension of its occupation zone to include the area around Lake Doiran (north of Salonika) and two regions in Serbia, for it believed that occupation would help to establish claims for later annexation of the territories.[29] Germany had declined the request then, but less than a month later had to ask in turn if Bulgaria would agree to a considerable temporary increase in its occupation area elsewhere.[30]

The Tsar was not enthusiastic about enlarging the Bulgarian occupation zone to include territories that Bulgaria could not reasonably expect to retain in a postwar settlement. Moreover, as these were territories in Serbia where partisan activity was increasing, occupation would add greatly to Bulgaria's already overstrained military responsibilities. Boris discussed the problem with Filov and Mihov and decided upon a limited extension of the occupation zone, provided that the troops would not have to go far from Bulgaria and that they would return to the original zone as soon as possible; dispersion was dangerous, they believed, as long as Turkey's attitude was uncertain.[31]

Germany now tried a different approach to obtain at least some Bulgarian participation in the war. Since Bulgarian forces needed to be as strong as possible, the Germans argued that Bulgarian volunteers should be allowed to join the Waffen-SS and be trained and equipped by Germany, thereby adding to Bulgaria's defense capabilities. In fact, though, only enough volunteers were expected to form a Bulgarian Legion of at most regimental strength; moreover, Germany offered no assurances that the force would be kept in the Balkans. Ribbentrop asked Beckerle's opinion of the plan and was told that Bulgaria would probably not object to the small group of Bulgarian *Volksdeutsch* joining the Waffen-SS, but other Bulgarians would probably not be allowed. Since the nationalist opposition would try to use the plan to embarrass the government, Ambassador Beckerle advised that the suggestion should not be pushed too hard unless the war situation became extremely serious.[32]

Internal Developments

The domestic situation in Bulgaria continued to be dominated by the fear that General Lukov and the nationalist opposition were planning a coup d'état. In a private meeting of nationalists in July 1942, Lukov had outlined his program, which included the active participation of Bulgaria on the Eastern Front, and had sharply criticized Bulgaria's "police regime, which lacks the support of the people."[33] During August, Boris received reports that Lukov, Ambassador Beckerle, and Colonel Pantev* were conspiring to overthrow the government and replace it with one more acceptable to Germany. The supposed plan called for Beckerle to assemble at a banquet those persons wanted for the new cabinet and to present the Tsar with a fait accompli. Boris was thus especially alarmed when he learned that Colonel Pantev was leaving for a trip to Germany, as this seemed proof of the conspiracy.[34]

---

* The chief of the Bulgarian police; the British had nicknamed him "The Black Panther."

Although such a plot probably never existed, Boris took the rumor very seriously and sank into a mood of deep depression, saying, "I've already been through this mess three times before!"* To forestall the plan he even considered asking Professor Tsankov to take power as soon as a coup appeared imminent. Boris believed that Hitler still supported him and his regime, but he feared that Nazi "party circles would be able to impose a change even against the will of Hitler." If this happened, Boris had decided that he would flee Bulgaria, for he was "determined not to play the role of the Danish King."[35]

The Tsar would have been less discouraged if he had known how pessimistic the nationalist opposition was at this time. Dr. Schmidt, Hitler's interpreter, made a trip to Sofia and heard the Legionnaires and others complain that Boris had succeeded in winning the support of the people. Moreover, many of the nationalists were also supporting the Tsar, since he was following a pro-German policy. Schmidt said it was unfortunate that Boris felt compelled to suppress the groups that were most pro-German, but they were a danger to the monarchy. Nevertheless, he said, "In this country our [German] authority is truly uncontested, and one does not find the intellectual doubt which prevails in Bucharest and Budapest."[36] This view was confirmed by Mohrmann, a German official who visited Sofia in September 1942; he reported that the Tsar had the people behind him and that the political situation was fairly stable. The only difficulties, he noted, were caused by a "few hundred out-of-work politicians whose activities did not amount to much."[37] In December 1942, when Lukov called for a mass meeting of the nationalist youth, only three hundred attended, and his harsh criticism of the government was embarrassing to the attending German and Italian ambassadors.[38]

The conflict with the nationalist opposition pointed up a major problem of Boris's regime—its lack of an ideology. After Bulgaria attained its revisionist goals, the country lacked any sense of purpose except loyalty to the Tsar, and this was considered insufficient in an age of ideology. The Tsar himself was disturbed by the apathy he

---

* "*Az tazi popara sum ya yal tri puti veche!*" He presumably was referring to the events of 1918, 1923, and 1934.

saw around him and remarked that even the army was lacking in spirit and idealism. This he attributed to the fact that Bulgaria, unlike the other states with which it had contact, had no official doctrine except opposition to party quarrels—the so-called *bezpartien rezhim*—and the government had been unsuccessful in elevating this doctrine to the level of an ideology. What the nation needed, Filov decided, was an idealistic program that could provide a rallying point against Bolshevism and a native alternative to foreign fascism.[39]

On September 15, 1942, Prime Minister Filov delivered an important speech at the Military Club in Sofia in which he attempted to set forth an ideological basis for the regime. Filov, though a distinguished scholar and archeologist, was not a gifted politician and his speech was a disappointment. He rejected the official creation of a single party, for this would have meant abandoning the basic principle of the bezpartien rezhim and would have led to the formation of opposition parties. The government's desire, he said, was for a society in which individuals rather than parties would play the leading role in the service of the nation. This, of course, ignored the fact that the bezpartien rezhim had long been a fiction: there was not one opposition bloc but three.

Filov's uninspiring ideology was hardly worthy of the name. He merely restated his April 15, 1942, declaration: "The main goal of our policy is to create a powerful and socially just national Bulgarian state in agreement with the principles of the new European order."[40] As Petko Stainov pointed out, there was nothing here that had not been said by every government since independence.[41] Yet there were two points in the speech that indicated the future policy of the government. First, the country was to unite around the person of the Tsar, who was to become the Bulgarian equivalent of the Duce and the Führer. This effort to use charisma instead of ideology had already been under way for a short time; references to the Tsar as the *Vozhd* or *Vodach*, in imitation of fascist titles, had lately become frequent. The opposition sharply criticized this practice because it was contrary to the Constitution and because it implied that the Tsar was abandoning his position of (theoretically) being above all politics.

Furthermore, the gesture was meaningless since the Tsar's powers were not changed, and his popularity could not be enhanced by giving him another title. What it did show was that Bulgaria was unable to create an original and effective ideology that could mobilize the people, and had instead committed itself to following the fascist patterns more closely. Second, the government was determined that Germany's strongest Bulgarian supporters, the Legionnaires and Ratnitsi, should be resolutely suppressed, although previously they had been tolerated because of their nationalism. They claimed they were not against Tsar Boris, but it was difficult to see what the Tsar's role would be in a state under their control.[42] General Lukov only commented that Filov's speech showed how afraid the government was, and he predicted that he would soon take power.[43]

Dimiter Peshev, Vice President of the Narodno Subranie, concluded in November 1942 that neither Filov's April declaration nor his September speech had produced any effect, for the regime still suffered from a lack of popular enthusiasm.[44] The problem was never really solved. The Tsar could at least be grateful that the Bulgarian people were more apathetic toward the enemies of his regime than they were toward the regime itself.

CHAPTER 9

The Jewish Question

ONE OF THE most revealing aspects of Nazi Germany's relations with its various allies and satellites was the extent to which these countries cooperated with Germany in her attempts to bring about a "final solution" of the Jewish question. The Jews in Bulgaria were numerically insignificant and—in contrast to other European countries—played little part in the country's academic, professional, or even economic life. As a result, anti-Semitism was virtually nonexistent; except for a few minor outbreaks around the turn of the century, there had been no pogroms in Bulgaria. The Legionnaires, Ratnitsi, and other nationalist groups adopted an anti-Semitic policy in imitation of the Nazis, but this position was generally regarded as of little relevance to Bulgarian conditions.

The Nazis and Bulgarian fascists produced statistics to discredit the Jews—for example, figures showing that the Jews did in fact have great economic importance and directly or indirectly controlled 35 to 80 percent of Bulgaria's trade. However, the only fact that could be convincingly shown was that the Jews owned larger amounts of stock per capita and had more money in the banks than the average Bulgarian, owing largely to their concentration in the cities. Dimiter Andreev, a Narodno Subranie deputy who collected many of these economic statistics, also tried to show that the Jews committed several times as many criminal acts per capita as the Bulgarians. The offenses selected for comparison were all in the economic category, based on incidents per 100,000 people over a four-year period. Since there were approximately 50,000 Bulgarian Jews, the most frequently cited figure of 4.95 incidents meant two Jews convicted for a particular offense during four years.[1]

The Nazi campaign against the Jews was linked with that against the Masons and other international organizations. As mentioned earlier, many or most of the leading government positions in Bulgaria were held by Masons, but these were men of many different political viewpoints and no Masonic "conspiracy" existed.* In May 1934, Germany had decreed that no member of the armed forces might belong to the Masons or other international secret organizations.[2] The Bulgarian fascists dutifully added to their program this opposition to secret societies and even included the Rotary Club and the Pen Club, which were not secret but international. In fact, Prime Minister Filov was then President of the Bulgarian Pen Club, and Slavcho Zagorov, a former minister of trade who replaced Draganov as Ambassador to Germany in 1942, was head of the Rotary Club. Nevertheless, under German pressure, Bulgaria ordered that the Masonic lodges should dissolve themselves in July 1940, and laws against the Masons and other international organizations were included in the subsequent legislation against the Jews.[3]

Legislation Against the Jews

In February 1939, about 6,000 Jews of foreign citizenship, many of whose families had lived in Bulgaria for generations, had been told that they would not receive extensions of their trade licenses and would be barred from making deliveries to the army and the public services.[4] In February 1940, however, Prime Minister Kioseivanov had reassured them that according to the Constitution all Bulgarians —including the Jews—were equal before the law.[5]

Then in September 1940, the Iron Guardists took control of Rumania and issued a number of Nazi-type decrees, including some placing restrictions on the Jews. "So as not to be behind Rumania in

---

* In 1936, for example, although the fascist Minister of War, General Lukov, was the only non-Mason member of the cabinet, two other fascist leaders, Alexander Tsankov and Todor Kozhuharov, were both Masons.

the expression of loyalty to Hitler," wrote Socialist politician Dimo Kazasov, "the Bulgarian Government proposed the 'Law for the Defense of the Nation.' "[6] In November 1940, a bitter debate erupted in the Narodno Subranie over the question of this comprehensive law against the Jews. Some of the supporters of the bill felt that even the fascist Professor Alexander Tsankov was not taking a strong enough line on this issue.*

Despite opposition by deputies Mushanov and Stainov, the law enacted was quite severe. As Raul Hilberg has pointed out, "In its effect, it was not exactly a mild law, for the Bulgarians did not start out with mildness. Restraint was applied only afterwards, when the prospects of a German victory began to fade."[7] Jews were forbidden to engage in a large number of occupations, and a *numerus clausus* was introduced to limit the percentage of Jews allowed to practice medicine, law, engineering, and a number of other professions, as well as to enter universities. Jews were not allowed to have gentile servants and were required to register their property and possessions; their dwelling places could not be changed, and money could not be sent out of the country.[8]

It should be pointed out, however, that the Bulgarian law was milder than might have been expected from the German models. First, the definition of a Jew was somewhat narrower than in the German edicts.[9] Second, Article 33 exempted the families of Jews who had been awarded medals for bravery, which meant that about one-tenth of the Jewish families in Bulgaria were freed from restrictions. This also affected the quota system, for it was decided not to include them in the *numerus clausus*, whose calculations were further modified by basing the percentages on the population of the cities rather than of the country as a whole. As a result, in Sofia the number of Jewish lawyers had to be reduced only from 20 to 18, engineers from 6 to 4, musicians from 14 to 8, and doctors from 21 to 13. Finally,

---

* A typical exchange in the Narodno Subranie went as follows. *Deni Kostov*: "Your place is in Palestine, Mr. Professor. I will send you there with the automobile of Zhak Aseov. You Jewish agent of Zhak Aseov!" *Alexander Tsankov*: "You are a bribe-taker! You have been in the service of Serbia! . . . You need to go to Palestine; I am a Bulgarian." XXV-NS, 2d reg. sess., 11th sitting, 15.xi.40, 1: 219.

though the law was passed by the Narodno Subranie in January 1941, it was not to go into full effect until six months later.[10] It should also be kept in mind that only one of the four sections of the "Law for the Defense of the Nation" dealt with the Jews; the others concerned secret organizations and conspiracies.

The plan to persecute the Jews met with widespread opposition from every corner of the nation. The Union of Bulgarian Lawyers described the law as "unnecessary, socially damaging, and contrary to our basic legal order"; the Doctors' Union declared that the purity of the nation could hardly be in danger; and the Union of Writers' petition, which included the name of the famous author Elin Pelin, warned that "this law would be very harmful" to the good name of the country.[11] Dimo Kazasov pointed out that it was strange to speak about the danger from a small number of Jews when there were 650,000 Turks and 70,000 Rumanians in the country who were the object of foreign propaganda, but no one was alarmed about them.[12] The Exarch Stefan, head of the Bulgarian Orthodox Church, described the sudden action against the Jews as "thunder from a clear sky" and told his priests not to refuse baptism to any convert who desired it.[13] The Tsar himself expressed dissatisfaction with the law and delayed signing it until February 15, 1941, on the grounds that he did not want to let such a severe law be enacted during the Christmas season.[14] In May 1941, when the Jewish Consistory sent its customary telegram of congratulations to the Tsar on his name day, he replied with a longer than usual note of thanks instead of ignoring the telegram as he might have done.[15]

Nevertheless, German insistence resulted in the enactment of many other regulations and restrictions on the Jews during the next eighteen months. Most important were the laws ordering (1) a special twenty percent tax on all Jewish possessions, and (2) the confiscation of mining property, pharmacies, stocks, insurance policies, and Jewish-owned houses except personal residences. Special permits were required for travel, although they were routinely issued until early 1942; radios were forbidden; and the yellow Star of David was to be worn.

To close any conceivable gaps in these laws, the government in June

1942 requested the passage of a special act giving the Council of Ministers the right to take any additional measures that might be deemed necessary. Interior Minister Gabrovsky said that such a law was needed because there had been many loopholes in the previous legislation and Jews were still operating freely in all spheres of Bulgarian life.[16] Docho Hristov, the main sponsor of the earlier Law for the Defense of the Nation, argued that the proposed law was really not as radical as it sounded, because the measures taken had to be approved afterward by the Narodno Subranie.[17] This bill encountered much opposition, even from many deputies who normally supported the government. Dimiter Andreev, a militant anti-Semite, said that whereas he favored strict laws against the Jews, the present bill was both unnecessary and dangerous; whenever the government desired any action on the Jewish question, he said, it should submit the request and let the Assembly vote, but there was no reason to rule by decree. Ivan Petrov and Krum Mitakov added that since the country was in no emergency, there was no justification for this dangerous precedent. Nevertheless, the "All Measures" law was passed by the Assembly in late June 1942 and was followed by a further series of severe restrictions on the Jews.[18]

Enacting laws was one thing, enforcing them was another. The best example was the law requiring Jews to wear a yellow star. Instead of requiring the Jews to make their own emblems, the government decided to have them manufactured; but the shortage of electricity considerably delayed production—or so the Germans were told. By October 1942, only enough stars had been made for twenty percent of the Jewish population; after a few days, many of those who had been given stars took them off. This disobedience was made possible, a German report said, by the "inactivity of the police and the complete indifference of the majority of the Bulgarian people." Many Jews had felt offended by the insignia at first but had received so much sympathy that they wore it proudly. Some even wore the yellow star alongside a picture of the Tsar.[19]

Opposition to the more extreme laws developed also among the leaders of the government, whose actions sometimes differed from their words. Perhaps the most striking example was that of Gabrovsky, the Minister of the Interior, who had been a sponsor of the anti-Jewish legislation. In September 1942, a group of 350 Jews gathered in front of the Ministry to protest its recent decisions. Gabrovsky saw them from his office and invited them into the courtyard where, to everyone's surprise, he talked to them for half an hour. The worst was over, he said, and they had no need to worry, for the government had foreseen everything. Then he stood at the gate and personally reassured each of the delegates that there was no danger. This incident caused consternation among the Germans and in the anti-Semitic Commissariat for Jewish Affairs.[20] That same day, Gabrovsky ordered the Bulgarian newspapers to make no mention of the Jewish question or the activities of the Commissariat; the situation was already determined, he said, and there was no point in alarming the people. He and Justice Minister Partov also informed Alexander Belev, the head of the Commissariat, that the Court and the Council of Ministers wanted some moderation in the action taken against the Jews; hence the Tsar had still not signed the law restricting the Jews to certain theaters and taverns.[21] Moreover, the Secretary of the Royal Court, Stanislav Balan, acting on orders of the Tsar himself, interceded directly with the Commissariat on behalf of a sick Jew who lived near the Tsar's summer palace.[22]

Doncho Uzunov, a deputy who had voted for the anti-Semitic laws, complained that their enforcement was frequently marked by cruelty and sadism, and said that some controls and supervision were necessary to prevent overzealous officials from exceeding the limits of humanity. The Exarch Stefan preached a sermon in which he said that God was punishing the Jews for their sins, but that God alone decided the fate of the Jews and man had no right to persecute them; on the contrary, it was the duty of all Christians to treat them as brothers and to help them in every way.[23]

Ambassador Beckerle, however, in his reports to Berlin denied that the government officials were lenient toward the Jews. One of the reasons that Bulgaria was reluctant to take action, he explained, was that many of the Jews were citizens of other countries, and these countries had protested against every restriction. (The foreign minister had collected these notes, which included several from Italy, Rumania, Hungary, Vichy France, and Spain, and had sent them to Belev and his Commissariat as a hint.) Beckerle, in defending the Bulgarian government from charges made by a disgruntled Bulgarian professor, stated that the idea that the Court was under Jewish influence was "stupid gossip."[24]

The Dannecker-Belev Agreement

Beckerle's report temporarily allayed suspicion in Berlin, but Bulgaria's future conduct would certainly be under close scrutiny. This was unfortunate, because the most important problem was yet to come —the German demand for "final solution" of the Jewish question. As early as December 1941, Hitler had informed Bulgaria and the other countries of Eastern Europe that Germany was willing to deport their Jews to the East (Poland, or later, occupied Russia) if they so desired. Bulgaria did not. In June 1942, Alexander Belev declared that the resettlement of the Jews would only be possible after the end of the war or when suitable land was taken from the allies in Africa or in the East, but he added that action could be taken sooner if Germany assumed the full responsibility for the task.[25] In this same month a new ordinance went into effect in the newly annexed parts of Macedonia and Belomorie (the Bulgarian name for Aegean Thrace) giving the inhabitants full Bulgarian citizenship unless they wished otherwise and left the country; Jews, however, were expressly denied the right to acquire citizenship. This suggested to some observers that the Jews would soon be deported.[26]

The first German move was to persuade Bulgaria to abandon its Jewish citizens residing in Germany. Hilberg says of this strategy, "The foreign Jews in the Reich were consequently used as a wedge. Once a foreign government had forsaken its Jews abroad, it was easier to induce it to give up its Jews at home."[27] Since only 30 Bulgarian Jews were then in Germany, Bulgaria saw no point in causing difficulty on this issue, even though both Italy and Hungary resisted similar demands. Germany had already deprived its Jews living abroad of German citizenship; about sixty were in Bulgaria, but the Bulgarian government never took any specific action against them.[28]

In September 1942, Ribbentrop ordered that all diplomatic efforts should be made to speed up the deportation of the Jews from the various countries of Europe, and he specifically mentioned Bulgaria. Beckerle reported that the Bulgarian government was delighted with the proposal but that there were certain difficulties; after all, if the government had been unable to deprive Jews of their Bulgarian citizenship, it was unlikely that more radical measures would be possible. Furthermore, he reported, because of the labor shortage in Bulgaria, Filov did not think that the adult male Jews could be spared from their present work of road construction; and the fee of 250 Reichsmarks that the Germans wanted to charge for every Jew "resettled" was considered much too high.[29]

It was now clear to the German government that the Tsar was reluctant to take drastic action against the Jews in Bulgaria, but the Nazis believed that he might be persuaded to allow the "resettlement" of the Jews from the newly annexed territories. In January 1943, SS-Hauptsturmführer (Captain) Theodore Dannecker came to Bulgaria as a special representative of Adolf Eichmann to negotiate with Belev for the deportation of the Macedonian and Thracian Jews. If some concession had to be made on the Jewish question, the Tsar preferred to sacrifice non-Bulgarian rather than Bulgarian Jews. Consequently, he gave his approval for the deportation but specified that he had "agreed only to the expulsion to the East of the Jews from the new lands. From the Bulgarian Jews themselves he wanted only a small number of Bolshevik-Communist elements."[30] The remaining Bulgarian Jews should be allowed to stay in the country because they were still urgently needed for road construction.[31]

This was the limit to which Belev was authorized to go, but during the treaty negotiations with Dannecker he made new computations and found that there were not 20,000 but only around 12,000 Jews in the new territories. To reach the desired quota, he needed to include 8,000 Bulgarian Jews in the deportation; he therefore marked out the limiting phrase "from the new Bulgarian lands, Thrace and Macedonia" from the draft copy of the treaty. Moreover, Belev decided that the Jews selected for the first deportation should be not the political activists, as the Tsar had directed, but rather the elite of each community.[32]

The Dannecker-Belev agreement was signed on February 22, 1943, and secret preparations were begun immediately to assemble the Jews in a few large camps. Border guards were increased to prevent escapes, for the authorities were aware that a few individual Jews had already learned of the plan. Indeed, the Jews of Skopie had been warned a few days earlier, although many had not believed it.[33] The plan called for the police in a given town to go to the homes of Jews in the early hours of the morning and order the families to pack their possessions within an hour or two. Then everyone would be assembled in some central place—in Skopie, for example, in an abandoned tobacco warehouse—where they could be kept for several weeks until deported.

The towns selected in Bulgaria proper were Plovdiv, Varna, Kyustendil, and later Sofia. The date was to be March 10, 1943. On March 2 the Council of Ministers, acting under the authority of the "All Measures" law, voted to deprive all Bulgarian Jews of their citizenship and to confiscate the property of those who had left the country.[34]

The Kyustendil Incident

The Kyustendil incident altered all the timetables.* One of Belev's officials, L. B. Panitza, had a Jewish mistress, whom he told of the plans for deporting the Jews of Kyustendil and other Bulgarian cities. She informed some friends in Kyustendil, who in turn contacted Yako Baruh, a Jewish lawyer in Sofia. Baruh and others then went to see Dimiter Peshev, Kyustendil's representative in the Narodno Subranie and vice president of that body.

Peshev had heard nothing about these plans and refused to believe the story until he had telephoned the chief of police in Kyustendil, who confirmed it. Peshev then hurriedly arranged a meeting with Interior Minister Gabrovsky to protest the deportation orders. Ga-

---

* The following account is based on a number of sources. The two most important are the typed statement of Yako Baruh (Archive of the Sofia Synagogue, folder 62) and Arditti, *Yehuday Bulgaria*, pp. 286–88, 294–96. See also report of Boris Tasey, representative of the Commissariat in Kyustendil, to chief inspector Popov, n.d., Archive of the Sofia Synagogue; and Filov, *Dnevnik*, 11.iii.43 and 15.iii.43.

brovsky at first denied the existence of such orders; but when told the details of the Kyustendil operation, he informed Filov and asked for instructions. Filov replied that the orders could not be changed. The delegation went home in despair.

The next morning, they learned that the situation had changed completely. The orders had been canceled; those orders that had already been sent out were countermanded and the Jews were released. The reasons for this change are still a subject of much controversy. The Peshev group knew only that Gabrovsky had left the Assembly at eleven that night; at midnight he had returned and without explanation had said that the orders were canceled. Beckerle reported that the deportation had been stopped on orders "from the highest authority," but he knew little else.

Many non-Communist historians, including Benjamin Arditti, have given the credit to the Tsar, for he made the final decisions in the country and it is unlikely that Filov would have dared to endanger relations with Germany on his own responsibility. Many of the Jews in Bulgaria and Israel today certainly believe it was the Tsar who saved them.[35] The Communists have never accepted this theory; they claim it was the protests of the Communist Party and the popular masses that averted the deportation, and in December 1966 staged an exhibition in Sofia to prove this point.[36]

Accounts of the incident differ enough to make a variety of interpretations possible, but the traditional view still seems the most probable. Boris did prefer to leave the unpleasant details to Belev's Commissariat, but one fact is beyond question—if the Tsar had wanted the Jews to be deported, they would have been. The anti-Jewish measures were certainly unpopular with the Bulgarian people, but this fact was as much an excuse as a reason for not deporting the Jews. The limits on the ability of the Bulgarian government to stave off the German demands were shown during the next few months.

Because the respite granted to the Jews was expected to be short-lived, Peshev began gathering support for his position among the members of the Narodno Subranie. On the morning of March 19, 1943, he presented Filov with a petition signed by 43 deputies, including a number very friendly toward Germany. Even Alexander Tsankov had signed the list. Filov was disgusted and said, "Now I really see how much influence the Jews have and how harmful they are."[37] Slaveiko Vasilev, a deputy in the Assembly and a former cabinet minister, led the opposition to Peshev's petition in the Narodno Subranie and accused Peshev of disloyalty and of bringing disgrace upon the Assembly.* After a long and difficult debate on March 24, 114 representatives voted their support for the government. Peshev himself was censured by a vote of 66 to 33.[38]

The Jews from Macedonia and Thrace, however, did not benefit from this short respite. They had been arrested on the night of March 3 and taken to deportation camps set up near a dozen large towns, from which they were sent by train and boat to the Treblinka death camp. Of about 11,400 deported, only about seventy ever returned.[39] One of the Tsar's advisers, Lulchev, said that Boris disapproved of the expulsions, for when the subject of the Skopie deportations came up in a conversation on June 1, Boris again became very depressed and repeated several times, "Here, take my head, take my head!"[40]

Beckerle reported to Berlin in early April 1943 that Bulgaria's determination to settle the Jewish question had not been affected by the Kyustendil incident and that the government's only concern was to deal with the matter as quickly as possible to avoid reactions from the world press.[41] Boris met Ribbentrop, however, and told him that permission had been given only for resettlement of the Jews in the new territories; the others he wanted to keep in Bulgaria to work on the roads. Ribbentrop decided not to push the issue but said only that Germany believed the radical solution was the best.[42]

Since the use of Jewish labor for road construction was Boris's justification for not immediately resettling the Bulgarian Jews, the Germans decided to investigate. At the time, 6,000 adult male Jews were in the construction crews, and another 8,000 were soon to be added, comprising almost all those capable of heavy labor. The German investigators reported, however, that the labor teams had accomplished

---

* Notes on the personalities: the Germans excused Tsankov on the grounds that he was only expressing a general opposition to the government; Slaveiko Vasilev later became a leading member of the Bagryanov cabinet of 1944; Dimiter Peshev was spared by the People's Court after the war because of his role in the Jewish affair and also his refusal to sign the execution order of Damian Velchev in 1935.

very little and that the crew members had to work only a few hours a day. In comparison, the few Greek labor teams worked twelve hours a day. The obvious conclusion, therefore, was that the Jewish labor service had little practical value and was merely a pretext for postponing evacuation.[43]

The Bulgarian government had been trying for several months to arrange for the Jews to be sent instead to Palestine, or at least for a group of 4,000 children to go there. (Former American Minister Earle had arrived in Istanbul as the new American naval attaché, and the Germans believed he was involved in the arrangements.) Germany had rejected the Palestine plan as early as February 15, 1943, before the signing of the Dannecker-Belev agreement, on the grounds that it would be used by British propagandists and would displease the Arabs.[44] The Rumanians had allowed a certain number of Jews to leave for Palestine, but over 750 were drowned when their unseaworthy ship sank near Istanbul. A few Rumanian Jews were allowed to transit Bulgaria, although the Bulgarian government had promised the Germans that this would not be permitted. Bulgaria had also told Germany that it had no intention of honoring its promise to the Swiss Red Cross that the Rumanian Jews would go to Palestine. Nevertheless, the Bulgarian government had provided transit visas and had asked a Swedish ship to stand by at the port of Dedeagach.[45]

The Germans were growing impatient. Dannecker complained that he had six ships waiting to assist in the deportation and that each day of delay cost 20,000 leva. Boris was also running out of excuses. Finally, toward the end of May 1943, he agreed to expel all but the privileged Jews from Sofia and place them in temporary camps, where they could be kept until deported. This order became known in Sofia on May 23, and on the 25th a large crowd gathered in front of the Royal Palace to protest. Sixty-three eminent Bulgarians sent an appeal to the Tsar, and the Exarch Stefan gave refuge to the Chief Rabbi of Sofia.[46]

The protests were to no avail: the Jews were herded into the provinces where their deportation was considered imminent. Bulgaria had given in to every German request except the last and most important —deportation of the Jews to the death camps. "It was as though the degree of involvement had already been predetermined. The operation was brought to a halt as if stopped by an invisible sign which said, 'So far and no farther.' "[47] Dr. Chapuisat of the International Red Cross visited Sofia and was assured that no Jews would be sent out of Bulgaria. His trip also had the effect of easing, for a time, German pressure on Bulgaria, because Beckerle and the German police attaché in Bulgaria, Otto Hoffmann, told Berlin, "for this reason, no pressure can at present be exerted on the Bulgarian Government to send Jews to the East." And they added, "On general political grounds and with regard for the Bulgarian mentality, the expulsion should be the desire of the Bulgarians themselves."[48]

The attitude of the German Ambassador to Bulgaria, Beckerle, toward the Jewish question is not completely clear. A dedicated Nazi who had been a member of the 1932 Reichstag and then head of the Frankfurt police, Beckerle had the high rank of Obergruppenführer (Colonel-General) in the SA at the age of 35. It therefore seems inconceivable that he would have had any but the most orthodox Nazi views concerning the Jews, although not surprisingly he has written to the author that he was responsible for saving the Bulgarian Jews from deportation.[49] Normally this claim would not be taken seriously. However, both Hannah Arendt and Gerald Reitlinger have stated that Beckerle's reports to Berlin discouraged Germany from putting more pressure on Bulgaria to persecute the Jews. It is true that many of the cables he sent during this period were the barest minimum that he could do and still keep the confidence of his superiors. Since the war, neither the Russians (who held him until late 1955) nor the Bonn government has been able to convict him for war crimes.[50]

The Sparing of the Jews

The sending of the Jews to the provinces caused food and housing problems in a country already troubled by both. The Germans therefore expected that the Bulgarians would be only too happy to see the Jewish problem quickly taken off their hands. Since many of the expellees were quartered in school buildings that would be needed again in the autumn, this seemed to put a limit on the time the "final solution" could be delayed.[51]

The possibility of an Allied landing in the Balkans caused the Germans to worry about the threat posed by 50,000 enemies located behind the German main lines of defense. This increased their desire to see the Jewish problem solved as soon as possible.[52] Bulgaria was also aware of the strategic situation, but for a different reason. It was widely believed in Bulgaria, as in Hungary, that Allied bombers had refrained from attacking the cities for fear of killing many Jews; with the Jews now out of the main cities, even more caution must be exerted to forestall Allied bombing.[53]

Germany sought the assistance of the Bulgarian air force to defend the Rumanian oil fields, which had recently been bombed, and also requested Bulgarian support in the propaganda campaign against the person of Stalin. The Germans felt that for the time being the final solution of the Jewish question should not be pursued, so as not to jeopardize these other requests. The death of Tsar Boris on August 28, 1943, also diverted attention from the Jewish question. It had become clear by then that Bulgaria would reject all further German demands concerning the Jews on the grounds that persecution would create internal complications. Thus, little more could be expected until Germany had gained some new military victories.[54]

For the remainder of the war, the Jews remained in villages and makeshift camps, living in uneasy tranquility. The less fortunate ones lived in such camps as Samobit, where the daily ration was 300 grams of bread and bean soup so watery that, in the words of one inmate, "the tiny beans could only be found with submarines."[55] More fortunate ones benefited from the sympathy of the neighboring peasants and ate much better than if they had remained in the cities. At least they were all spared the air raids that struck Sofia during the latter part of 1943 and early 1944. The Jews continued to fear that Germany would one day remember the Jewish problem —there were panics in February 1944 and in the summer of that year—but the Germans apparently had forgotten about the Bulgarian Jews. Perhaps by then they had other things to worry about.

CHAPTER 10

The Allied Threat

❧

GERMANY'S POSITION at Stalingrad at the beginning of 1943 had become so critical that even the strongest Bulgarian Germanophiles were alarmed. Filov himself was disturbed. On January 26, 1943, he wrote: "I am convinced that sooner or later the Germans will cope with the situation, but I am afraid of the political reverberations, not only in our country, but especially in Rumania and Hungary." Despite his general optimism, he admitted that recently he had had "several sleepless nights."[1] At the beginning of February 1943, the German Sixth Army at Stalingrad finally surrendered. The Tsar, who usually became despondent at the slightest setback, took the news with surprising calmness.[2] The full significance of Stalingrad was not immediately perceived; it was recognized as a serious setback, to be sure, but was not considered a permanent one. Even in Germany, one diarist wrote, "The masses have taken the disaster calmly. Only a very few are capable of appreciating the full implications of the tragedy. The official communiqué is so tersely worded that only those in the know can interpret it correctly."[3] The Bulgarian Minister of War, General Mihov, met Hitler in mid-February and returned to Bulgaria with little anxiety about the defeat at Stalingrad; when Boris talked with Beckerle a few days later, his only comment was praise for von Kleist's "military masterpiece" of a withdrawal.[4]

Another reason for the Tsar's continued confidence may have been the belief—shared and perhaps inspired by Hitler—that the alliance

between Moscow and the West was built on such irreconcilable differences that it would soon come apart, particularly if the Soviet
Union began to seem a greater threat than Germany. Thus Stalingrad could conceivably work to the benefit of the Axis. Filov remarked, "It would not surprise me if after some great Russian successes the British reduced or stopped shipment to Russia" in order
to prolong the war and exhaust both the continental powers.[5] By the
end of March 1943, however, the Tsar's ephemeral optimism had
evaporated and he once again was convinced that Germany had
already lost the war.[6]

Stalingrad marked a turning point in the war, and this gradual
realization had an enormous effect upon Bulgaria during the coming
months. The Communist Party, which had shriveled in the autumn
of 1941, slowly began to revive. Yet it would be wrong to exaggerate
the impact of Stalingrad on the Bulgarian government at this time.
Perhaps the government should have been more concerned, but the
available evidence indicates that it was not. The main cause of Bulgarian anxiety during this period was not the danger from the Soviet
Union, but the threat of Allied intervention through Turkey. The
Allies had defeated the Germans in North Africa and had large forces
poised in the Mediterranean to open a second front, whereas the Red
army still seemed far away on the steppes.

In early January 1943, General Mihov had gone to Germany to discuss the defense of the Balkans with Hitler and to reach an agreement on the German-Bulgarian command structure in the event of
an Allied invasion. Bulgaria would need German divisions if invaded, but the Bulgarian government did not want to give Germany
complete control of military operations.* The two parties had finally
agreed that if Turkey should attack Bulgaria, Bulgaria would direct
the combined forces and German troops in the area would come under Bulgarian command; if the attack were made by Britain on the
Aegean coast, as was more likely, Germany would have the supreme
command. Germany had a low opinion of the Bulgarian generals,

---

* To make certain that no unfavorable commitments were made, the Tsar had sent
his close friend and adviser, Yordan Sevov, to the conference disguised as a captain.

but since it regarded an attack from Turkey as unlikely, this concession to Bulgaria's national pride was acceptable.[7]

The German evaluation of the Turkish situation was summarized by Morrell, the air attaché in Ankara: (1) the Turks would like to stay neutral; (2) they have an enormous fear of Russia, which is "out for their hide" (*das ihnen ans Leder wolle*); (3) they will fight if we invade; (4) they would not fight if England undertook to do something in Turkey.[8] It was this fourth possibility that alarmed Bulgaria, for during January 1943 Prime Minister Churchill and Turkish President Ismet Inönü met in Adana, Turkey, and agreed on the so-called "Adana lists," which included a provision that "Even should Germany not attack Turkey, Turkish interests may dictate that she intervene in the Balkans to prevent anarchy. Such a condition could arise as a result of increasing German weakness, trouble in Bulgaria, a quarrel between Rumania and Hungary over Transylvania, or more extensive Greek or Yugoslav resistance." There were also reports of an increasing number of British and Americans entering Turkey, presumably to prepare the way for the basing of Allied aircraft in that country. Numerous long-range bombers were reportedly stationed at Aleppo, Syria, giving credibility to the report that the Allies were planning to bomb a Balkan city that spring. (German Intelligence did not yet know which city, but the name was said to begin with the letter "S," meaning either Salonika or Sofia.)[9]

While in Germany, Mihov had assured the Germans that the Bulgarian army was well trained and in good spirits but woefully ill equipped; he feared panic might result if the Allies attacked. The Bulgarian government therefore began an intensive effort to persuade Germany to send more arms—especially tanks, planes, and heavy weapons.[10] Bulgaria also passed along the rumor that Stalin had recently demanded the opening of a second front in the Balkans, although even the Bulgarian Ambassador admitted that this rumor was not credible. Furthermore, Bulgaria pointed to the British-Turkish military negotiations in Ankara and the arrival of the former American Minister to Bulgaria, Earle, as American naval attaché to Turkey. The Tsar believed that Turkey could be trusted for the time being because of the war situation, but he did fear an Allied landing on Crete and the Peloponnesus.[11]

A preemptive attack on Turkey was still a popular idea in Bulgaria. Hitler told Boris at their meeting on March 31, 1943, that Germany remained firmly against such an attack despite believing that Turkey would move closer and closer toward Great Britain.[12] Fear of Russia was expected to keep Turkey cautious about involvement in the war, but Bulgaria had little confidence in Turkish neutrality and erroneously regarded the Turks as the main threat to Bulgarian security.[13]

The Allied Conditions for Peace

The German reverses in Russia and North Africa and the expected invasion of southeastern Europe prompted a number of Bulgarian officials independently to seek contact with the West to sound out the possibility of Bulgaria's leaving the war. They did not believe the war was necessarily lost but thought it desirable to ascertain the Allied attitude "just in case." The Germans knew the Bulgarians well enough to expect them to contact the Allies as soon as Axis fortunes began to wane, and the fact that Germany had broken the Bulgarian diplomatic code in 1942 proved useful in confirming this suspicion.*

In 1943, for the first time, Germany began asking questions about the activities and movements of certain high Bulgarian officials. For example, the Tsar's confidant, Yordan Sevov, made an official trip to Istanbul early in 1943 ostensibly to investigate the intentions of the Turkish government toward Bulgaria, but rumors circulated that he had actually gone to meet a representative of the Allies, Angel Kuyumdzhiisky. This man, who had been a prominent Bulgarian financier before the war, was acting as a representative of the Allies with the rank of colonel in the United States Army. It is doubtful, however, that Sevov met him or any other Allied representative at this time.[14]

---

* The Germans periodically circulated copies of important intercepted messages in a top secret brown booklet nicknamed "The Brown Friend."

Allen Dulles, the American intelligence chief in Switzerland, was in contact with the Bulgarian Consul in Geneva, M. H. Milev, and tried unsuccessfully to use him to reach the Ambassador, former Prime Minister Georgi Kioseivanov. Milev informed Sofia of the developments and reported that "Kioseivanov had categorically rejected all attempts to enter into connection with him"; but, he suggested, "it would be useful for us to know what the Americans are thinking and what their intentions are concerning relations with Bulgaria, and at the same time to let them know our problem."[15]

It must be said that the Allies themselves were making no great effort to encourage Bulgaria's defection from the Axis. Two issues were important obstacles to a Bulgarian settlement with the Allies: the Allied demand for unconditional surrender, and their unwillingness to promise that Bulgaria would retain its territorial gains. At the Casablanca conference in January 1943, Churchill and Roosevelt had agreed that unconditional surrender should be required of Germany and Japan, although there was some sentiment for excluding Italy in order to encourage the breakup of the Axis at its weakest link. The British War Cabinet, however, decided that "it would be better to include Italy, because of the misgivings that might otherwise be caused in Turkey, the Balkans and elsewhere."[16] Thus, no exceptions to that policy were to be allowed.

Also, no concessions were offered on the territorial issue. The U.S. Secretary of State, Cordell Hull, informed the American representative in Ankara:

The Department has received an increasing number of reports indicating the desire of various of the so-called "satellite states" to establish contact with official or unofficial representatives of the U.S. All of these reports have one common element: the individuals desire assurance that their territories will be maintained at the end of the war.

... Although the Department has no direct reports, it is clear that a number of Bulgarians are endeavoring to do the same thing in Turkey.

The Department has uniformly declined to permit discussions, although it has not interfered with the gathering of information from these, and other enemy nationals, by the Intelligence service.[17]

The British government was no more enthusiastic about talks with the Bulgarians, for in April 1943 a note to the U.S. Department of State contained this passage:

His Majesty's Government have hitherto received no indications of peace feelers from the Bulgarian Government. If any approaches are made in the future it will be open to His Majesty's Government to decide on their merits whether or not they should be pursued. It should be borne in mind, however, that any negotiations between His Majesty's Government and the Bulgarians would at once arouse the deepest suspicion on the part of the Greek, Yugoslav and Turkish Governments.[18]

The American reply to the above note summarized the official attitude in Washington that the contacts made so far by the Bulgarians were not serious enough to warrant more encouragement:

The general tenor of reports reaching the Department indicates that the Bulgarian people, as compared with the Huns, are less ready to admit the mistakes of their Government's policy, or to take the positive action which would be necessary if they are to make any effective contribution to the defeat of the Axis. It may be suspected, in whatever peace-feelers may have been made thus far, of emanating from official quarters. The Department therefore believes that the agencies concerned with the state of public opinion in Bulgaria should intensify their efforts to bring about a change in Bulgarian mentality, preliminary to any indication of interest in anything Bulgarian spokesmen may have to say.[19]

The Germans were unaware of the contents of these notes, but they were concerned about a trip to Turkey in March 1943 by a man named Lyuben Pulev. German intelligence sources had discovered that Pulev had used a diplomatic passport and suspected that he had gone to confer with Earle. Tsar Boris denied that the trip had any significance or that Pulev was a figure of any importance; Pulev's diplomatic passport, he said, dated from an earlier period.* This and the Sevov incident earlier in the year showed that Germany was at least somewhat concerned about the loyalty of its Balkan partner.

---

* Exhaustive inquiries by the Germans soon revealed that Pulev had been a close friend of Earle and was thought to be an Allied agent, possibly with access to an airplane belonging to the Bulgarian commercial attaché in Bucharest. Ribbentrop-Boris talks, Berlin, 4.iv.43, SSF, T120 255.173890–91; Beckerle, Sofia, 21.iv.43, SSF, T120 255.173902–3.

But surprisingly, during the next year and a half, Germany made few attempts to protest or prevent Bulgarian contacts with the Allies. By the end of 1943, these contacts were common knowledge, and by mid-1944 they were carried on almost openly. Yet Germany did not interfere.

One explanation might be that Bulgaria was trusted so much that these contacts were not taken seriously. But former Ambassador Beckerle has hinted at another explanation: "These contacts with the Allies were known to us and took place with the consent of Hitler, who wanted thereby to test certain possibilities."[20] This unfortunately raises more questions than it answers, and at present no more is known, but the point should be kept in mind during the remaining chapters.

The summer of 1943 saw a renewal of interest in peace negotiations. In July, the former Bulgarian Ambassador to Great Britain, Nikola Momchilov, who had resigned in protest against the Tripartite Pact in 1941, sent a letter to Purvan Draganov recommending that Bulgaria join Great Britain at once in driving Germany from the Balkans. Draganov said he could not act on this matter himself since it would be treason, but he did forward the letter to Filov, who in turn rejected all responsibility for it but passed it on to the Tsar. There it seems the matter ended.[21] The former British Ambassador to Bulgaria, Sir George Rendel, did not have much more success with Kioseivanov. After a three-and-a-half-hour talk with Filov, Kioseivanov informed Rendel that Filov still believed in a German victory. The Allied refusal to guarantee Bulgaria's new frontiers remained a major obstacle, and after the meeting Kioseivanov declared, "We are unable to make any deviations from our policy, which is guided by our aspiration for national unity."[22]

The Bulgarian government, however, did authorize its diplomatic mission in Switzerland to use a Swiss official to contact Allen Dulles's group in that country. It hoped that perhaps the Americans would be more sympathetic to Bulgarian irredentism and more willing to recognize its territorial acquisitions. This did not prove to be the case. The Americans replied that no guarantees could be made before a peace conference, except that Bulgaria's right to the Southern Dobruja might possibly be recognized.[23]

These attempts to find a basis for negotiations were adversely affected by the extremely hard line the Allies took against the regime of Tsar Boris. The magnitude of this hostility toward Bulgaria is illustrated by an Aide-Mémoire from the British Embassy in Washington to the U.S. Department of State: "His Majesty's Government therefore regard Bulgaria's inclusion in the Axis as the result of a deliberate decision taken with full knowledge and warning of the consequences. They refuse to recognize the annexation by Bulgaria of Greek and Yugoslav territory and *they regard themselves in no way committed to the survival of the sovereign Bulgarian state* [emphasis added]."[24] British Ambassador Rendel had repeatedly warned Boris against joining the Axis, and now the Tsar was to pay for his actions. The British plan suggested the creation of a South East Europe Confederation that would include Bulgaria, but no assurances were to be given that Bulgaria would be allowed to participate as a national entity. This confederation would also take care of the problem of dealing with the Bulgarian monarchy:

As regards His Majesty's Government's attitude towards the Saxe-Coburg dynasty, it will be recalled that the present war is the third occasion on which a member of this House has been party to a treacherous attack on one of its neighbors. The responsibility in the present instance cannot be transferred from the King to the Bulgarian Government, who are regarded by the Bulgarian people as the creatures of their King, and are so in fact. If the future of South East Europe is on a federal basis, there will, moreover, be no place for a Bulgaria ruled over by a member of the present royal House because of the natural and justified feelings of rancour with which he could be regarded by the neighbouring states, and particularly the royal Houses of Yugoslavia and Greece. *His Majesty's Government therefore cannot have any dealings with King Boris, whose fate they regard as a matter of indifference, any more than they can have with the present government* [emphasis added]. The King is a man of no little ability and cunning, but morally weak and incapable of courageous decision, a true son of his father. Any attempts to give him support in the hopes of detaching Bulgaria from the Axis would probably fail and we should merely compromise ourselves in the eyes of our Balkan allies and the world besides laying up for ourselves incalculable difficulties in our plans for the future of South Eastern Europe.

... We can make no promises and give no undertakings regarding the future of Bulgaria, and the Bulgarian people must trust that by honourable capitulation they will find the only way out of their present misery.[25]

Thus there was little basis for negotiations between Bulgaria and the Anglo-Americans. It is understandable that Bulgaria was not enthusiastic about the Rumanian suggestion on August 16 that the two countries should allow the Anglo-Saxons to take over the Balkan peninsula to save it from Bolshevism.[26] When former Foreign Minister Ivan Popov went to Filov in August and told him that the seriousness of the international situation made it incumbent upon Bulgaria to have at least some contacts with the Allies, Filov replied that it was "still early" for this.[27]

The Threat of an Allied Invasion

In the summer of 1943, Bulgaria was filled with rumors of an imminent Allied invasion of the Balkans. The French General Giraud had established a pro-Allied government in North Africa in March 1943 and Axis resistance ceased there in May. The Allies were expected to strike north from Africa sometime during the summer. The Allies had encouraged the belief that they would land in the Balkans because they wanted to distract Germany's attention from Sicily, the actual site of the planned operation. The British "Operation Mincemeat," involving the placing of misleading documents on the body of a British military officer supposedly drowned off the Spanish coast, successfully deceived German intelligence about the location of the next Allied attack. On May 14, Admiral Doenitz wrote: "The Führer does not agree with the Duce that the most likely invasion is Sicily. Furthermore, he believes that the discovered Anglo-Saxon order confirms the assumption that the planned attack will be directed mainly against Sardinia and the Peloponnesus."[28] Hitler remained so certain that even two weeks after the Allied landings in Sicily he still believed them a feint and sent Field Marshal Rommel to Greece to take command of the troops there.

With an invasion of Greece expected, Germany wanted to dispatch all available troops to the threatened area. When Boris again visited Hitler at the beginning of June 1943, he was requested to extend Bulgaria's zone of occupation once more to free German troops for the defense of the Peloponnesus. Bulgaria put aside its fear of Turkey and hesitantly yielded to the German request. General Mihov, despite his firm sympathies with Germany, worried that Bulgaria's forces were so overextended that the request should have been declined. Filov discounted this objection, for he said that Bulgaria's compliance on this issue would strengthen a later claim to German military support.[29]

Germany wanted Bulgaria's help not only in the occupation of the Balkans but also in the defense of the entire peninsula. The Italians were uneasy about the military situation in the Balkans, and to reassure them Ribbentrop promised that "at the moment the Anglo-Saxons would undertake an invasion of the Balkans, Bulgaria would jump in line with us with twenty-eight divisions."[30] Despite this promise, the Bulgarian government had not changed its intention of remaining out of the war.[31]

On July 10, 1943, the Allied forces invaded southern Europe, not in the Balkans, as expected, but in Sicily. Rome and Naples were attacked from the air, and by July 22, half of Sicily had fallen to the invaders. Then on Sunday, July 25, came the news that Mussolini had been overthrown by a group of his closest supporters and that Marshal Badoglio had formed a new government. Three days later, the Fascist Party was dissolved. Badoglio assured the Germans that Italy would continue to honor its obligations, but his government was actually preparing to make a separate peace. Bulgarian officials were much relieved by Badoglio's statement of continued loyalty to the Axis, but the Tsar himself realized that the change in government was no mere palace revolution. The Italian fascist regime had collapsed, and Boris did not believe that Italy would continue the war any longer than was necessary.[32]

The Rumanian dictator, Marshal Ion Antonescu, was greatly alarmed by the events in Italy and sent a proposal to Bulgaria that the two countries should prepare for the joint defense of their territory. Antonescu explained that this would in no way change relations with Germany, but it was evident that he no longer had complete faith in German protection. Filov informed Beckerle of the offer, including Antonescu's assurance that it would not affect either country's attitude toward Germany. Beckerle replied that discussions on Balkan defense measures might be useful, but Ribbentrop was clearly not pleased by the plan. Bulgaria seemed less concerned about the merits of Antonescu's proposal than about the opportunity it provided to win favor with Germany by revealing Antonescu's intentions. Filov told Beckerle on this occasion that "our relations with Germany are radically different from those of Hungary and Rumania with Germany.... There is much similarity in the character and mentality of the Germans and Bulgarians ... and the Government cannot undertake anything in foreign policy without Germany."[33]

The Murder of General Lukov

During the first half of 1943, the internal situation in Bulgaria altered considerably. The nationalist opposition, which had been a major concern for the Tsar, declined sharply in importance owing to the death of its leader, while the Communists once again became a nuisance, if not yet a threat. On February 13, General Hristo Lukov, the extreme Germanophile and leading member of the nationalist opposition, was shot dead by unknown assassins. The police believed that he had been killed by the same person or persons who had recently murdered a police agent, as both men were reportedly killed by the same gun. Despite a substantial reward of 300,000 leva, the usually efficient Sofia police were baffled by the assassination.[34]

The initial assumption was that the Communists were responsible for the murder, and since the war they have claimed the credit, but speculation quickly arose concerning the incident. One theory, which was accepted by British Intelligence, was that Lukov's murder was the result of his initial support but subsequent betrayal of Georgiev, Velchev, and Zaimov in the 1934 coup, for which he had been rewarded with the post of Minister of War under Kioseivanov. Lukov was also believed partly responsible for the arrest and execution of General Zaimov in 1942, although there is no evidence that he was in any way involved.[35] A more popular theory was that the murder had been carried out by agents of the Tsar, and this suspicion increased as the days passed without an arrest. Lukov had been a source of considerable anxiety to Boris, and no one benefited more than the Tsar from his death. The Legionnaires and Ratnitsi themselves believed that the assassination was the signal for a full-scale purge directed against them, and during the next few days they made frantic efforts to prepare for action.[36] Assassination had been so common in recent Bulgarian history, especially during the turbulent interwar period, that this belief did not seem unreasonable.

Filov told Boris four days after Lukov's death that public curiosity could not be satisfied merely by saying that the murder had been committed by a "foreign hand" or "enemies of Bulgaria." People were beginning to ask questions, he said, and suspicion would fall on the government unless the true killers were found. Filov believed that there was no question but that the Communists were responsible because of the evidence of the gun, but this had to be proved irrefutably. "We need to use this killing," he said, "to strengthen the fight against the Communists and likewise against the Jews."[37] The Tsar and Sevov believed that the assassination had been the work of the Turks, with the help of the British, since Lukov was known to be so violently anti-Turkish that he had delighted in throwing pork down Turkish wells.

On April 15, 1943, another assassination occurred. Sotir Yanev, the chairman of the Foreign Affairs Committee in the Narodno Subranie and a leading supporter of the regime, was shot down by two people in front of his Sofia law office only a day after he had delivered a strongly pro-German speech. Some two weeks later terrorists struck again, killing Colonel Pantev (the "Black Panther"), the former director of police who had become head of the Sofia Military Tribunal. He had had close ties with Lukov and had been suspected by the Tsar of planning a coup in 1942. Two suspects were arrested by the police, but could not be connected with the affair.*

The government could hardly delay taking drastic measures to find those responsible for the murders. On May 5, the entire city of Sofia was blockaded and a house-to-house search conducted. Fifty known Communists were discovered in hiding, including some who had been sentenced to death in absentia, but the government was unable to connect any of them with the recent events. Then on May 10, an attempt was made on the life of Kulcho Yanakiev, a relatively minor official who was an adviser on radio matters to the Director of National Propaganda working on the jamming of foreign broadcasts. He was only slightly wounded, but both of his assailants were captured: a man and a woman belonging to a Communist terrorist group. On May 25 Yanakiev was attacked again. This time he escaped harm, but his would-be killer was shot down by the police after a long gun battle. The flurry of police activity and the blockade discouraged the Communist efforts at urban terrorism: "After these actions, the position of fighting groups in Sofia became much more difficult. Only in Sofia did individual fighters remain."[38]

The government was also facing the challenge of renewed militant street demonstrations, owing to the improvement of Communist morale after Stalingrad. The anniversary of the 1878 Treaty of San Stefano and Bulgaria's liberation from the Turks was on March 3. On the previous evening, the Bulgarian Communist Party ordered the Russian memorial and other monuments to be decorated with flowers and banners. It also distributed mimeographed leaflets bearing such slogans as "Long live our liberator—the Russian people," "Not one soldier for the Eastern Front," and "Down with the government of Bogdan Filov." The next day a crowd of two thousand people gathered in the area between the University and the Narodno Subranie building, where they were met by police with drawn pistols

---

* The details and even the dates of these killings vary considerably in different accounts. Pantev's murder was on May 3, not in April as some have said. Details on ballistics and pattern of attack are quite unclear, owing partially to the frequent confusion in Bulgarian accounts of the Lukov killing with that of Yanev.

who tried to force them back. One medical student who had been an active Communist for eleven years was killed, and 300 other people were arrested. It is interesting, however, to note the leniency with which those arrested were treated by the courts. Of the 300, six were sent to provincial villages (the so-called "domestic exile") and fifteen to camps in Thrace; all the rest were merely booked and released.[39]

Also in 1943, for the first time since 1939, there was a large May Day demonstration in Sofia. In fact, Communist historians claim that the demonstration was so large and menacing that the Tsar was forced to flee the city.* The March and May demonstrations were a portent of what could happen if Bulgaria's international position continued to decline, and were a warning that more drastic police measures would be needed in the future. At this time, for example, there was still no prohibition against listening to foreign broadcasts, although the Russian-based "Hristo Botev" radio station was attracting a growing number of listeners.[40] Also, pro-Communist students had benefited from the government's policy of maintaining the "political purity of the army," which had exempted them from military service. In February 1943, however, the government finally decided that these students could perhaps be kept under closer observation if they were in the army, and many of them were inducted.[41]

A consistent policy seems to have been lacking in the government's treatment of arrested Communists. On the one hand, a surprising number of Party members and even captured partisans were able to secure their release from prison, usually through the intercession of their Narodno Subranie representative, who in many cases was a person of unquestionably anti-Communist views. It is still not clear how this procedure worked or why the government tolerated it.[42] On the other hand, captured Communists were often treated with great brutality by the police, who paid little attention to the niceties of the law. Execution was a favorite means of dealing with partisans: prison-

---

* The Tsar left Sofia for Plovdiv during the last week in April; almost certainly he did not come back to the capital until the Monday or Tuesday following the May Day weekend. Thus, the dramatic account of his flight from the city is probably false: see *Utro* (Sofia), 1.v.43 and 5.v.43.

ers were shot or burned alive in special furnaces under the Sofia headquarters. Suspects were held without charge much longer than the
statutory six months. Brutality toward the Communists increased
sharply with the revival of the partisan movement in mid-1943, and
before long it became standard practice to cut off the heads of killed
or captured partisans and bring them in for a reward.[43]

CHAPTER II

The Bulgarian Occupation of Macedonia

꙾

No WORD HAD more magic for the Bulgarian people than "Macedonia." This rugged and barren territory in what is today southern Yugoslavia and northern Greece was a principal reason for Bulgaria's involvement in two unsuccessful wars—the Second Balkan War and the First World War—and was a major factor in Bulgarian politics during the 1920's and early 1930's, when political groups were killing each other in the streets of Sofia over it. Yet, when Bulgaria finally occupied Macedonia in 1941 after Operation Marita, that long-contested land became merely another provincial area in the Bulgarian state.

Some important differences between Macedonia and the rest of Bulgaria nevertheless remained. Macedonia was an ethnic patchwork, with many inhabitants who did not regard themselves as Bulgarians; as a result, the occupiers made energetic efforts to "Bulgarize" them, either by propaganda or—especially in Aegean Macedonia, where the population was overwhelmingly Greek—by expulsions and executions.* In addition, the boundaries of the "new lands" were not permanently fixed; as the Germans reduced their own forces in the Balkans, the Bulgarian occupation zone expanded on several occasions—and Bulgaria expected that Germany would formally recog-

---

* Aegean Macedonia (Egeiska Makedoniya), the area between Salonika and the Turkish border, was not a part of the territory traditionally considered Macedonia. Europeans generally called the area Aegean Thrace; Bulgarians often referred to it as Belomorie or Belomorska Trakiya, based on their term for the Aegean (*Byalo more* = white sea).

nize the annexations at the end of the war. The occupation of Macedonia also touched off a bitter internecine conflict between Bulgarian and Yugoslav Communists over control of the Macedonian Party, and this conflict had considerable postwar significance.

The Occupation of Vardar Macedonia

When German troops advanced into Vardar (Yugoslav) Macedonia in April 1941, the Macedonians greeted the victors with great enthusiasm. Crowds in Skopie, the provincial capital, displayed a banner which, paraphrasing the German slogan, hailed the unification of Macedonia and Bulgaria: "One people, one Tsar, one kingdom."[1] The citizens gave an even more tumultuous welcome to the Bulgarian troops that entered Macedonia on April 19, 1941.[2] The warm reception accorded the Bulgarian soldiers was in large part the result of Macedonian resentment at three decades of Serbian dominance. "Administrative brutality, Serbian chauvinism, political corruption, and economic exploitation were more flagrant in Macedonia than in any other part of Yugoslavia."[3] It was therefore not surprising that many Macedonians cheered the entering Bulgarians. One resident of Skopie later explained, "Of course we cheered; we had no way of knowing then that the Bulgarians would just repeat all the mistakes the Serbs had made."[4]

Disillusionment came quickly. Bulgarians, not Macedonians, replaced the expelled Serbian officials, and "even the returning Macedonian exiles seemed strangers."[5] All matters of importance were decided in Sofia, and the local authorities seemed determined to make the region into an indistinguishable part of Greater Bulgaria. The officials sent to Macedonia were rarely Bulgaria's best. Because the primitive conditions of the region made it an undesirable place in which to serve, the administration was staffed by castoffs from other governmental agencies. A German intelligence report in October 1942 observed: "The Macedonians, who during the period of Yugoslav rule had regarded everything Bulgarian with admiration, now are exceedingly disillusioned after becoming acquainted with a completely corrupt as well as incompetent Bulgarian administration."[6]

Even if the officials had been better, the conditions they encountered would have severely tested their endurance. A leading opposition member of the Narodno Subranie, Petko Stainov, complained in June 1942, "What outlook and spirit do you expect from officials who for five months have eaten only bread and beans?"[7] The occupation troops had adequate food, sent from Bulgaria proper, but they acted just as harshly and arrogantly toward the local population as did the officials. Instead of acting as "liberators," the troops behaved as conquerors. This was remedied somewhat after higher authorities became aware of the problem, but the bitter impression remained. The army that had been greeted with such enthusiasm became an object of disgust.[8]

Those Macedonians who had expected cultural and linguistic autonomy were especially disappointed. The authorities rejected all claims to Macedonian cultural uniqueness and "treated the natives as somewhat backward Bulgarians."[9] Heavy emphasis was placed on education as a means of Bulgarization. (Prime Minister Filov was also minister of education.) Delegates to a teachers' conference in Skopie were told that their highest duty was the "preservation of the territorial unity and independence of the Bulgarian state."[10] The new curriculum in the Macedonian schools strongly emphasized Bulgarian topics and discouraged the use of the Macedonian language, which the Bulgarian authorities regarded, rightly or wrongly, as only a dialect of Bulgarian. A typical weekly schedule included seven hours of Bulgarian, three hours of Bulgarian history, and one hour of Bulgarian church history. This compared with only three hours for mathematics, three for a modern language, and one hour for Russian (which was available only in grades five and six).[11]

The Bulgarians, to their credit, did enact a series of laws providing for tax relief and economic assistance in the new territories, including Southern Dobruja. They also established 800 new schools in Macedonia and presented Skopie with a library, a museum, a national theater, and, in December 1943, a university named after the recently deceased Tsar Boris.[12] Many Macedonians, however, regarded these endowments as further evidence of Bulgarization. The use of the Bulgarian

language in schools aroused increasing opposition and became a rallying point for dissident Macedonians irritated by other aspects of the
occupation. In 1943 and 1944, the opposition reached such a level that
in many areas attendance was maintained only by coercion, and some
schools were unable to operate at all.[13]

Bulgarization was not limited to secular institutions. On May 3,
1941, the Bulgarian Holy Synod assumed control over the Orthodox
churches in occupied Yugoslavia and Greece. Four new eparchies
were established, and several new bishops and metropolitans were
designated.[14] Under government direction, the Synod brought in
priests from Bulgaria proper, ordered services conducted in Bulgarian
rather than Macedonian, and appointed a church commission to remove all vestiges of non-Bulgarian culture.[15] On June 10, 1942, the
Narodno Subranie imposed Bulgarian citizenship on all persons of
"Bulgarian" descent living in Vardar and Aegean Macedonia. All
others still residing in these areas on April 1, 1943, would become citizens unless they declared themselves otherwise, in which case they
would be required to leave the country. Those who made this choice
would have to leave penniless because the Bulgarians froze all bank
accounts in Macedonia. On the other hand, those accepting Bulgarian
citizenship were promised exemption from all taxes and levies.[16]

IMRO and Ivan Mihailov

The Internal Macedonian Revolutionary Organization (IMRO)
was no longer an important factor in Macedonian affairs. This famous terrorist organization, founded originally in 1895 to fight for
Macedonia's liberation from the Turks, had made Bulgaria its base
after the incorporation of most of Macedonia into Yugoslavia following the First World War. From Bulgaria it waged a guerrilla campaign against Yugoslav—and particularly Serbian—domination of
Macedonia. Bulgarian Prime Minister Stambolisky had attempted to
curb IMRO activities and to establish better relations with Yugoslavia,
but his efforts only contributed to his overthrow and death in 1923.
For a decade IMRO operated freely—almost as a state within a state—
administering Bulgarian (Pirin) Macedonia and assassinating those

who opposed its goals. Although IMRO was divided between those who favored Macedonian autonomy and those who desired unification with Bulgaria, ideology was often less important to the organization than was financial support from various interested countries, notably Bulgaria and Italy. The organization's excesses gradually lost it much of its popular support, and in 1934 the Bulgarian government finally took decisive action against it. It then shriveled to a small remnant around its leader, Ivan Mihailov.[17]

Even though IMRO had little significance during the war, many individuals who had been linked to the organization held positions of responsibility in Bulgarian agencies, particularly in the "new lands."[18] Mihailov himself retained a certain amount of influence. There are reports that he was twice considered by the Bulgarians and Germans as a possible governor of Macedonia. In October 1942, according to these accounts, the Tsar became so concerned about the deteriorating situation in Macedonia that he sent the head of his court intelligence service to Zagreb, where Mihailov was a guest of Ante Pavelich, the *Poglavnik* (ruler) of Croatia. Mihailov reportedly criticized the Bulgarization campaign in Macedonia, and the meeting came to naught.[19] In 1944, when unrest in Macedonia reached crisis proportions, Mihailov was contacted by both the Bulgarians and the Germans; the latter are said to have considered him for *Gauleiter* of Macedonia in the event of the collapse of the Bulgarian occupation. These talks also came to naught.[20]

The Occupation of Aegean Macedonia

The Bulgarian occupation in Aegean Macedonia was considerably harsher than in Vardar Macedonia, where the population was largely Slavic. Whereas the Bulgarian policy in the latter was to win the loyalty of the Slav inhabitants, the policy in the Aegean littoral was to Bulgarize forcibly as many Greeks as possible and to expel or kill the rest. Bulgarian colonists were encouraged to settle on land expropriated from Greeks, in the hope that a Bulgarian majority in the region would insure permanent Bulgarian control.[21]

During the first few months of the Aegean occupation, the Bulgarians made an effort to gain the support of the local inhabitants. They conducted an extensive propaganda campaign, established Bulgarian schools, and distributed food and milk to Greek children.[22] It quickly became apparent, however, that this approach had little chance of success. The occupation authorities therefore resorted to more drastic measures. The Bulgarians closed Greek schools and expelled the teachers, replaced Greek clergymen with priests from Bulgaria, and sharply repressed the Greek language: even gravestones bearing Greek inscriptions were defaced. Bulgarian families were encouraged to settle in Macedonia by government credits and incentives, including houses and land confiscated from the natives. The authorities also confiscated Greek business property and gave it to Bulgarian colonists. In the town of Kavalla, for example, over seven hundred shops and other enterprises were expropriated. Large numbers of Greeks were expelled, and others were deprived of the right to work by a license system that banned the practice of a trade or profession without the express permission of the occupation government.[23]

A revolt broke out in the city of Drama on the morning of September 28, 1941, and quickly spread throughout Greek Macedonia. In Drama a crowd attacked the city hall and killed four Bulgarian policemen; in Doxato the entire Bulgarian police force of twenty men was massacred; in Choristi armed Greeks seized the town and called on other towns to join them; and in many other villages there were clashes between Greeks and the Bulgarian authorities.[24] The rebellion was short-lived. On September 29 Bulgarian troops moved into Drama and the other rebellious cities and seized all men between the ages of 18 and 45. Over three thousand people were reportedly executed in Drama alone; in the countryside entire villages were machine-gunned and looted. An estimated fifteen thousand Greeks were killed during the next few weeks.[25]

The Drama revolt had hardly ended before rumors spread that the entire rebellion had been instigated by Bulgarian agents provocateurs. Although conclusive evidence of Bulgarian provocation is lacking, present-day historians, both Greek and Bulgarian, continue to voice their suspicions. One Greek writer relates examples of Bulgarian provocations and describes the rebellion as still "*une affaire obscure*"; a Bulgarian historian admits "the Drama events have still not been thoroughly investigated."[26] Whatever its origins, the revolt allowed authorities to justify the subsequent atrocities by claiming "military necessity."[27]

The massacres precipitated a mass exodus of Greeks from the zone of Bulgarian control into the German occupation zone. Bulgarian "reprisals" continued after the September revolt, adding to the torrent of refugees. Villages were destroyed for sheltering "partisans," who were in fact only the survivors of villages previously destroyed.[28] (There were some Greek partisans in Macedonia, but they were of little significance.[29]) The terror and famine became so severe in the region that the Athens government considered plans for evacuating the entire population of Aegean Macedonia to German-occupied Greece.[30]

The exodus of many Greeks and the settlement of Bulgarian families in Belomorie altered the ethnic composition of the region. The Sofia newspaper *Zora* clearly approved: "The Greeks have now been expelled forever from these Bulgarian regions; our Thracian brothers return in masses to their ancient homes. By means of the repopulation of these regions by Bulgarians, which is being carried out on a large scale, and by the 'Bulgarization' of Western Thrace, these territories of Southern Bulgaria are colonized for a fourth time by those who have lived there for centuries."[31]

Although the Bulgarian government considered Macedonia an integral part of Bulgaria from the first, the territory's status was not so clear to Germany. Hitler had privately indicated that Macedonia should eventually be granted to Bulgaria, but the official German position was that "the fate of the various regions belonging to Yugoslavia will not be settled definitely until later, at the conclusion of peace. At present, therefore, no statements can be made regarding the future boundaries of Macedonia."[32] When Bulgaria formally annexed the occupied portions of Macedonia on May 14, 1941, however, Germany raised no strong objections. With the invasion of the USSR only a month away, Germany could not spare the soldiers necessary to garrison the entire Balkan region and thus needed to rely on Bulgarian and Italian troops to police the newly conquered territories. Therein lay conflict, for Italy also had designs on Macedonia.[33]

The Italians wished to expand from their Albanian enclave into western Macedonia to avail themselves of the mineral wealth of the region—chromium, tin, manganese, antimony, and molybdenum—and to enlarge the Roman imperium. The German government realized, however, that obtaining these war-essential minerals for itself would be easier if Bulgaria rather than Italy controlled the region. The boundaries of the Bulgarian occupation zone announced on April 17, 1941, were thus reasonably favorable to Bulgaria—although many Bulgarians were disappointed—and were expanded on May 15 to include the ancient Bulgarian shrine of Ohrid on the Albanian border.* On April 24, 1941, Clodius, the German emissary for economic affairs, secured a concession from the Bulgarian government giving Germany mining and railroad rights in the territory assigned to Bulgaria.[34]

In Greece the Bulgarians reacquired their former territory of Belomorie, extending along the Aegean coast from the Struma (Strymon) River east of Salonika to Dedeagach (Alexandropoulis) on the Turkish border.[35] Bulgaria looked longingly toward Salonika and western Macedonia, which were under German and Italian control, and established propaganda centers to secure the allegiance of the approximately 80,000 Slavs in these regions. The Bulgarian plan was to organize these Slavs militarily in the hope that Bulgaria would eventually assume the administration there. The appearance of Greek partisans in western Macedonia persuaded the Italian and German authorities to allow the formation of Slav security batallions (*Ohrana* units) led by Bulgarian officers.[36]

The heavy losses on the Eastern Front, the collapse of Italy, and the growing partisan movement in Yugoslavia forced Germany in 1943 to thin its forces in the Balkans. In late 1942 Germany had first requested increased Bulgarian participation in Balkan occupation duties (see Chapter 8), but Bulgarian assistance now became a necessity.[37]

---

* The University of Sofia is officially named after the great religious leader Kliment of Ohrid.

Hitler raised the problem at a meeting with Tsar Boris in August 1941, urging the Bulgarians to occupy northeast Serbia and an additional section of Greek Macedonia. The Tsar agreed in principle but postponed a decision pending "consultations," during which he vacillated between territorial avarice and the fear of further involvement in partisan-infested areas to which Bulgaria had little valid claim. His death left to his successors the task of expanding the Bulgarian occupation zone in Serbia.[38]

The net result of the Bulgarian occupation of both Macedonian areas was misery and bitterness. In Vardar Macedonia, these feelings were caused by the emphasis on giving Macedonian Slavs a sense of Bulgarian identity, even if unwanted. In Aegean Macedonia, it was the policy of extermination and expulsion that only increased the hatred Greeks felt toward Bulgarians. And the Greeks blamed the Germans for inflicting the Bulgarians on them.[39]

The Conflict Between the Yugoslav and the Bulgarian Communists

The Bulgarian occupation of Macedonia produced a major conflict between the Yugoslav and the Bulgarian Communists: who was to be responsible for Macedonia? The majority of Bulgarian Communists, like the rest of their countrymen, believed that Macedonia was rightfully Bulgarian. A leading theoretician of the BKP, Todor Pavlov, circulated a letter in April 1941 denying that the Macedonians were a separate people; a Macedonian himself, he stated that throughout history they had always considered themselves Bulgarians, albeit with certain customs and traditions of their own.[40] Traicho Kostov, using the name "Grigorov," argued that the ethnic question was in any case irrelevant: since Bulgaria was occupying the region, the BKP should be responsible for operations there.

Both the Bulgarian and Yugoslav parties urged resistance to fascism; but for the former, resistance apparently meant political opposition to the Tsarist regime, whereas to the latter it meant an armed struggle against the Bulgarian domination of Macedonia.[41] The head of the Macedonian Communist Party, Metodi Shatarov ("Sharlo"), was pro-Bulgarian. Despite his Bulgarian and Macedonian national-ist sympathies, Sharlo had been named Secretary of the Macedonian Party in February 1940 in an attempt by the Yugoslav Communists to gain greater support in the region. After the Bulgarian occupation in April 1941, he refused to take orders from Tito and the Yugoslav Party. Tito advocated partisan resistance to the Bulgarians, but Sharlo ignored his orders to conceal weapons from the Bulgarian authorities and to prepare for armed resistance.[42] The BKP set up a committee to oversee the integration of Sharlo's Party into the Bulgarian Party, and Anton Yugov attempted in April 1941 to reach an agreement with the Yugoslavs. Tito, however, refused to sanction the loss of Mace-donia; in fact he had hopes of extending his own control to embrace Pirin (Bulgarian) Macedonia. Near the end of May 1941, he sent Lazar Kolishevski, a Macedonian, to take control of the Macedonian Party from Sharlo and to organize armed resistance to the Bulgarian occupation.

On June 25, 1941, a few days after the German attack on the USSR, Tito sent a letter to the Macedonian Party declaring Sharlo and the entire Macedonian Central Committee expelled. Sharlo replied on July 2 with an appeal for a "Soviet Macedonia" and declared his in-tention of remaining the leader of the Macedonian Party. This ex-change brought the conflict to the attention of the Comintern in Moscow, where Tito was in a strong position because his call for resis-tance against the Axis now coincided with Soviet policy after the German invasion.[43] The Comintern's decision in August 1941 was in favor of Tito and his position of armed resistance in Macedonia. The BKP accepted this decision and recalled Sharlo to Bulgaria, although they objected to his being described as a "class enemy."[44] On August 25, Kolishevski established a regional committee for Macedonia and immediately set to work organizing resistance to the occupation. The BKP sent Peter Bogdanov, succeeded by Boyan Bulgaranov in Oc-tober 1941, to maintain liaison with Kolishevski, but the relationship was not a cordial one. The pro-Kolishevski group was openly hostile to the Bulgarians and condemned the BKP's continued reluctance to support any form of resistance stronger than sabotage.[45]

Kolishevski persisted in his effort to create partisan units, particularly in the regions of Kumanovo (25 km northeast of Skopie) and Prilep. On October 11, 1941, his forces had their first encounter with the Bulgarian army and were virtually wiped out. Shortly afterward, Kolishevski himself and a number of his lieutenants were captured and were imprisoned in Bulgaria for the rest of the war.[46] The resistance movement after Kolishevski's arrest reverted to Bulgarian control. Throughout 1942 and part of 1943, it was weak and sporadic. There was considerable opposition within the BKP to committing scarce resources to a hopeless struggle against Bulgarian occupation forces, which, along with the I Corps in part of Serbia, amounted to five divisions during this period. Indeed, it was argued that those who fled into the mountains were doing the authorities a favor, because they were easier to catch there and could do less damage to the regime than if they were engaged in revolutionary agitation. According to this view, the Party should avoid a violent confrontation with the government until it gathered enough strength to assure success.[47]

The Yugoslav Communists, fighting for their lives, were unsympathetic to this argument. The Bulgarian Communists, however, pointed out the differences between the situations of the two parties: in Bulgaria, the government apparatus and the army remained intact, and despite propaganda about German control there was no alien occupier against whom national anger could be directed; in Yugoslavia, the army and the government had been destroyed and Axis troops were in occupation.[48]

Until late 1942 the partisan movement in Macedonia had few successes, although the continued sabotage acts in German-occupied Serbia were a frequent topic of conversation in Sofia. The Bulgarians feared that unless this unrest was put down swiftly, it could spread to their occupation zone in Macedonia. Partisan activity was therefore discouraged by the tactics of the Bulgarian Fifth Army, which took vigorous action against the partisan units by acting "without mercy, not respecting military law."[49] Armed resistance, as well as popular passive opposition, increased during 1943, but less so in Macedonia than in adjacent regions. By January or February 1943, partisan units had grown strong enough to attack in company strength. On September 20, 1943, a serious revolt broke out in Lerinsko and Kichevo, near the Albanian border; a soviet republic was proclaimed and the red flag raised throughout this area before the revolt was crushed by Bulgarian troops.[50] This was one of the first partisan incidents in Macedonia serious enough to merit the attention of the government in Sofia.[51]

The year 1943 also marked the reemergence of Tito in the Macedonian Communist debate. On January 16 he sent a note to the Macedonian Communist Party in which he condemned autonomist tendencies and declared that the Macedonian Communist Party could attain success only in association with the Yugoslav Party. At the end of February 1943, he sent Svetozar Vukmanovich ("Tempo"), a Montenegrin well acquainted with Macedonia, to assume control of the Party organization. Tempo immediately made a number of changes that improved the partisan situation: he transferred the center of operations from the strongly occupied eastern portion of Macedonia to the western area near the Albanian border, established a working relationship with the Albanian and Greek Communist partisans, and reorganized the partisan units to take full advantage of the growing popular discontent.[52] From then on, the Bulgarian Communists had little or no influence on Macedonia. Boyan Bulgaranov, the chief BKP representative in Macedonia, returned to Bulgaria in early 1944 to command the First (Sofia) Resistance Zone. The meeting of the Yugoslav Communist Party at Jajce in November 1943 recognized Macedonia as one of the six Yugoslav republics—an arrangement the Bulgarians did not like but were powerless to change.

The victories of the Red army and the capitulation of Italy turned the tide, and thereafter Tito's partisans went from victory to victory. The BKP was hard-pressed to create its own partisan campaign in Bulgaria proper, which even in the summer of 1944 was only mildly successful.* The triumph of Tito's program put the BKP on the defensive because of the great prestige that came to the Yugoslav leader.

---

* See Chapter 16 on the Bulgarian partisans.

There was even a possibility that he would be able to detach Pirin Macedonia from Bulgaria to add to his Macedonian state, despite the vigorous opposition of the Bulgarians.[53]

Hermann Neubacher, the special economic envoy attached to the German Embassy in Bucharest during the war, wrote in 1956: "It was a serious political mistake for Bulgaria to enter Serbian and Greek territory as an occupier, in order to spare German troops."[54] Elizabeth Barker has summarized the result for the Greeks as follows: "Although the Greeks were relieved by the belated Bulgarian withdrawal, they were left with an overpowering hatred of all Bulgars, whether pro-German or Communist."[55] This occupation, for which Bulgarians had so long dreamed, succeeded only in creating a legacy of hatred that lingers to this day.

CHAPTER 12

The Death of Tsar Boris

B Y LATE SUMMER 1943, Bulgaria's international position had become critical. The fall of Mussolini had dramatically altered the Axis position in the Mediterranean, and rumors again circulated of an impending Allied invasion of the Balkans. On the Eastern Front, the German army had been unable to regain the territory lost during the winter and was facing another Stalingrad at Kharkov. Hitler ordered von Manstein to hold that city at all costs because, he said, "its fall would produce an unfavorable effect on the attitude of Bulgaria and Turkey."[1] Those Bulgarians who had minimized the importance of Stalingrad and El Alamein now overcompensated by exaggerating the seriousness—or at least the imminence—of the Allied threat, and many privately compared this period with the disintegration of the Central Powers in the autumn of 1918.

There are many indications that Tsar Boris was planning to take his country out of the war in 1943, but conclusive proof is lacking. Even the Communist accounts, which generally portray him in the most unfavorable light, state that Boris had lost faith in Germany and was "prepared to form a new government, whose main task was to get Bulgaria out of the war. He entered into negotiations with his father-in-law, the Italian king, hoping that together they could defend the institution of the monarchy with the help of the Anglo-Americans."[2] Former Ambassador Rendel noted: "It was Bulgaria's surrender in the First World War that had been the first step in bringing hostilities to an end. There seems to be some reason to believe King

Boris may have hoped that history would repeat itself and he still might be the means of bringing the war to an end by a compromise peace."³

A cabinet change could not be postponed much longer. Prime Minister Filov was having trouble controlling his cabinet and was on very bad terms with the minister of the interior, Gabrovsky, and the minister of trade, the Agrarian politician Nikola Zahariev. Georgi Kioseivanov seemed the likeliest candidate to replace Filov, and there were rumors that his new government would include some members of the opposition and would have the express purpose of taking Bulgaria out of the war.⁴

In his reports to Berlin, however, Beckerle denied that conditions in Bulgaria were deteriorating. He pointed to improvements in the economic situation and to police successes against the partisans, and he denounced the rumored installation of a pro-Allied government as merely propaganda spread by Anglophile circles.⁵ On the other hand, the SD officers in Sofia reported to Berlin that the next premier would probably be Nikola Mushanov or Ivan Bagryanov, both of whom were thought to be sympathetic to the Allies. A high official in the Bulgarian Ministry of Foreign Affairs was quoted as saying that there was no longer any doubt of Germany's final defeat and Bulgarian policy must now be aimed at driving the Germans out of Bulgaria in order to come to terms with the British.⁶

Hristu Pastuhov, the Social Democratic leader who had long opposed the alliance with Germany, revealed later that in the summer of 1943, the Tsar had approached him about forming a new government and had promised that there would soon be a shift in Bulgaria's foreign alignments.⁷ It is now also known that in early August a special representative from Boris went to see one of the leading opposition politicians, who was then confined to a remote village, and asked if he would be interested in taking a cabinet post. The matter was to be kept absolutely secret, for in a few days Boris was flying to Germany and he did not want any complications on this trip. The person in question was so well known for his pro-Allied views that his appointment to a ministerial post could only have been interpreted as a significant change in Bulgaria's policy, even if some Germanophile ministers had been retained.[8] Another story, more questionable, is that Boris telephoned his sister Evdokiya shortly before the trip to Germany, and said that he expected Hitler to demand Bulgarian troops for the Eastern Front. Boris allegedly said he had no intention of agreeing to this and told his sister of his plans for leaving the war as soon as his father-in-law, Victor Emmanuel, asked the Allies for an armistice.[9]

These stories are especially significant because of their possible connection with the mysterious death of Tsar Boris in late August 1943. On August 3, Hitler invited Boris to a conference at Rastenburg in East Prussia; on the 14th, he sent his personal airplane to fly Boris and General Mihov to the one-day meeting. Boris returned to Sofia the following day in good health and went to his mountain retreats at Tsarska Bistritsa and Chamkoriya for several days, during which time he and several others ascended Mount Musala (9,596 ft.), the highest mountain in the Balkans. On August 23, three days after this mountain-climbing expedition, he telephoned his sister around seven o'clock in the evening. She noticed that he sounded unusually tired; when asked about this, he replied that he was having difficulty breathing and felt pressure in his chest. A few minutes later he complained that he had never felt so bad, and with great effort he went up to his bedroom, where he fell unconscious.[10]

The first diagnosis was a gall bladder attack, but this was obviously unsatisfactory. The Tsar's physician, Dr. Sajitz, was flown back from Berlin, and several distinguished German doctors were sent to Sofia at the request of the Bulgarian government, because "the Bulgarian doctors are not able to make the right diagnosis."* The next day there was a slight improvement in the Tsar's condition, but the weakness of his heart became a new concern. By August 26, though, there had been such improvement that it was hoped the Tsar might pass the crisis within a few days. That same afternoon, however, his condition once more declined. According to Dr. Sajitz, the Tsar was fully aware

---

* The Queen's version differs from this account in a few details, but she was not summoned back to Sofia until the night of Wednesday, August 25.

of the seriousness of his illness and did not expect to live. Boris himself believed he had angina pectoris, which he attributed to his excursion up Mount Musala.

To prevent any dissident elements in the country from taking advantage of the Tsar's condition to create unrest or stage a coup, the illness was kept so secret that outside court circles only Filov and General Mihov were informed. Even the doctors were confined to the palace. But the banning of traffic from the palace area and other measures gave rise to rumors; therefore, shortly before midnight on August 26 the Royal Court decided to issue a terse statement for the morning newspapers: "His Majesty the Tsar has been seriously ill for three days. His treatment is in the hands of the best medical specialists." The second communiqué, issued on the morning of the 27th, said only: "The position of H. M. the Tsar continues to be serious. The doctors are making every effort for his improvement."

Later that morning the Tsar was said to be much better, but since the doctors were gravely concerned that complications might affect the brain, an eminent neurologist was summoned from Berlin. Incredibly, Dr. Sajitz, the royal physician, thought the illness was only anemia, but the others considered the situation so serious that detailed instructions were issued on the ceremonies and procedures in case of the Tsar's death. Filov said that the Tsar spoke only a few words for his bodily needs, but "during the whole illness he neither expressed a desire, nor gave an order, nor asked to see anyone." Most of the time the Tsar was under heavy sedation, but he still slept restlessly.

On the morning of August 28, his lung congestion was reported to be persisting and the inflammation spreading. At 4:22 that afternoon, the Tsar died.

Rumors and Suspicions

Even before Boris was dead, rumors spread that he was the victim of foul play. The fact that he had recently returned from a visit to Hitler gave rise to the suspicion that the Tsar had stood up to the Germans and had been killed for it. The popular theory, as Kazasov vividly described it, was that Boris "had been poisoned by the one who had drowned the world in blood."[11] The Tsar was thought to be too young and healthy to have suffered a heart attack, and the complicated diagnosis made the internal disintegration of his body seem massive: "Thrombosis arteriae coronirae sinistrae, pneumonia bilateralis, et oedema pulmonium et cerebri."* The secrecy that had surrounded the illness added to the drama and encouraged wild speculation. The BBC announced that Boris had probably been killed by Hitler; the *New York Times* said that a police inspector had fired several shots at him in a train station near Sofia; Hungarian sources reported that he had been killed by one of his own bodyguards.[12]

The Germans were also suspicious of the cause of the Tsar's death. When Beckerle asked three of the doctors if, in their opinion, a death by poisoning was possible, they replied that it looked like a "typical Balkan death."[13] An autopsy was necessary to determine the exact cause of death, but the Queen refused to allow an autopsy or even an examination of the brain. Shortly afterward, the doctors were told by someone (not the Queen) that an autopsy would be allowed but only after the body had been embalmed. Embalming, however, would have made it virtually impossible to detect poisons other than those with a metallic base, such as arsenic.[14] There is considerable controversy over whether an autopsy was actually performed against the wishes of the Queen. She has maintained that there was an autopsy, and other writers have agreed with her but have disagreed about its findings. For example, von Papen, the German Ambassador to Turkey, stated: "From the cursory examination they [the doctors] were able to make, they were convinced that the King's death could not possibly be due to any of the causes suggested by the Queen. They noted signs of complete decomposition of the internal organs, which could only be due to some form of poison."[15] On the other hand, Constant Schaufelberger, the tutor to the heir apparent, was told by one of the doctors that the autopsy fully confirmed the official diagnosis of heart failure, double pneumonia, and an infection of the brain.[16]

Filov assured the Germans that this diagnosis was correct and that there was no evidence of poisoning, although he admitted to having

* It was printed in Latin in the Bulgarian newspapers.

suspected "foul play" at first. In his opinion, the exhaustion resulting from the climb of Mount Musala had caused the heart attack, and he had warned the Tsar beforehand that such a trip was irresponsible.[17] The Queen heard none of the results from the autopsy, if there was one. She did remember that the Tsar had complained of feeling ill while hunting a stag shortly after his climb, but the feeling had not persisted and no one had worried at the time.[18] Wolfgang Bretholz, the anti-Nazi former editor of the *Berliner Tageblatt* who visited Sofia in late September 1944, reported that no normal organic trouble had been found by the autopsy and that instead there had been "traces of an unknown and slow-working poison that caused the heart to stop."[19]

Public opinion was less informed but more unanimous: Boris had been murdered, probably by the Germans. This opinion remains unchanged in Bulgaria today.[20] However, a number of important questions remain to be answered. One, what happened at the Rastenburg meeting between Boris and Hitler? Two, was there anything suspicious about the flight back to Sofia? Three, how was the health of the Tsar during the week between his return and the advent of his illness? Four, what was the course and nature of the illness itself? Five, what measures were taken to ascertain the cause of death after Boris died? Six, what were the reactions of various individuals and groups to the Tsar's death? And seven, how did his death affect the future of Bulgaria? Some of these questions have already been touched upon, but a few of the key points will now be examined more closely.

No official transcript exists of the Rastenburg conference, but the general outlines of the discussion can be pieced together from a number of sources. First, Hitler expressed his concern about the Italian situation and sought assurance from the Tsar that Bulgaria, too, was not planning to defect from the Axis camp. Second, he and Boris discussed the contribution that Bulgaria would be able to make to the war effort, and the conversation on this point reportedly became quite heated.[21] It is still the general belief in Bulgaria today that Hitler demanded the Tsar send troops to the Eastern Front—a demand Boris refused on the grounds that Bulgarians would never fight their liberators. Boris's secretary, Pavel Gruev, later dramatically related the

Tsar's comments on the outcome of this argument: "I had to fight for hours against Hitler and his cronies in order to tear Bulgaria from their claws but finally I succeeded. I am willing to pay with my life to keep them from bringing my fatherland to ruin."[22] It is questionable whether Boris ever made such a remark, and the present evidence is that Hitler made no strong demand for Bulgarian troops to fight in Russia.

General Mihov's diary unfortunately is available only for the period after he became Regent (September 1943), but Prime Minister Filov's diary gives a full account of this incident. The Tsar told him that Hitler had not discussed the Soviet Union in much detail except to indicate that Germany was confident of coping with the problem. However, after his audience with the Tsar on August 15, Filov wrote in his diary that the Tsar was very discouraged: "He is not at all satisfied with his trip today.... On his return he even wished to encounter an enemy airplane which would finish him off. Actually there is not any reason for such pessimism. The Germans wanted two of our divisions for north Greece and eventually Albania, in order to protect the rear of the German troops in Greece and on the Albanian coast. They considered that there was not now any danger from Turkey."[23] The Tsar had agreed in principle to this request, but had wanted a military mission to discuss the details before he gave his final approval.[24] (Prince Kiril later confirmed this in his testimony before the People's Court.[25]) Unless additional evidence is forthcoming, therefore, we can conclude that Boris's meeting with Hitler was very strained, but that the more colorful stories about it are apocryphal.[26]

Theories About the Return from Rastenburg

The greatest number of theories concern the Tsar's flight back to Sofia after his visit to Germany. It was in Hitler's personal aircraft on this return flight, many people have said, that Boris was marked for death. One theory even states that the Tsar was dead on arrival and that the accounts of his activities during the following week were fabrications. Basically, however, there are three theories concerning the flight. The first is that some slow-acting, lethal gas was administered to the Tsar through his oxygen mask. The most frequently mentioned gases are chloroform and a "too strong dose of oxygen," although obviously neither of the two fits the above description of the Tsar's actual symptoms. Prince Kiril himself favored this theory.[27] A second version of the flight is given by the German pilot, Flug-kapitän Hans Baur. He claims that he was ordered to climb to 8,000 meters, dive to treetop level, climb back to 6,000 meters, dive again, and so forth until the altitude changes, combined with poison in the oxygen mask, had weakened Boris's heart. (A slightly different version says the oxygen mask was also defective.[28]) The third theory is that of former Ambassador Rendel, who said that Boris was a poor air traveler and usually took airsickness pills before a flight. This time he was given another drug, which, combined with the great height flown by the plane over the Carpathian Mountains, led to his later heart attack. The pilot, Baur, also suggests poison, but says it was administered in a cup of coffee.[29]

The first theory is difficult to accept for a number of reasons. Neither of the gases mentioned would have damaged Boris's internal organs in such a way that he would notice nothing wrong for a week and then collapse. Oxygen would have been harmless; chloroform would have had to be administered in such a heavy dose that he would have needed to be carried off the plane. Yet we know that he was in good health when he arrived in Sofia, for he had several conferences that evening. There is no known poison gas that would have such a delayed action. Furthermore, the oxygen masks were not assigned to the passengers but were picked up at random, so there was no certainty that the Tsar would pick up any particular one.

An elaborate arrangement can be imagined that would have allowed the Germans to circumvent this problem; but rather than make extensive alterations to Hitler's private plane on a day's notice, it is more likely that they would have resorted to some simpler method of killing the Tsar. Baur himself said that the weather was perfect that day and that Boris was delighted with the trip, which hardly sounds as though he spent the journey in discomfort or in a doped stupor.[30]

As for the second theory, even in the unlikely event that the other passengers had endured a "roller coaster" ride without question, the Tsar would not have. His strong mechanical interest and considerable flight experience would have caused him to grow suspicious. The only justification for a pilot to have flown a lumbering Junker-52 like a dive-bomber would have been to take violent evasive action against an enemy attack, but it is known that—despite the Tsar's wish—no enemy planes were encountered. If Baur had in fact flown the way he later claimed, Boris would certainly have lost faith in him. Yet the day after he returned to Sofia, Boris took a present to Baur at the airport and discussed technical matters with him for a long time while the young prince and princess climbed all over the plane. Only the Queen's maternal fears kept Boris from allowing the two children to go with Baur for a flight around the city.[31] Finally, none of the other passengers on the trip, including General Mihov and the court adviser Stanislav Balan, commented adversely on the journey or suffered any undue effects from it.

The third theory, Rendel's suggestion of an airsickness pill, is more reasonable than the other two, because a pill could have been administered with less difficulty and could conceivably have been made with a delayed-action effect. If a seasoned flier like Boris had taken a drug for a flight in perfect weather, why was this fact not mentioned by some of those closer to the court than Rendel? Although a poison pill is more plausible than a poison gas, there really is no evidence to support either theory; and the "roller coaster" theory was taken seriously neither by the Queen nor by anyone else close to the events. If the Tsar was indeed poisoned, it is highly unlikely that the deed was done on the flight from Rastenburg.

The German Reaction to the Tsar's Death

As mentioned earlier, the German records reveal no plots or conspiracies but show, on the contrary, that everything possible was done to diagnose the illness correctly and, afterward, to ascertain the exact cause of death. Two other points must now be discussed for a better understanding of the German view. First, it is important to note that

Germany regarded Boris's death as a disaster for the Axis, regardless of the fact that he may have been secretly planning to leave the war. Germany considered Bulgaria a loyal, if somewhat obdurate, ally, and consequently had given the Tsar much freedom of action. This appraisal did not change during the summer of 1943. Beckerle has written: "There is no question of the King playing a double role. King Boris knew very well that he had bound his fate completely with that of Germany and there was no backing out.... Between Hitler and King Boris there was a relationship of close confidence until the last."[32]

The day before Boris's death, German Staatssekretär Baron Steengracht described the Tsar as one "who in the eyes of the people was less a monarch than a Führer and who represented in his person the symbol of Bulgarian unity.... The Bulgarian people, who are in a certain respect leaderless and unsure without the King, could fall to a considerable extent under the influence of the Communist and Anglophile opposition."[33] Von Papen in Ankara was even more emphatic: "Only the determined and adroit personality of the King could have guided the future course of affairs. It must have been a long-term aim of the enemy, rather than of Hitler, to obtain his removal from the scene."[34] In Berlin, Goebbels's reaction was, "King Boris of Bulgaria is dead. An important pillar of our Balkan position has gone."[35]

The second point is that the German leaders apparently knew as little about the Tsar's death as everyone else. They were certain that he had been murdered, probably by some kind of poison, but they did not know by whom. Hitler believed that the Queen and her Italian relatives were responsible. This suspicion seems to have been almost entirely the result of Hitler's distrust of anything connected with Italy because of that country's recent defection. The Queen of Bulgaria was the daughter of the Italian King, and her refusal to allow an autopsy was considered an indication that she feared something sinister might be discovered. There were also stories that her marriage had been unhappy from the beginning, thereby providing another possible motive. Hitler's anger reached such a height that he wanted to have her arrested and brought with the young Tsar Simeon to Germany, but the German air attaché in Sofia, General Schönebeck, and others dissuaded him from so rash an action.[36]

Hitler then decided that the main culprit was the Queen's sister, Princess Mafalda, although she had not arrived in Sofia from Italy until the day after Boris's death. What could not be done to the Queen was done to this princess: she was lured to Germany shortly afterward and put in the concentration camp at Buchenwald, where she died during an air raid in August 1944. The Germans remained so suspicious of an Italian plot in Bulgaria that when Ribbentrop went to Sofia for Boris's funeral, he would not eat any food except that prepared by special German chefs.[37]

If neither the Germans nor the Queen killed Boris—and it seems almost certain that they did not—who did kill him? No one has ever claimed that the Communists were involved. Although the popular image of the Tsar martyred for resisting the Germans has long hindered Communist efforts to depict him as a German agent, Communist historians have reluctantly accepted the view that he was killed by Hitler.* A theory that has found some favor is that the Bulgarian fascists and/or the SS agents in Sofia took immediate and drastic action against the Tsar, without the approval of Hitler, to prevent Bulgaria's withdrawal from the Axis. The various German organizations often had their own special policies (*Sonderpolitik*) differing from the official position, and the SD had tried for years to undermine the Tsar's position by sending unfavorable reports on him to Berlin.

The SD report of August 16, 1943, or perhaps some other report that claimed that the Tsar was planning to follow Italy's example, might have led certain groups or powerful individuals to decide even without consulting Hitler that Boris must be killed without delay. Himmler and Schellenberg are suspected by some; Göring and General Schönebeck by others. Ambassador Beckerle has said that the SS would have liked to create a situation in Bulgaria similar to that in Rumania, but that because of the close relationship between Hitler

* See *Istoriya Bolgarii*, p. 294. A recent change in this view is discussed on p. 147, below.

and Boris any Sonderpolitik had to be concealed. However, Beckerle has stated emphatically that "it was out of the question that the SS circles could have thought about the murder of the King." Therefore, such a conspiracy theory must remain a mere conjecture, attractive only because alternative explanations are so unsatisfactory.[38]

A Possible Solution

There is, however, one explanation that has been almost completely ignored and yet would provide a reasonable answer to nearly every one of the puzzles surrounding Boris's death. In particular, it would answer the main question of who killed him. The answer? No one—he died of a heart attack just as the official diagnosis said.

Most of the other theories have their origin (1) in the feeling that his death at this time of crisis must have been planned, and (2) in the secrecy surrounding the whole affair, which created the impression that everyone had something to hide. In fact, the recent history of Bulgaria had been but one long series of crises; the Tsar's death at any point in his reign of almost 25 years would have come at some important time when circumstances would have made it seem suspicious. The secrecy around the episode was perfectly understandable, and was largely owing to the desire to keep enemies of the state from taking advantage of the leadership vacuum caused by the Tsar's indisposition. The Royal Court tried for as long as possible to play down the seriousness of his condition, and even the Queen was told for two days that there was no need for her to come to Sofia. Her later refusal to allow an autopsy, though unfortunate, could easily have been the natural reaction of a distressed wife and need have no sinister significance.

The Tsar was, after all, not as young as some have made him seem. He was only five months short of his fiftieth birthday and had lived a life that would make any man a perfect candidate for a coronary thrombosis. The disorders of 1918, the turmoil of the Stambolisky period, the coups of 1923 and 1934, the terrors of IMRO, and the delicate diplomatic balancing between the major powers had hardly given him a life of peace and rest. His people knew him as a vigorous leader and a healthy outdoorsman, but he was also given to excessive drinking and had damaged his health by dissipation in his youth; he suffered constantly from a digestive problem and was of an extremely nervous temperament.[39] The exhausting climb on Mount Musala must have brought on both his heart attack and the accompanying pneumonia, and it is known that he briefly felt ill even before he left his mountain retreat. There is, therefore, no need to believe that Boris was poisoned or otherwise deviously killed, when the evidence for it is so vague and contradictory.*

The conspiratorial theories are probably too firmly entrenched now to be shaken by a mere lack of evidence, and the legend of the martyred Tsar satisfies a psychological need regardless of its truth or falsehood. This legend has enabled many Bulgarians to avoid feelings of guilt for being on the Axis side during the war and has provided the non-Communists in Bulgaria with a popular hero. Indeed, it is somewhat surprising how highly Boris is praised today by those former politicians of the Bulgarian democratic parties who spent a lifetime in opposition to his policies. And among average Bulgarian citizens one often hears the expression, "Everything might have turned out differently if the Tsar had lived."[40]

This view is extremely optimistic, of course, even if the Tsar was seriously planning to follow Italy out of the Axis bloc. He had been kept well informed of developments in Italy and knew that the Badoglio government would request an armistice from the Allies in early September. Italy's defection was expected to have a much greater effect on the war than it actually had; and Boris was one of the many who thought that Italian and Bulgarian withdrawal from the war could make 1943 a repetition of 1918. In mid-August, there were large-scale movements of Bulgarian troops to the vicinity of Sofia under

* The latest official history of Bulgaria has introduced the new theory that Boris's death was due to a heart attack "as a result of systematic abuse of alcohol." This differs from the Communists' previous acceptance of the theory that he was killed by the Germans, and is preferable to ignoring the issue completely, as is done in many Bulgarian textbooks. One tends to suspect that the change is the result of political concerns rather than the discovery of new evidence. The document cited is at present classified (TsDIA, f.456, op. 1, a.e. 18, 1.59), and there is no indication of what it might represent; one wag has suggested that it might be the Tsar's liquor bill. See *Istoriya na Bulgaria*, p. 405.

the guise of maneuvers. Their real purpose may have been to guard against a Nazi coup if Filov's government were to be replaced within a week or two. According to the Queen, these maneuvers were a main topic of conversation in the meetings Boris had with General Mihov, with the Bulgarian Ambassador in Berlin, Zagorov, and with others he consulted in the week before his illness.[41]

Because of his cautious nature, it is unlikely that Boris would have thrown himself on the mercy of the Allies immediately after Italy did, since he would have sought certain guarantees for his regime and some assurance that the Allies would intervene to protect Bulgaria from German reprisals. More probably he would have wanted to wait several weeks until contacts with the West could be reestablished and until he had a chance to observe the success of the Italian venture. What he would have seen would not have been encouraging, and the intransigence of the Allies would have made any attempt at cooperation virtually impossible. Boris would have been more flexible about changing sides in the war than his successors were. Had he lived, however, it seems doubtful that he would have been able to accomplish much more than they did; and the fact that the British government held him personally responsible for Bulgaria's policy might have proved a major difficulty in negotiations. Tsar Boris's death brought some changes, of course, but it had much less long-term effect than one might have expected, for Bulgaria's fate was now being determined more and more by international military and political factors beyond its control.

PART THREE

September 1943-September 1944

CHAPTER 13

The Regency and Bozhilov

※

PROFESSOR Bogdan Filov had originally been chosen for the premiership because he was expected to be a "glittering court ornament" and a "ready tool of the King."[1] After the death of Tsar Boris, however, he suddenly emerged as the leading political figure in Bulgaria. The opposition leaders also became more important as the country grew disenchanted with the government's pro-German policy; it was expected to be only a matter of time before they came to power. But just as Filov and other government and opposition personalities were achieving greater prominence within Bulgaria, the fortunes of war steadily diminished their ability to influence events outside the country. Allied air raids, the Russian advance, and the anticipation of an Allied attack on the Balkans became the major factors determining Bulgaria's fate.

The Formation of the Regency

When Boris died, his young son, Simeon, was only seven years old. According to Articles 27 and 143 of the Bulgarian Constitution, a special election should have been held for a Veliko Narodno Subranie —a Great National Assembly—to elect a Council of Regents to govern the country during the new Tsar's minority. Filov was not eager to see an election campaign that might call government policy into question and endanger the stability of the state. He also desired that the dead Tsar's brother, Prince Kiril, be named one of the Regents, even though the Constitution specified that they should be selected only from leading government officials or people distinguished in public service.[2] Although realizing that the election of Kiril to the Regency might be unconstitutional, Filov argued that in a country which had been dominated from its inception by strong monarchs the presence of a member of the royal family on the Council of Regents would add greatly to the Regency's prestige and authority.

Attempting to resolve these two issues, Filov consulted four of the former prime ministers: Alexander Tsankov and General Pencho Zlatev were against holding elections and favored Prince Kiril; Kimon Georgiev was for elections and strongly against Kiril; and Nikola Mushanov was for elections but was noncommittal about the Prince. With counsel divided, Filov chose to ignore the Constitution and follow his own inclination for he was confident of sufficient support in the Narodno Subranie.[3] However, since the parliamentary opposition was certain to protest when the matter came up for debate, Filov decided to resolve all the details beforehand so that the government could present a solid front. There were to be three Regents: Filov himself, Prince Kiril, and a third as yet unnamed.

The leading contender for the remaining position and, alternatively, for the premiership, was the Ambassador to Switzerland, Georgi Kioseivanov. Despite his previous undistinguished performance as prime minister (1935–40) and his Western education, the Germans favored his candidacy.[4] However, he had alienated the Macedonians in 1937 by concluding the friendship pact with Yugoslavia, and it was suggested that Filov considered him to be more valuable in Bern because of his contacts with the Allies.[5] Even more important, Filov had grown fond of power and was not eager to share it with the ambitious Kioseivanov. Filov finally selected General Nikola Mihov as the third Regent. Mihov, Minister of War since April 1942, was German-educated, an able officer, and not overly concerned with politics; in addition, he had recently been described as the "most sincere advocate of cooperation with the Germans."[6] Filov favored Mihov because he sought not only the support of the army but also "full agreement between two Regents in order to counter possible influences over the Prince"—especially the influence of Kiril's sister, Evdokiya.

The choice of Mihov was popular with the army and with the Narodno Subranie representatives, who did not want to see Kioseivanov returned to high office.[7]

On September 8, 1943, a special session of the Assembly decided that a Veliko Narodno Subranie should be postponed because of the war and the possibility of unrest. Bowing slightly to constitutionalism, the deputies stated that a Great National Assembly would be convoked after the war, or as soon as conditions permitted. When they met the following day to elect the Regents, however, a stormy debate broke out anew on this issue. Mushanov declared that there was no better time for the election of a Veliko Narodno Subranie to unify the Bulgarian people; and he read a statement by the various opposition leaders calling for unity, domestic tranquillity, and cooperation.* Tsankov replied that an election would divide rather than unify the country; Dr. Peter Shishkov pointed out that the British government had also postponed elections for the duration of the war. Finally, Dr. Ivan Vazov, who was soon to become minister of trade, argued that the manner of selecting the Regents was less important than the need for making an immediate choice. A vote was then taken and Filov, Mihov, and Prince Kiril were accepted by the Narodno Subranie.[8] The opposition denounced this election as illegal and refused to cooperate with the new government.†

The weak man in the Regency was Prince Kiril. He had a reputation as a Don Juan and was always surrounded by women who made use of his name and helped him spend his money. He was still heavily in debt from the time he had lived in Vienna after World War I, for both his father Ferdinand and his brother Boris had refused to set a precedent by paying off his debts. He had no interest in politics, but like his brother he was intrigued by mechanical things, especially racing cars. He and Boris were on very good terms, but the Tsar com-

---

* The signatories were Dimiter Gichev, Konstantin Muraviev, Vergil Dimov, and Nikola Petkov (Agrarians); Atanas Burov and Hristu Pastuhov (Social Democrats); Kimon Georgiev and Petko Stainov (Zveno–Fatherland Front; and Nikola Mushanov (Democrat).

† These statements were to embarrass many of them a year later when they accepted a mandate to form a new government from the "illegal" Regents.

plained that "Prince 'Kiki' will never amount to anything because he shows an interest in absolutely nothing."[9] After becoming a Regent, Kiril completely neglected his official duties. Filov had to remind the irritated General Mihov that the Prince "has not acquired the habit of prolonged and concentrated work."[10] They finally decided that the only way to deal with him was to agree beforehand and then confront him with a prepared opinion. As for Kiril's feelings toward Germany, Beckerle reported in August 1943, "I believe that he has no particular opinions of his own, but that he can be described as friendly to Germany since this is the attitude around him. I see no grounds for saying he has Nazi tendencies."[11]

The first tasks of the newly elected Regents were to appoint a prime minister and form a cabinet. To what extent did the Germans try to influence these decisions, and what was their reaction to the composition of the new government after it was formed? Just after Boris's death, for example, Ribbentrop had ordered Staatssekretär Steengracht to go to Sofia and to "stay as long as you deem it necessary in order to bring your influence to bear upon the composition of the Regency Council and the appointment of the prime minister....I consider it very desirable that Tsankov should become premier, if this is possible....At any rate, Tsankov ought to be given a decisive share in the shaping of future Bulgarian policy."[12] Yet the available evidence indicates that the Germans did not significantly influence the selection of the new government or even make a determined effort to do so; and their predictions about its composition were so wrong that it seems likely they were not even consulted.

Ivan Bagryanov, an Agrarian who had resigned from the government in early 1941, was considered by the Germans the leading contender for the premiership; they rated two little-known officials second and third. In fact, Filov had briefly considered Kioseivanov and Gabrovsky, although they had little support. The candidacy of Alexander Tsankov was never even in question. Filov was believed to be seeking the weakest person possible for the premiership so that he himself would be the undisputed leader of the government. Bagryanov was therefore eliminated because he was too independent and ambitious.[13] Instead, Filov chose Dobri Bozhilov, the minister of finance since 1938. Bozhilov was fairly competent in his former post, but he was not qualified for higher office. He had been a high-level Freemason and was suspected of doubting a final German victory, but he was expected to be as much a tool of Filov as Filov himself had once been of Boris. All indications were that Bulgarian policy would continue unchanged.[14]

With the exception of Tsankov, however, Germany had not expressed a strong preference for any individual and was generally satisfied with the appointments. Goebbels's reaction to the Bozhilov government, which Heiber cites, confirms the impression that Germany was not displeased: "His government consists exclusively of the friends of former Prime Minister Filov, who is now a Regent. As a whole we can be satisfied with this government. It has certainly no distinctive and strong face, but is nevertheless outspokenly pro-German."[15] Beckerle described the cabinet as "not unpleasing" and expressed satisfaction at the exclusion of certain questionable persons. Although the Germans remained concerned about this first wartime government not directed by the Tsar, they considered Filov's continued leadership the best guarantee that Bulgaria would remain pro-German.[16]

The cabinet was composed mainly of intelligent specialists rather than prominent political personalities. Foreign Minister Sava Kirov was perhaps the only eminent individual, for he had been Ambassador in Ankara, but within a month he was replaced for "defeatism." Docho Hristov, who had been a relatively unimportant member of the Narodno Subranie, replaced the disliked and discredited Gabrovsky as minister of the interior. It was certainly the most colorless cabinet in many years.

The Aegean Campaign

The Bulgarians had expected an Allied invasion of Europe through the Balkans since the spring of 1943. The Allies were considering several such plans. One called for a landing on the Dalmatian coast in order to establish contact with the Yugoslav partisans and open supply ports for them; it would make use of British troops not needed elsewhere. Another envisaged an attack at the head of the Adriatic directed against the Ljubljana Gap connecting Germany with the Balkans.[17] To President Roosevelt, however, Balkan operations seemed to be British schemes with more political than military significance, and he feared that they would cause difficulties with Russia. In his opinion, the cross-Channel attack ("Overlord") deserved absolute priority. In November 1943, the Allied Combined Chiefs of Staff drew up a statement aboard the battleship U.S.S. Iowa that established Allied policy toward the Balkans:

Recognizing that (1) the Balkan–Eastern Mediterranean approach to the European fortress is unsuitable, due to terrain and communication difficulties, for large-scale military operations, (2) the implementation of our agreed strategy for the defeat of Germany will require all available military means, and (3) our experience shows that the acceptance of limited objective operations, however attractive in themselves, invariably requires resources beyond those initially anticipated, we are agreed that our strategy will be best served by causing Germany to dissipate her defensive strength in maintaining her position in the Balkans–Aegean area.

So long, therefore, as the present strategic situation in this area remains substantially unchanged, operations in the Balkans–Eastern Mediterranean region will be limited to: (a) the supply of Balkan guerrillas by sea and air transport, (b) minor action by commando forces, (c) the bombing of vital strategic targets.

We agree that it is desirable to bring Turkey into the war at this time but this must be brought about without diversion of resources that would prejudice our commitments elsewhere.[18]

Two months earlier, in September 1943, Churchill had managed to persuade the American Chiefs of Staff to accept the British plan for an attack on the Dodecanese Islands in the Aegean. This offensive, he had argued, would employ troops currently inactive in the Mediterranean area, would secure strategic airfields and bases, would damage German prestige, and hopefully would encourage Turkey to declare in favor of the Allies. It was thought that the German garrisons on these isolated islands would be unable to offer much resistance; an easy Allied victory was therefore expected. British troops seized Castelrosso (a tiny island east of Rhodes) on September 10, occupied Cos on the 12th, and then landed on Samos. Soon a number of islands had been taken and Churchill was pressing for an attack on Rhodes. In October, however, the Germans retook Cos, which "showed beyond all question that despite heavy commitments elsewhere, the Germans were determined upon bold counter-measures in the Aegean."[19] The British campaign came to an ignominious end with the evacuation of Samos. Great Britain had lost over five thousand men, one hundred planes, six destroyers, and one submarine. Further Allied intervention in the Balkans was effectively discouraged.[20]

Bulgaria was naturally concerned about Allied activity so near at hand, and the newspapers reported the situation with alarm. On October 18, the Regents and Dimiter Shishmanov (the newly appointed foreign minister, who replaced Sava Kirov) went to Germany for their first meeting with Hitler since taking office. If Hitler had doubted them before, he was reported after the meeting to be "slightly reassured." The Bulgarians, however, were not as satisfied with Hitler. Even the staunchly pro-German Filov had begun to harbor occasional doubts about Germany's ability to remain indefinitely in the Balkans.[21] Hitler had pointed out that the line from Trieste to Rhodes was as long as the Eastern Front, and he had frankly admitted that there was no possibility of defending the whole area. Instead, he hoped to fortify only the most likely beaches and keep a mobile reserve of two German divisions at Skopie. Overlooking the fact that there were only a limited number of suitable landing areas in the Balkans, the Bulgarian delegation pessimistically concluded that an Allied invasion force could land, dig into strong positions, and build up considerable strength before Axis forces could intervene. Filov noted in his diary that "in general the Germans are not speaking of a decisive victory but more of a successful defense." The only encouraging news Hitler could offer was that in the coming spring Germany would have new wonder weapons that would make a dramatic change in the war.[22]

Filov's attitude had changed significantly from that of only a month before, when he had intervened personally to persuade reluctant Bulgarian officials to recognize Mussolini's so-called Salò republic. Since Mussolini's deposition on July 25, 1943, Bulgaria and the other Axis states in Eastern Europe had maintained loose relations with the new Badoglio government, which officially was carrying on the war as before; but on September 8, 1943, Italy announced that it had signed an alliance with the Allies. On the 12th, a German airborne unit led by Otto Skorzeny carried out a dramatic rescue of Mussolini and took him to Salò in northern Italy, where he set up a government in opposition to the one in Rome.[23]

The Germans immediately urged their satellite-allies to recognize the Salò government, but the prestige of Germany had declined so drastically that these countries preferred a more cautious attitude until they could ascertain the effect of Italy's withdrawal from the war. The Bulgarian Foreign Minister, Sava Kirov, was encouraged by Hungary's reluctance to recognize Mussolini and attempted to fend off the German demand for as long as possible. This angered Filov, who still believed that Bulgaria's future lay with Germany and that delay in recognition would only undermine German confidence in the new Regency. Kirov, Filov said, "is undoubtedly a defeatist, lacking in courage and afraid to take responsibility.... For him Germany has already lost the war.... I doubt that he will be able to remain minister much longer."[24] As we have seen, he did not.

Kirov may have been aware of rumors reaching Bulgaria that certain high German officials—notably SS-General Kaltenbrunner—had advocated building up a strong fascist Albania and Serbia rather than wasting any more time with "soft" Bulgaria.[25] Frightened, Bulgaria finally recognized Mussolini's government on September 28, but it took no action against those Italian diplomats in Sofia who supported the Badoglio regime and did not freeze their bank accounts as Germany had requested.[26]

Despite the German recovery of the Aegean islands that the British had temporarily held, Bulgaria never quite regained confidence in Germany's ability or willingness to hold the Balkans at all costs. Hitler met Prime Minister Bozhilov on November 5, 1943, and made little effort to paint a rosy picture of the military situation. Instead, he told the Bulgarian leader that there was no choice but to support Germany; the only alternative was the Bolshevization of the Balkans. The recent Moscow Conference, Hitler said, had placed the Balkans in the Soviet sphere of influence and had given Stalin a political veto over any Anglo-American military operations there. Thus, there could be no hope of averting Soviet domination by letting in the Western Allies, as some had advocated.[27]

The Bulgarian government decided to contact Turkey about military and political cooperation to counter the Soviet threat to the Balkans. Precisely what could be accomplished by this was never clear, but the Bulgarians at least wanted to reduce their dependence on Germany. Turkey was disturbed about the danger from Russia but had no wish to aggravate matters by allying with an Axis member. This would have been grist for the Soviet propaganda mill, which was already criticizing Turkey for not declaring war on Germany.

The Turks were hoping, as were many Bulgarians, to wait until the Allies were close at hand before turning on the Germans; they "suspected that the Russians wanted to push them into a disaster so that they would not be able to evade the Russian clutch after the war."[28] Endeavoring to avoid any participation in the war, Turkey merely reassured Bulgaria that it had no intention of changing its policy of neutrality. In fact, though, the Turks had expressed a willingness to join the Allies but had made such impossible demands for arms and equipment, as well as for an impenetrable air defense system around Istanbul, that the British calculated that it would require over a year just to transport the material to Istanbul.[29]

The Fatherland Front

The decline of German military prestige coupled with the political and diplomatic uncertainty following the death of Boris provided the Bulgarian opposition groups, including the Communists, with a new opportunity to participate in the political life of the country. Whereas the Nazi-Soviet Pact of 1939 had divided the opposition, leading the Communists to make bitter attacks on the pro-Allied democratic groups, the German invasion of the Soviet Union in June 1941 had once again provided the anti-fascist parties with a common enemy. Shortly after the beginning of Operation Barbarossa, the BKP had tried without success to organize a coalition of the anti-Nazi groups. Perhaps the memory of the BKP's propaganda campaign against the Western Allies inspired the general reluctance among the democratic opposition leaders to participate; certainly the Communists' demand for control of the coalition irritated the other parties. Attempts at cooperation during 1941 had finally collapsed when the leading members of the Communist Party were discovered and arrested by the police.

During the first part of 1942, however, a few secret meetings occurred between Kiril Dramaliev, a representative of the Communist Party, Kimon Georgiev of Zveno, and Nikola Petkov, a leader of the Agrarian Pladne wing. In June 1942, these three were joined by the Social Democrat Grigor Chesmedzhiev in forming the Fatherland Front (*Otechestven Front*). On July 17, 1942, the "Hristo Botev" radio station in the USSR broadcast what the Soviets demanded be the Front's political dogma. The nonnegotiable character of this program for the Fatherland Front proved a serious obstacle in gaining the cooperation of other parties.

When the Vrabcha Agrarians were contacted about joining the Front, the Vrabcha leader Dimiter Gichev suggested that they mutually devise a compromise program to unite all those opposed to the pro-Nazi regime. The Communists, however, refused to negotiate their Moscow-dictated program and told Gichev that he would have to accept it as it stood or be branded as a fascist. Thereupon Gichev replied, "We are not going to be the fifth wheel of the cart," and broke off discussions.[80] The non-Communist opposition was clearly reluctant to join with the Communists, however much they might deny it. The electoral coalition of 1938 had been successful but not harmonious, and the Communist line during the period of the Nazi-Soviet Pact had caused much antagonism. Furthermore, it was expected that Tsar Boris would switch to the Allied side as soon as the opportunity presented itself; this created a wait-and-see attitude during the first half of 1943. Finally, many Agrarians were unable to forget that certain members of the Fatherland Front, particularly Kimon Georgiev and Damian Velchev, had participated in the 1923 coup against Stambolisky and had led the 1934 coup against the governing Agrarian coalition.[31]

The Democratic leader, Nikola Mushanov, was contacted twice during 1942 by the Fatherland Front, but he insisted that he could give no definite answer until he had toured the country to discover what the people were thinking. The Front then turned to the leader of the Radicals, Stoyan Kosturkov, but he fled abroad shortly afterward. Hristu Pastuhov, the Social Democratic leader, and Atanas Burov, leader of the small Narodnik Party, refused even to meet representatives of the Fatherland Front. In March 1943, the Front was able to arrange another appointment with Mushanov, but he cancelled it because he believed that Boris was planning an imminent change of policy.[32]

Despite these failures to broaden the Front by including prominent non-Communists in it, in June 1943 a Directorate (*Rukovoden Tsentur*) of the Fatherland Front formed at a meeting that included Kiril Dramaliev (Communist), Grigor Chesmedzhiev (Social Democrat), Nikola Petkov (Pladne Agrarian), and Dimo Kazasov (Independent). The other leaders were represented by deputies because the government had them in confinement. Petkov, in fact, was released just in time to attend the meeting that established the Directorate, and Kimon Georgiev remained in "domestic exile" confined to Burgas.

The various party leaders who adhered to the Front really had little popular following. Georgiev had the support of certain army officers, and Petkov had inherited some of the prestige of his brother (who had been assassinated in 1924), but these leaders alone were still too weak to be an effective opposition. Thus, another attempt was made to persuade men like Gichev and Mushanov to join the Front. Gichev persistently refused to participate alongside Georgiev and the

Zvenoists because of their role in the coups of 1923 and 1934, and the Fatherland Front was equally adamant in demanding that he accept the platform of July 1942 without discussion. Nikola Mushanov urged the Front to wait until the Allies were able to facilitate the Tsar's withdrawal from the war; in the meantime, he felt there was no point in causing unnecessary suffering that could have but little result. He also opposed the plan for strong political agitation in the army, for he thought that it would potentially endanger the stability of the state. Once again, no basis for agreement could be found between the Fatherland Front "activists" and these democratic opposition "passivists."[33]

Boris's death destroyed all hopes for an early Bulgarian withdrawal from the war but did not reduce the reluctance of most opposition leaders to join the Fatherland Front. They now hoped for some form of Allied intervention—a hope encouraged by British operations in the Aegean, the rumors of an impending Balkan invasion, and the news of the Tehran and Cairo conferences. These moves by the Anglo-Americans disturbed the Fatherland Front, which preferred that Bulgaria be liberated by the Soviets. As long as two centers of opposition existed, "the Front did not have sole monopoly of political opposition and so could not claim sole right to rule the country when the Germans left."[34] As a result, on November 19, 1943, the Communist Party (not the Front) sent identical letters to Mushanov and Gichev offering them a four-point program and renewing the request to join the Front. The four proposals were fundamentally unobjectionable and were a partial compromise with Gichev's objection to the Moscow-dictated 1942 platform.* The Communists even sent Dr. Ivan Pashov to meet Gichev when they received no answer to their letter. Gichev offered the usual objections, including the inadvisability of partisan activity at that time, and added that he personally disapproved of the prominence given to Nikola Petkov, who had no following and should be treated as a private person. Pashov coun-

---

* The proposals were (1) driving out the Germans; (2) concluding peace with Great Britain and America, and alliance with Russia; (3) withdrawing troops from Yugoslavia and Greece; and (4) sweeping out the fascist regime and creating a truly democratic administration.

tered that Gichev could not seriously object to cooperation with groups such as Zveno, since he had participated in the Agrarian coalition in the early 1930's with some of the very people he now called the murderers of Stambolisky. Furthermore, said Pashov, the gravity of the situation warranted special efforts to achieve cooperation among all those opposed to the government's policy.[35]

Of course, Gichev's specific objections were less important than the general reluctance of the non-Communist opposition leaders to submerge themselves in the Communist-dominated Fatherland Front. They did not object to cooperation with the Communists, for Gichev made a counterproposal involving an agreement between the Communists and the Agrarians alone. This would have separated the Communists from their allies and allowed the Agrarians to be equal partners with the BKP rather than just another party in a Communist front. Nevertheless, it is clear that the opposition demanded terms to which they knew the Communists could not agree.

Near the end of 1943, Gichev was contacted by Peter Vranchev* and was once more asked to participate in an opposition cabinet in which he would be the prime minister. Gichev listened attentively to this idea of an underground government, but insisted that a government without territory was not a government. He agreed to participate only if the partisans could occupy enough territory to provide a secure base for the government; otherwise, a clandestine government had no chance of survival. He was well aware that the partisans were weak and fighting for their very existence; there was no possibility that they could seize and hold any considerable piece of territory. Moreover, Gichev and many of the opposition leaders objected to the partisan movement because they believed it accomplished little except to provoke government reprisals on innocent villagers who were usually members of the Agrarian Party. Only those people who were pursued by the police or who had escaped from the concentration camps should take up arms in the mountains, Gichev said.†

---

* A Communist who was made a general after the September 1944 coup.

† In the trial of Nikola Petkov after the war, the Communist Dramaliev testified that the partisan issue was the main point of disagreement between the Agrarians and the Communists. The Agrarians favored a coup at a decisive moment rather than a

Negotiations of this sort continued between the Fatherland Front and the other opposition groups, but the results remained unchanged. Mushanov, Gichev, and the others never did join the Fatherland Front, and as we shall see, they were never forgiven by it.

protracted partisan campaign. *The Trial of Nikola D. Petkov*, pp. 331–32, 339. Petkov's trial was a farce, but this particular piece of testimony seems in accord with other accounts. Interview, Bulgaria; Kazasov, *Burni godini*, pp. 749–50.

CHAPTER 14

Bombs and Peace Feelers

꿍

W HEN BULGARIA declared war on the United States and Great Britain in December 1941, the declarations were described as merely symbolic gestures to placate the Germans, thereby compensating for Bulgaria's failure to participate actively in the war. Britain's military power was said to be virtually destroyed; America was far away and unprepared for war. By September 1943, however, when Bozhilov became prime minister, the tide of war had turned against the Axis. Allied bomber attacks on Bulgarian cities were expected at any time. These attacks, when they finally came, had a devastating effect on Bulgarian morale and compelled the Bulgarian government to consider peace negotiations.

The Allied Bombing of Bulgaria

Until the summer of 1943, Bulgaria had been largely unaffected by the war. The British had made several air attacks on the country during the German invasion of Greece in 1941, but only a few planes had been involved and little damage had been done. Then, on August 1, 1943, the Allies sent a fleet of bombers over Bulgarian territory to attack the Rumanian oil fields at Ploesti. The bombers were tracked by a German radar station in Bulgaria, and Bulgarian fighter planes attempted to intercept them. The Bulgarian air force was mainly equipped with obsolete, Czech-made Avias, which had neither radios nor oxygen equipment. The Avias were unable to reach the bombers flying at 15,000 feet; three Allied stragglers returning from the target, however, fell victim to a Bulgarian squadron of modern Me-109s. For this exploit, three Bulgarian officers were decorated by the Tsar,* but Bulgaria minimized its role in this defense of Ploesti for fear of provoking Allied reprisals.

The Germans anticipated further attacks on Ploesti and provided the Bulgarian air force with 120 captured French fighters; these aircraft were only slightly less outmoded than the Avias, however, and were soon swept from the skies by the P-38s that escorted the Allied bombers.[1] In late October 1943, the Allied Combined Chiefs of Staff suggested to General Eisenhower that Bulgaria should be given a "sharp lesson"; "the quickest way to promote resistance in Bulgaria and possibly to bring the country out of the war [is] to open a large-scale bombing attack upon it."[2] Eisenhower accepted the suggestion. On November 14, 1943, 91 B-25s, escorted by a large number of P-38s, attacked Sofia. The marshaling yards and airfield were heavily damaged and 187 buildings in the city were reported destroyed. Casualties were not heavy, but Sofia was thrown into panic.[3] The myth of Bulgaria's "symbolic war" was destroyed.

Two further air attacks were directed against Sofia before the end of the year. Bad weather prevented either from being very successful, but the Germans were irritated that such light and infrequent raids were able to paralyze the Bulgarian capital. There were several reasons for the disproportionate psychological effect of the bombings. First, unlike the Germans, the Bulgarians were not accustomed to air raids. Their initial reaction was to flee the city, and those who were unable to leave sent their families. This resettlement dislocated life in Sofia and caused confusion, overcrowding, and inflation in the villages. The government enacted legislation to curb the exodus, but the laws were generally evaded. Second, Sofia then had a population of only about 300,000 concentrated in a fairly small area. A hundred bombers could thus have relatively more effect on such a city than could a thousand on a city like Berlin. Third, Bulgarian antiaircraft defenses were weak and the most elementary civil defense measures were lacking.

---

* Two of the three were later killed by the Communist government of Bulgaria; the third retired as a colonel in 1956.

As a result, morale in Sofia was lowered by the knowledge that Allied planes could attack the city with impunity and that the hurriedly built air-raid shelters were inadequate to protect the population. Prime Minister Bozhilov angrily denounced the Allies for killing "defenseless people who did not wish evil on anyone." Citizens of Sofia, however, began to blame the government for bringing such misfortune on the country.[4]

The Allied air attack of January 10, 1944, impressed even the Germans. Several thousand people were killed, water and electrical connections were broken, many homes and buildings were reduced to rubble, and fires broke out all over Sofia. The railroad stations and roads were clogged with refugees, as what seemed the entire population of Sofia tried to flee the city. Filov, who had been out of the city at the time of the attack, said that on his return he passed "endless lines of cars with baggage; some people were carrying all their household possessions."[5] This attack made all the previous ones look like mere practice raids. Filov described it as "the first great terror raid on Sofia." This was the coldest time of the year and it was virtually impossible to find food and lodging in the countryside for the additional thousands of people; the living conditions of the refugees in many of the villages were shocking. A full week passed before even state employees could be induced to return to their work and before the basic public facilities could be restored. The government was overwhelmed by the magnitude of the disaster; it could neither prevent the raids nor do much to help the people after they occurred. Germany's prestige also suffered because of its demonstrated inability to protect its ally. Filov proposed to the German General Warlimont that Germany make a massive air attack somewhere, perhaps on Istanbul, to restore the prestige of the Luftwaffe, but the Germans were not enthusiastic about the plan.[6]

The raids, of course, made excellent propaganda for those who were actively opposed to Bulgaria's alliance with Germany. The BKP issued several statements describing the devastation in Sofia and urged the "immediate conclusion of peace with England and America"; it was implied that a revolution would be needed, for "our fascist government will not do this."[7] The Soviets also attempted to take advantage of the political crisis created by the bombing. The Soviet Minister, Lavrishchev, told Bozhilov that the USSR was prepared to intercede to stop the bombing if Bulgaria would agree to withdraw its occupation corps from Macedonia and Thrace. The Bulgarian government declined for fear of antagonizing Germany. Filov, however, tried to use this Soviet offer to alarm the West and to show that the bombings were "water for the Communist mill."[8] He requested that the Turkish government act as an intermediary to convince the British and Americans that a withdrawal of the occupation corps would not be in the Western interest because it would help Tito. His naïve efforts met with no success, and Bulgaria nervously awaited the next aerial onslaught.[9]

On March 16, 1944, the Allies dropped incendiary bombs on Sofia. Eight days later, the royal palace at Vranya was deliberately attacked and burned to the ground.[10] Then, on March 29 and 30, the Allies launched a massive firebomb attack on Sofia. Strong winds fanned the flames, and the heat was so intense that books caught fire in buildings that were not afire themselves. The conflagration destroyed several of the ministries, the National Theater, the Holy Synod, and the city arsenal. Public services were interrupted for several weeks, and everywhere there were pleas for food. The plight of the evacuees outside the city had already become an open scandal; their condition now deteriorated even further as they were joined by thousands of new refugees.

The confusion in Sofia after the March 30 raid was intensified by rumors that the Communists were planning to attack the city the next evening. The government was completely disorganized, and all communication lines with the rest of the country had been severed. The partisans had lately increased considerably in numbers, although they were still weak; if they had made a maximum effort, they might have been able to seize the city temporarily. Filov was now convinced that the West and the Communists were in close cooperation: "The air attacks cannot be just terrorist actions. It is obvious that they have another purpose and this is probably the weakening of the home front and the strengthening of partisan activity in order to support their eventual connections through Serbia and the people of Tito."[11]

Sofia was not the only Bulgarian city to fall victim to Allied air attacks; other incidents generally went unreported by the newspapers, but information could be pieced together from such sources as the reports on public contributions to relief funds. Plovdiv was the second largest city in Bulgaria and a key communications point, but it was spared until April 18, 1944. Even before the attack the city had been described as panic-stricken, and many thousands of its citizens had fled to the mountains. The bombing inflicted little damage and only about sixty people were killed, but the morale of the city was shattered.[12]

As a result of the Allied air raids, the people of Bulgaria lost nearly all their faith in German power, and the Bulgarian leaders were discredited for having made the alliance with the Axis. The late Tsar Boris was not included in this public abuse because it was believed that he had wanted to remove Bulgaria from the war at the first opportunity. His successors seemed all the more inflexibly pro-Nazi. Although the Regent Mihov optimistically claimed that "the bomber squadrons are like flocks of birds who peck at the grains one by one but are not able to take the land," it was already apparent that Bulgaria was once again on the losing side of a war.[13]

Peace Feelers

Bulgaria urgently needed an armistice to spare the country from the bombings and the approaching Red army. A major problem in negotiating any settlement, however, was that the Western Allies and the Bulgarian government had quite different views of the effect an armistice would have on Germany. If and when the Bulgarian government decided to seek peace from the Allies, it wanted to have a large Allied military force near at hand to protect the country from German reprisals. The Allies, on the other hand, had no desire to send troops to the Balkans; their strategy was to force the Germans to do so. If Bulgaria could be bombed out of the war, Allied planners expected that Germany would then have to occupy the country with troops urgently needed elsewhere. This plan is clearly evident in a report by Air Marshal Sir John Slessor:

The best service we in this theatre can perform for Overlord is really to create hell in the Balkans by any means, air, land, and sea, that can be made available without embarking on major operations involving bridgeheads that have to be covered and supplied. . . .

It appears certain that if the Balkan satellites are knocked out, the effect on German strategy would be catastrophic; and therefore, if heavy bombing seems likely to put them out, which I believe it would, the Hun would have to occupy them or accept their collapse, and he could not afford to do the latter.[14]

This does not excuse the Bulgarian government for its reluctance to negotiate or support the contention that the Allies were hypocritical; but certainly an armistice would have been militarily embarrassing to the Allies.

The Bulgarian government was maintaining contact with the Allies through M. H. Milev, the Bulgarian diplomatic representative in Geneva, and Ambassador Balabanov in Turkey, but little could be accomplished until the leaders in Sofia decided on a change of policy. Bulgaria was unwilling to surrender unconditionally, to withdraw from Macedonia and Thrace, to antagonize the Germans, or even to admit that the war was lost. The American OSS (Office of Strategic Services, the American equivalent of the British SOE), which was working in Istanbul to detach Bulgaria from the Axis, informed Balabanov on December 18, 1943, that it would listen to any proposals. Balabanov reported this to Sofia and on January 10, 1944, recommended that Bulgaria should "decide how we can get out of the war with the least damage in case of (God forbid!) a German defeat."[15] No progress was made, however, until Balabanov went to Sofia at the beginning of February 1944 to speak with government and opposition leaders. Upon his return to Turkey, he informed the American mission that everyone had agreed that Bulgaria must withdraw from the Axis. The Americans suggested that a Bulgarian delegation be sent to Istanbul to open immediate discussions on "the conditions under which the Bulgarian Army would join the Allies as a combatant force." To expedite negotiations, Balabanov requested that the United States guarantee the national existence of Bulgaria and stop bombing for ten days until the delegation could reach Istanbul.[16]

Despite Balabanov's efforts, his government did not respond to the Allied offer of negotiations. The late Tsar's friend and adviser, Yordan Sevov, arrived at Istanbul at the end of February 1944, prompting speculation in the Turkish press that he would negotiate an armistice. Sevov had not come to Turkey for this purpose, but Balabanov was now desperate and asked the Allied mission "whether if for any reason his [Balabanov's] Government found it inadvisable to send two qualified persons to Istanbul, he and Sevov would be acceptable."[17] The Americans realized that this delay indicated that Sofia was not eager for negotiations and was not then contemplating a radical change in policy. They also were aware that Bulgaria was unwilling to relinquish its territorial gains. Feeling in Bulgaria on this issue was so strong that the American mission predicted, "The Bulgarian people at this time would be likely to turn against their leaders if they abandoned the still holy cause of unification." The Allied demand for unconditional surrender and the proximity of German troops were other obvious obstacles to an armistice.[18]

Filov was losing faith in a German victory and had concluded that in the event of military operations against Turkey or on the Aegean coast, Germany would "not be able to give us any significant help." Nevertheless, he had an almost suicidal determination to keep Bulgaria in the Axis alliance. "We have to remain loyal to Germany to the end, because we will have need of it, even if it is bolshevized, and because a small government has to preserve its honor; the Italians not only did not gain anything but now are even held in contempt by the Anglo-Americans. The matter may come to an unconditional surrender, but it is necessary to be honorable."[19] There was still considerable pressure on Filov to maintain this attitude. Mihov remained confident of a German victory and pointed to the failure of Finland's attempt to leave the Axis. "The Finns see that with the Russians it is not possible to have an agreement, and negotiations have been broken off."[20] Slaveiko Vasilev, a former cabinet minister, declared in the Narodno Subranie that the Axis was still strong; and as proof he pointed to the Japanese, who in their last campaign had inflicted 8,000 casualties on the enemy while losing only 260 men as prisoners.[21]

Hitler himself invited the Regents to Salzburg and told them that an unconditional surrender would place Bulgaria at the mercy of the Communists and the Western plutocrats.[22] Anthony Eden further stiffened Bulgarian resistance by stating in the House of Commons that "there is no question of offering Bulgaria any Greek or Yugoslav territory as an incentive to come out of the war."[23] On the other hand, there was a growing demand for progress toward an armistice. The newspaper *Mir* provided excellent coverage of the war during this period and—despite the censorship—left little doubt that the Axis was destined for defeat. Kimon Georgiev (of Zveno and the Fatherland Front) and Ivan Bagryanov (an Agrarian leader who had been personally close to the late Tsar) joined forces long enough to send Bozhilov a letter advocating an end to Bulgaria's participation in the war. A government supporter in the Narodno Subranie proposed that Bulgaria make a concession to the Allies by withdrawing troops from that part of Serbia to which Bulgaria had no claim—"a policy which will get Bulgaria out of the war will surely save Bulgaria from Bolshevism."[24]

Pessimism extended even to the strongest government supporters. Lazar Popov, for example, appealed to Mihov that it was imperative to improve relations with Moscow and to bring men like Mushanov into the government. Mihov received these suggestions coolly, and likewise rejected letters from the opposition that in his opinion were "recommendations which cannot be fulfilled. It is as if the whole world revolved around us and anything we want will come true.... Who does not want to have good relations with the Soviet Union, but the prior condition is that we become a Bolshevik republic."[25]

No progress had been made toward the negotiations with the Allies. A Bulgarian industrialist, Georgi Kiselov, arrived in Istanbul on March 24, 1944, ostensibly for trade talks with the Turks, but he claimed to have conferred with Filov, Foreign Minister Shishmanov, and Prime Minister Bozhilov before leaving Sofia. Kiselov's main purpose was apparently to convince the Allies that the bombing was hurting their cause, as well as opening the way for a German occupation and enabling the Russians to draw Bulgaria into the Soviet orbit. He argued that Bulgaria would open immediate negotiations as soon as the Allies landed in the Balkans; but until then, the Germans could prevent Bulgaria from leaving the war.[26]

Balabanov was deeply discouraged over his government's failure to take advantage of the opportunity for negotiations. Officially he followed government policy on the pernicious effect of the bombings and Bulgaria's inability to act as long as Germany dominated the Balkan peninsula; the impression he conveyed to American representatives, however, was much more critical. He declared that his government "was fumbling and undecided and afraid of what happened to Hungary.... The members of the Government lacked qualities of leadership and rather than take action are hoping for a miracle."[27]

Bulgaria's unwillingness to withdraw prematurely from the war is understandable. Tsar Boris had joined the Axis above all to avoid a German occupation, and the fate of other Balkan states that had been invaded and occupied had convinced the Bulgarians that this policy was correct. The country's autonomy had been preserved, and the social order remained intact. Bulgaria had attained its territorial goals, and despite the bombings it had suffered far less from the war than its neighbors. The Bulgarian leaders had no wish to jeopardize these gains by accepting an unattractive Allied offer of unconditional surrender and national humiliation, particularly since the Allies could not promise to protect the country if it withdrew from the Axis. The ultimate reason for the failure of negotiations was the attitude of the Bulgarian leaders, especially Bogdan Filov. Prime Minister Bozhilov was said to favor a break with Germany, but he was a poor leader whose days in office were numbered. A strong premier, if one could have been found, might have been able to gather enough support to withdraw Bulgaria from the war early in 1944.

CHAPTER 15

The Bagryanov Government

—※—

THE GOVERNMENT that had ruled Bulgaria since September 1943 had failed to solve any of the major problems facing the country —Allied air raids, inflation, political disunity, and the threat of invasion. Whereas Tsar Boris had been opportunistic and flexible, especially in regard to Bulgaria's relations with Germany, his successors were unimaginative and dogmatic Germanophiles. The Bulgarian people had supported the pro-German policy when it gave them the Southern Dobruja and Macedonia, but by mid-1944 they universally regarded the alliance with Germany as a millstone around the nation's neck.

The Red army was advancing steadily toward the Balkans, prompting many Bulgarians to remember their traditional pro-Russian feeling. The Bozhilov government had established limited contacts with the Allies but felt no sense of urgency about negotiations; months had passed without any significant progress. Inflation had increased to disturbing proportions, with both raw materials and consumer goods in short supply. The partisan movement, though it had so far suffered heavy casualties without much success, was growing increasingly troublesome. The opposition groups, including the Fatherland Front, had gained the tacit support of much of the population and had substantial influence even in the bureaucracy. Time was running out for Bulgaria, and the government's options had shrunk almost to the vanishing point.

Bagryanov and His Cabinet

Ivan Bagryanov seemed the ideal candidate for prime minister at this difficult time. He had been a close friend of the Tsar for over two decades and was highly regarded by the Royal Court. Because of his resignation from the government in early 1941, which the Allies had interpreted as a protest against Bulgaria's adherence to the Tripartite Agreement,[1] he was not tainted by collaboration with the Germans. Yet he was also acceptable to the Germans, who regarded him as intelligent and pro-German; he had been educated in Germany and had commanded a German artillery battery on the Western Front in World War I. Moreover, he was also an Agrarian politician with a large following among the peasants—although the party leaders contemptuously called him a demagogue and an agent of the Tsar. Bagryanov, therefore, had considerable freedom of action in his dealings both with the Allies and with the Germans.

The new prime minister tried to be all things to all men; thus his personal views are not clear. He did realize the necessity of Bulgaria's leaving the war and, according to Lukacs, had advocated such a move in a letter to Filov in February 1944. However, skeptics recalled the 1941 theory that his resignation from the government was prompted by Tsar Boris's desire to hold him in reserve in case Bulgaria's pro-German policy had to be changed.[2] The men whom Bagryanov selected for his cabinet, however, were closely linked with the previous pro-Axis governments. The foreign minister was Purvan Draganov, who had been Ambassador to Germany and was reputedly the late Tsar's half brother. Minister of the Interior Alexander Stanishev was a Germanophile who had once been associated with IMRO. The Minister of Justice, Alexander Stalisky, had been a follower of Tsankov and had later founded his own nationalist party. Perhaps the most influential member of the new cabinet was Slaveiko Vasilev, former President of the League of Reserve Officers, who had been a leading participant in the coup against Stambolisky in 1923. He was bitterly hated by the Agrarians, who accused him of personally torturing and killing some of their members.[3] As recently as March 23, 1944, in a speech in the Narodno Subranie, he had expressed his confidence in an Axis victory and had praised the Japanese war effort.

Bagryanov had tried to persuade several members of the democratic opposition to join his government; for a week or two he even left vacant several cabinet posts (including that of foreign minister) in the hope that the opposition would eventually accept them. However, the democratic politicians refused to serve with men like Vasilev, hoping to avoid the mistake of Alexander Malinov, who had compromised himself in 1918 by accepting power too soon.* Bagryanov's only success was in persuading Professor Doncho Kostov to become minister of agriculture. Kostov was a biologist who had spent three years in the United States and had been a researcher in Leningrad University until 1943, when he returned to Bulgaria. His inclusion in Bagryanov's cabinet was intended to be a conciliatory gesture toward the USSR, but when the Fatherland Front informed Kostov that his participation in the cabinet would aid the fascists, he resigned "for reasons of health."[4]

The Bulgarian Communists were somewhat confused about the attitude they should take toward Bagryanov. He told the Communists privately that he intended to take Bulgaria out of the war and establish friendly relations with the USSR. He also tried to induce the BKP to participate in his cabinet by promising both to name a Communist as director of police and to abolish the concentration camps. This so impressed the BKP representatives that they informed him that he would also be their choice for prime minister.[5] Plans for cooperation between Bagryanov and the Communists ended almost immediately, though, when the "Hristo Botev" radio station in the Soviet Union broadcast an article by Georgi Dimitrov that stated: "The Bagryanov government is a pro-German government. . . . The Fatherland Front exposes all kinds of illusions relating to this gov-

---

* The case of Malinov made a strong impression on Bulgarian politicians. In May 1944, Bozhilov had asked Ambassador Kioseivanov to become foreign minister in a new cabinet he was trying to form. Kioseivanov referred to the fate of Malinov and said that it was both "too early and too late" to take office.

ernment and calls with renewed force for a complete strengthening of the national liberation fight against the Hitlerists."[6]

The Communists now would not be satisfied with any government not nominated by the Fatherland Front and complained that Bagryanov only sought to silence their criticism by "implicating them in his crime." They were right: Bagryanov had no intention of allowing the Fatherland Front or the Communist Party to influence decisions of his government. Bulgaria's international position was so precarious that he wanted to remove any threat from his domestic opposition, particularly from the armed Communist partisans. The BKP complained that he promised a democratic change in internal policy but was at the same time trying to crush the partisans.[7]

On June 1, 1944, shortly after the new cabinet was formed, the Regents assured Beckerle that there would be no change in Bulgaria's foreign policy toward Germany. Bagryanov was a stronger man than Bozhilov, Filov told Beckerle, and would therefore be able to break off relations with the Soviet Union, as Germany was demanding.[8] For this reason, the Germans completely misinterpreted Bagryanov's inaugural address of June 3. Full of platitudes and equivocal phrases, the speech was based on the theme that "the fate of Bulgaria is entirely in the hands of Bulgarians." Opponents of the war assumed—probably correctly—that this was an assertion that Bulgaria would henceforth pursue an independent foreign policy. The Germans, however, strangely assumed that other vague phrases, such as "trying to create a new world of more truth and justice" and "our fatherland will take its place with dignity in the world," meant that Bulgaria was planning to break relations with the USSR.[9]

Consequently, Germany remained favorably inclined toward the new government. The *Neues Wiener Tageblatt*, for example, described Bagryanov's previous success as minister of agriculture and asserted, "The personality of the new Prime Minister Ivan Bagryanov is a significant guarantee for the conduct of the Bulgarian nation"; Bulgaria would be as firm an ally as it had been in the First World War, and the Bulgarians "will defend with rifles, ... prepared for all eventualities, as they have often done in their history."[10] The

precedent of Bulgaria's staunch defense in World War I greatly influenced Germany's evaluation of the political situation and soon led
to a serious miscalculation.[11]

Bagryanov hoped to remain on good terms with the Germans
while working behind the scenes for an armistice with the Allies.
Like his predecessors, he faced the problem of how to take Bulgaria
out of the war without provoking a German occupation. Bagryanov's plan apparently was to arrange the armistice with the Allies but
to refrain from consummating it until the Germans began to withdraw from the Balkans. Bulgaria would then change sides and mobilize its 25 divisions along the border to discourage either German or
Russian interference. If the Bulgarians could make their move at exactly the right time, the two Great Powers might be so concerned with
fighting each other that they would not wish to fight the Bulgarian
army as well. If the move were made too early, the country would be
occupied first by the Germans and then by the Russians; if it came
too late, the Russians would sweep into Bulgaria and treat it as an
enemy. Bagryanov's plan was not new, but he was the first Bulgarian
prime minister who had a reasonable chance of implementing it.

However, he made at least two important mistakes. First, he over-
estimated the amount of time he had available to carry out his plans,
and therefore he did not act with sufficient haste to reach an agreement with the Allies. The Soviet army was still fighting on its own
territory and all of Rumania lay between it and Bulgaria. The Bulgarian General Staff thought it possible that the Russians would not
reach the Bulgarian border until the end of 1944, and a few generals
(including General Mihov) believed that stiffened German resistance might delay the Russians until the summer of 1945. Bagryanov
was not so unrealistic, but he did believe that for the next few months
his task would be to avoid offending the Great Powers rather than
to take positive action. His second mistake was to assume that he
could remain head of an Axis state, preside over a cabinet of German sympathizers, collaborate with the Germans, and still be acceptable to the Allies. As discreetly as possible, he tried to convince
the Allies that his government was markedly different from the pre-

ceding ones, but he was too subtle and too half-hearted in his actions.

Soon after coming into office, Bagryanov launched an ambitious (his opponents said demagogic) economic program to win the support of the people. Since wartime inflation had inflicted severe hardship on those with fixed salaries, especially civil servants, he ordered wages for government employees to be increased 30 to 50 percent. Pensions were raised proportionately a few days later. This was hardly a cure for inflation, and most of his other plans similarly had more glitter than substance, but he was trying to stave off popular unrest as long as possible. Bagryanov also halted the shipment of food to Germany on the grounds that it was needed to supply the enlarged Bulgarian army. This move slightly improved the economic situation, gained popular support, and was interpreted abroad as the first action against the Germans.[12]

Bagryanov also took steps to reduce Germany's use of his country as a military base against the USSR, a major concern of the Soviet government. German trains crossing Bulgaria to Rumania were reduced from eight a week to one, and the remaining one was to be eliminated. Bulgaria ordered the Germans to remove all their operational forces from the ports of Varna and Burgas and made arrangements for Soviet diplomats to verify the withdrawal (in fact, many German ships and support troops remained in the ports). Filov agreed to these actions and felt them "justified by the new situation in the Black Sea, in order to avoid if possible a new conflict in the Balkans with Russia and eventually also with Turkey, which will probably intervene if Russia breaks with us."[13] The Soviets had given Bulgaria a virtual ultimatum about the German use of the Black Sea ports, and Draganov cabled the Bulgarian minister in Moscow that "an evasive answer will lead to a breaking of our relations with Russia, which is neither in our interest nor that of Germany and will cause a disaster in the Balkans." He therefore formally requested Germany to evacuate the ports and thus "give Bulgaria the possibility of escaping the catastrophe with Russia."[14] Germany complied without protest. This did not undermine Germany's confidence in Bagryanov: "The new government is doubtlessly stronger both in composition and also in the country itself than the Bozhilov government; it can therefore make urgent decisions with more energy and consideration."[15] Germany remained confident that "the sympathies of the majority of the people are on the German side."[16]

Negotiations with the Allies

The Western Allies expected that as soon as Bagryanov came to power he would attempt to lead Bulgaria out of the war. Bagryanov did place some limitations on the Germans, as we have seen, but he was very slow in contacting the Allies. On June 20, 1944, the Bulgarian Consul in Istanbul, Ivan Stanchov, was authorized to begin discussions with Dr. Floyd Black, who had been president of the American College in Sofia since 1926, and with another American professor. Stanchov asked for a definite Allied promise that Bulgaria would be allowed to keep the Southern Dobruja and a large portion of Macedonia, would not be subjected to Allied occupation, and would not be asked to drive out the Germans. He requested an immediate reply from the Allies.[17]

Final Allied terms were extremely generous in comparison with those in the earlier British draft version. They demanded that Bulgarian troops withdraw from all the territory occupied by Bulgaria since January 1, 1940 (which included the Southern Dobruja), but promised that this would be "without prejudice to the ultimate settlement of the disputed territorial claims." Bulgaria would also be required to accept Allied occupation, to "make such reparation and restitution as the United Nations may require," and to provide the Allies with war materials, transportation, information, and archives. Bulgaria would not be accorded the status of cobelligerent. The surrender would be unconditional, but the Allied negotiators were authorized to offer certain inducements: a guarantee of Bulgarian independence, assurance that neither Yugoslav nor Greek troops would participate in the occupation, and the retention of the Southern Dobruja. No compromise was offered on Thrace or Macedonia because of the great difficulty this would cause with Greece and Yugoslavia; the British position was that the Bulgarian claims were "by no means convincing." These were regarded as maximum concessions and would only be offered if Bulgaria defected from the Axis and surrendered the Germans on its territory. "If, on the other hand, Bulgaria should delay surrender until the defeat of Germany is imminent, the United Nations should make no concessions to Bulgaria except with respect to the ultimate restoration of its independence."[18]

The Allied terms were reasonable but not very attractive. Bulgaria had expected to be able to change sides at the last possible moment and still avoid being treated as an enemy by the Allies. At worst, it expected to be required to participate in the war on the Allied side; at best it might be able to remain neutral. Bagryanov now found that the Allies wanted him to withdraw from the war immediately, even though he believed that this would be national suicide, and they would only offer him terms that he regarded as humiliating. Most important was the territorial issue: as long as the Allies would not guarantee that the newly acquired lands would remain a part of Bulgaria, Bagryanov was reluctant to make a final settlement.

It was clear to the Bulgarians that Greek and Yugoslav pressure would have much more effect on the British and Americans after the war than would the claims of a former enemy state. Bulgaria, therefore, had to obtain all the concessions possible while it was in a strategic position and still had bargaining power. Bagryanov decided to postpone a formal acceptance of the Allied offer in the hope that better terms could be obtained later. In the meantime, he sought to show the Allies that Bulgaria sincerely wanted to break away from the Axis as soon as possible.

On July 20, 1944, Nikola Balabanov, Bulgarian Ambassador to Turkey, brought from Sofia a note for the Allied negotiators in Istanbul outlining the general policy of the Bulgarian government. He attached great importance to this document and requested that it be kept absolutely secret to prevent the Bagryanov cabinet's being replaced by one that was more pro-German. According to this note, the purpose of the government was "to get Bulgaria out of the war as soon as conditions make this purpose possible." It claimed that German activities in Bulgaria had been sharply curtailed, especially along the Black Sea coast, and that internal pacification had been largely achieved. Furthermore, the note suggested that Bulgaria was planning to withdraw military forces from Serbia (but not from Macedonia), to declare a general political amnesty, and to repeal the anti-Jewish legislation. The note concluded with the assurance that Bagryanov was "doing everything possible to get Bulgaria out of the war," and said that the American government could help by offering its views on "the position of Bulgaria in the future political arrangements in the Balkans."[19] Thus, after almost two months in power, Bagryanov had still not reached agreement with the Allies and seemed unlikely to do so until international events made it unavoidable.

The Soviet Union and Turkey

While dealing with the West, the Bulgarian government was also concerned about two threats from the East—Turkey and the USSR. Bulgaria was not at war with the Soviet Union, but the Soviets had expressed considerable dissatisfaction with Bulgarian policy. Bagryanov determined to improve relations with Moscow by reducing German military activity in Bulgaria, and this he did. The Soviet government was not satisfied, however, and demanded that Bulgaria allow the reopening of the Soviet consulate in Varna, which had been closed after a year of German pressure in 1942. They claimed this would wipe out the stain on Bulgarian honor caused by the unexplained killing of a Soviet diplomat there earlier in the war; but the real reason they wanted the consulate was to observe German naval movements in the port, where in June 1944 there were over 60 German vessels.[20] Bagryanov's restrictions on the Germans had only limited their "offensive" activities; their "defensive" activities—if such a distinction can be made—were increasing as the Red army advanced toward the Balkans. Because such activity worsened relations with the Soviet Union, which was not Bagryanov's intention, he conceded on July 29 to the reopening of the Soviet consulate in Varna and announced that everything incompatible with Bulgaria's position of neutrality had now been swept away.[21]

Bulgaria's neutral neighbor, Turkey, had cooperated with Germany throughout the war: it had made regular shipments of chrome ore to the Reich, and as recently as June 1944 had allowed German naval vessels to pass through the Straits. In the middle of July 1944, however, Bulgarian newspapers reported that Turkey was negotiating with the British and the Americans. By the end of the month, Turkey was engaged in discussions with the Soviets as well, and Bulgarian intelligence reports indicated that Turkey would make a major change of policy within a day or two. On August 2, 1944, the Turkish parliament, influenced by Allied pressure and the fear of being diplomatically isolated in the postwar world, voted to break off relations with Germany.[22]

The Change in Policy Stalled

On that same day, August 2, Prime Minister Churchill made a speech in the House of Commons strongly criticizing Bulgaria and implying that it, like Rumania, would have to make its peace primarily with the Soviet Union. Churchill made no distinction between the Bagryanov government and the previous pro-German governments, and indicated that Bulgaria would not fare well at a future peace conference.

Thrice thrown into war on the wrong side by a miserable set of criminal politicians, who seem to be available for their country's ruin generation after generation, three times in my life has this wretched Bulgaria subjected a peasant population to all the pangs of war and the chastisements of defeat. . . .

The moment of repentence has not passed, but it is passing swiftly. The whole of Europe is heading irresistably into new and secure foundations. What will be the place of Bulgaria at the judgement seat, when the petty and cowardly part she has played in this war is revealed, and when the entire Yugoslav and Greek nations, through their representatives, will reveal at the Allies' armistice table the dismal tale of the work the Bulgarian Army has done their countries as the cruel lackeys of the fallen Nazi power?[23]

This accusation elicited a reply from a young member of the Narodno Subranie, Nikola Minkov, who quoted part of Churchill's speech and emphasized that some thought should have been given to the suffering of Bulgaria at the hands of the Greeks and Serbs. Bulgarian territorial claims, he said, were fully in accord with the principle of nationality, and Bulgaria still had a strong army.[24] The pressure on Bulgaria to negotiate, however, was growing stronger. At the beginning of August, the Allied forces in the West broke out of the Normandy beachhead and advanced rapidly across France. On the other side of the continent, Soviet forces were poised for an advance into the Balkans that German and Rumanian troops would find impossible to stop.

On August 12, a group of opposition leaders presented the Bulgarian government with a petition—the first since 1942 that contained the names of both Communist and non-Communist party leaders. The petition demanded that the government end the war with Great Britain and the United States, open genuinely friendly relations with the Soviet Union, withdraw troops from territory not claimed by Bulgaria (but not from the annexed territories), respect democratic rights, and form a representative and constitutional government.[25]

The main difficulty remained the territorial question, on which neither the Bulgarians nor the Allies would yield. Milev, the Bulgarian Consul in Geneva, informed Foreign Minister Draganov that the most that could be expected from the Allies, even if Bulgaria immediately left the war, was the pre-Marita (1941) boundaries. "They do not want to even hear about Thrace and the outlet to the Aegean. Now the Greeks are *les infants gâtés* and in no case will their territorial integrity be impaired."[26] Bagryanov tried, however, to resolve the conflicting pressures by taking half measures, as he had been doing for over two months. On August 14, he removed former Prime Minister Bozhilov from his new position as Director of the National Bank. Although the official reason given was Bozhilov's "ill health," the move was taken to placate those who had complained that the present government had too many ties with the previous ones. Bagryanov also removed some of Bozhilov's closest associates in the bank, including the administrator and assistant administrator.[27]

Two days later, Bagryanov, Draganov, and Filov met to discuss the proposed secret treaty with Turkey, by which they hoped to avoid a conflict between the two countries and prevent Bulgaria's complete diplomatic isolation. A treaty with Turkey meant an alliance with a state that was at least technically allied with Britain. Furthermore, Bulgaria and Turkey shared a fear of a Soviet domination of the Balkans; the final text of the treaty included the sentence "The two Governments consider that a true and lasting peace in the Balkans will be possible only if established on a fair basis which leaves the Balkans to the Balkan people."[28]

The Germans were aware of Bulgaria's desire to dissociate itself from the Axis, and many of the German officers in the country regarded the situation as highly unstable. The German Commander-in-Chief in the Balkans, Field Marshal von Weichs, believed that Bulgaria would suddenly change sides in the war, as Italy had done, and he warned against too much dependence upon the Bulgarian army for the defense of the Balkans. He therefore recommended to Berlin that the army be disarmed so that it could not be turned against the Germans at a critical moment.[29] The official German attitude, however, continued to be influenced by the history of Bulgaria's determined stand during World War I, when the small country had held at bay an expeditionary force of French, British, Serbian, and Russian divisions. Bulgaria was expected to do the same if Allied troops again appeared on the country's border, and the two dozen Bulgarian divisions could greatly assist in Germany's defense of the Balkans.

For this reason, despite the objections of a number of military and intelligence officers, Germany decided to send additional weapons and equipment to the Bulgarian army, including much equipment badly needed by the German army. When 50 assault guns and 88 Mark IV tanks were sent to Bulgaria in early August, Colonel von Jungenfeldt, the chief training adviser to the Bulgarian army, made a strong objection to the Inspector General of Panzers, General Guderian. As a result, Guderian ordered that these armored vehicles be diverted to the 4th SS Division in the Balkans. At Hitler's headquar-

ters, however, General Jodl countermanded this order and directed
that the original instructions be followed. Not until August 25 did
Germany begin to take "certain precautionary measures" against the
possibility of Bulgaria's defection from the Axis.[30]

Finally, on August 17, Bagryanov officially repudiated the policies
of his predecessors. In a speech before the Narodno Subranie, he described the disasters that had been brought upon the country by following "the bloody path of chauvinism and war"—a policy he called
shortsighted and "contrary to the will of the people." He announced
that henceforth Bulgaria would follow a policy of strict neutrality,
and he promised a full political amnesty.[31] The Assembly greeted the
new policy with the same tumultuous applause it had given the former pro-German policy. Newspapers devoted considerable space to
the speech, and their headlines conveyed the impression that it was
much more explicit than it actually was. The newspapers also dis-
closed that the former President of the Assembly, Stoicho Moshanov,
had been sent to Cairo to negotiate a formal peace settlement.[32] (Actually, Moshanov went to Ankara, not Cairo.)

Bagryanov thus attempted to take Bulgaria out of the war not by
surrendering, but simply by declaring the country neutral. Although
it was doubtful that this would satisfy the Allies, Bagryanov's alternatives were so unpleasant that the gamble seemed worthwhile. Nevertheless, some Narodno Subranie representatives criticized him for
going too far. Alexander Tsankov argued that Bulgaria's fate was
bound up with that of Germany, and that the Reich would never
capitulate; Lazar Popov objected to Bagryanov's claim that he had
saved the country by becoming premier and to the implication that
Germany had lost the war; Dimiter Peshev, former Vice President
of the Narodno Subranie, urged that no compromise be made on the
territorial question, for Macedonia and Thrace were "not just dreams
—they are national needs"; and former Prime Minister Nikola Mushanov said that Bagryanov should have adopted the more popular and
realistic course of relying on Russia, although it was not clear to
Mushanov or anyone else how this could be done.[33] Of greater importance was the unfortunate remark of Foreign Minister Draganov

that Bulgaria had been justified in joining the Tripartite Pact in 1941 and that "if Bulgaria found itself in the enemy's camp, much of the blame lies with the Allies." Draganov's remark may have contained some truth, but it did throw doubt on Bulgaria's sincerity and had a detrimental effect on the Moshanov peace mission.[34]

On August 14, Stoicho Moshanov approached the Counsellor of the British Embassy in Ankara with a request to speak to the Ambassador, Sir Hughe Knatchbull-Hugessen. The Counsellor told Moshanov that the British position on Bulgaria was quite clear, but Moshanov replied that he was bringing entirely new set of proposals. The British Foreign Office authorized Sir Hughe to listen to Moshanov's proposals but advised him to take no action except to report them to London.

At the subsequent meeting with the British, on August 16, 1944, Moshanov stated that the Bulgarian government now desired to leave the war and wished to know the Allied conditions. Two factors affected the timing of the armistice, he said. One was the necessity of gathering as much of the harvest as possible beforehand, in case of German reprisals. The harvest was good but late, and most of the army reservists were working in the fields. The other factor was the need to secure unity in the country, which he claimed would take another week or two.

Knatchbull-Hugessen replied that time was running out; the war would not stand still until mid-September when Bulgaria gathered its harvest. Moshanov acknowledged that Bulgaria's defection from the Axis would have significant military impact but objected that "it would be impractical to ask Bulgaria to break off relations with Germany and withdraw troops from Serbia and Greece at this stage." In the meantime, he proposed that Bulgaria could show its sincerity by releasing Allied prisoners (mostly captured airmen) and by sending an emissary to Cairo not later than the end of August.[35]

The British vacillated on the strategic advisability of an immediate Bulgarian break with Germany. An Aide-Mémoire from the British Embassy in Washington to the U.S. Department of State dated August 20, 1944, indicated that the time might not yet be ripe for such a break; another Aide-Mémoire, from the same source on the same day but dealing with Turkey, proposed that the Turkish and Soviet governments present Bulgaria with an ultimatum that "unless they expel the Germans from Bulgaria forthwith, sever relations with Germany and withdraw their troops from Allied territory they have occupied, Turkey and the Soviet Union will declare war on Bulgaria." The plan stressed, however, that it was complementary to, and not in conflict with, the effort to reach an agreement with the Moshanov mission.[36]

Moshanov and the Bulgarian industrialist Georgi Kiselov presented their credentials to the Allies in Istanbul on August 23 and urged them to act immediately on the Bulgarian request for peace. Kiselov argued that the Bagryanov government had already taken considerable risks in attempting to dissociate itself from Germany and that German military intervention in Bulgaria remained a possibility. The Bulgarian emissaries, attempting to play the West off against Russia, emphasized that the Soviets would probably offer Bulgaria better terms but that Bulgaria was willing to make some sacrifice to ensure its "future status as a free democratic state." They warned, however, that if the West proposed overly harsh terms the Bulgarian troops would turn to the Soviet Union and the government would be unable to resist.[37]

The Results of Rumania's Defection

Events in Rumania gave the Bulgarian negotiations added urgency. On August 20, the Russians launched a massive attack on German and Rumanian defenses along the Rumanian border. By noon of that day, Russian tank-mounted infantry were reported to be penetrating the Rumanian sections of the line and meeting almost no resistance. Marshal Antonescu, the dictator of Rumania, went to the front in an attempt to rally the dispirited forces. Upon his return to Bucharest on August 23, King Michael summoned him to report on the military situation and demanded that he come to terms with the Soviet Union. Antonescu refused and was immediately arrested on orders of the King, who thereupon ordered the arrest of the cabinet and the chief of the German military mission. Rumania's defection from the Axis left only four German divisions between Bulgaria and the advancing Red army. When word of the King's coup reached Berlin, German units in Rumania were immediately ordered to occupy strategic areas and reinforcements were flown into the country. In the meantime, the Luftwaffe made aimless attacks on the Rumanian capital. But German strength was inadequate to resist the Russians and punish the Rumanians at the same time. The German reprisals only provoked the Rumanians to declare war on Germany on the 25th.[38]

On August 23, Bagryanov announced that Bulgaria was withdrawing completely from the war. Three days later, Draganov informed the Soviet chargé d'affaires in Sofia that all German troops fleeing into Bulgaria from Rumania would henceforth be disarmed and that German troops already in the country would be asked to withdraw immediately or be disarmed. The Western Allies, learning of this, requested that the Soviet government not encourage the Bulgarians to believe that neutrality would suffice in place of vigorous action against Germany. Moscow responded by opening a violent radio and press campaign against the Bagryanov government.[39]

Moshanov returned to Sofia for instructions on the night of August 24, while Kiselov remained in Turkey to urge the British and the Americans not to lose the opportunity to help Bulgaria out of the war. The Red army might appear on the Danube at any time, he stated; or a Communist regime might replace the present one in Bulgaria; or the Germans might intervene and prevent Bulgaria from leaving the Axis. The Allies and the Bulgarians blamed each other for the delay in reaching an accord. Draganov asked the Turks on August 25 to intervene diplomatically in order to hasten the armistice negotiations: "The Russians are approaching the mouth of the Danube.... The British and Americans are acting much too slowly. To arrive at an understanding, speed is now essential."[40]

In an attempt to expedite matters, the Allies decided to conduct the initial negotiations in Ankara, rather than in Cairo, and declared that in the meantime they would look favorably upon any pro-Allied actions taken by the Bulgarians. Specifically mentioned were the release of Allied prisoners, the cessation of hostilities against the Allies (although this had already been done), the severing of diplomatic relations with Germany, and the expulsion of German troops from Bulgarian territory. These measures formed the basis of the official armistice terms that the Allies were now ready to present to Bulgaria. In addition, Bulgaria was required to withdraw from Greek and Yugoslav territory, to provide for the trial of Bulgarian war criminals, and to make reparations for war damage inflicted on the Allied nations. Bulgaria would, however, be given an oral promise that its independence would be respected, and Greece and Yugoslavia would merely assent to the treaty rather than participate in the signing.[41]

The negotiations now moved to Cairo, as originally planned; on August 30, Moshanov and Colonel Zheleskov (former Bulgarian military attaché in Istanbul) flew there, to be joined soon by the diplomat Ivan Stanchov and the pro-American former Director of Bulgarian Railways, Lyuben Boshkov. The Bulgarian representatives pointed out that the Bagryanov government had taken additional measures to prove its sincerity: almost five thousand German troops from Rumania had been disarmed, the Gestapo had been expelled from the country on August 27, the other Germans stationed in Bulgaria had been given a deadline of August 31 to leave, all anti-Jewish laws had been abrogated, and the Bulgarian occupation corps was being withdrawn from Serbia. Furthermore, Allied prisoners would soon be released, and the Narodno Subranie was to be dissolved in a few days. No action had been taken to break off relations with Germany, the delegation said, because this would not be in keeping with Bulgaria's avowal of strict neutrality.[42]

The Bulgarians were aware that Germany knew of these moves and were apprehensive during the last week of August that the Germans would resort to military action against Bulgaria. Sofia was in panic and rumors spread that the city would be bombed. On the day of the Rumanian surrender, an Allied air raid on the Danube crossings greatly alarmed the Bulgarians, who thought that the Rumanians and the Red army were invading Bulgaria. Bulgarians were also worried because it was known that the German troops leaving Bulgaria proper were taking up positions in Macedonia with the obvious intention of defending the Vardar and Morava valleys. Ambassador Beckerle, who had angrily left Bulgaria earlier in the month, returned on August 27 in a much calmer mood and said only that the Bulgarians would regret their mistake.

Germany could not permit Bulgaria to defect from the Axis, for this would cut off the units in Rumania and imperil Germany's position in Greece and Serbia. To prevent this, the Germans had a contingency plan—appropriately called "Operation Hundessohn"—to be led by an SS police division. A Bulgarian puppet state would be created under Tsankov. (The Germans also briefly considered Ivan Mihailov, the leader of IMRO, for the role of administrator of Macedonia.)* But insufficient time and the rapid advance of the Red army made it impossible for Germany to carry out this operation with the small forces then available.

Moscow's Double Game

The USSR was not at war with Bulgaria but had been consulted by the Western Allies about the peace negotiations and requested to send an observer. In mid-March 1944, Molotov had told U.S. Ambassador Harriman that he believed it was premature to discuss terms for a Bulgarian surrender because Allied forces were still too far away to support Bulgaria if it tried to leave the Axis. Western diplomats were still uncertain about Russia's attitude toward Bulgaria and suspected that the Soviets might be planning to use Bulgaria to extend its influence into the Balkans.† A report prepared for the American Under Secretary of State, Edward Stettinius, summarized this possibility: "The Slavic tie between Russia and Bulgaria and Russia's traditional ambition to have a dependable access to the Mediterranean combine to create interesting possibilities as regards the Soviet role in deter-

* Tsankov was soon to become the leader of a Bulgarian government-in-exile in Germany; at the end of the war, he fled to Argentina. Mihailov remained in Croatia for another few months, then went to Germany himself; after the war he set up a clandestine headquarters in Italy, where he reportedly lives today.

† It was this same fear in 1878 that prompted Great Britain and the other powers to overturn the treaty of San Stefano and hold the Congress of Berlin, which greatly reduced the territory of Bulgaria.

mining the disposition to be made of Bulgaria. Will the Soviet Government, for example, insist on an enlarged and strengthened Bulgaria, reviving Bulgarian claims to North Dobruja and championing Bulgaria's longstanding insistence upon an outlet on the Aegean?"[43]

The Soviets reportedly told the Bulgarians that a strong Slavic bloc would be created that would be the dominant force in world politics, and Bulgaria was advised to join while there was still an opportunity. The Soviet chargé d'affaires in Sofia was in close contact with the Fatherland Front and also met openly with the opposition leaders Mushanov and Gichev, who were adopting a favorable attitude toward Russia. Even the official Bulgarian government radio began once more to broadcast Russian music.

However, the evidence was growing that, in the words of one Western report, "Russia is playing a double game in Bulgaria."[44] The Soviet government had accepted Bagryanov's declaration of neutrality of August 17, but the Soviet Legation in Sofia had denied to the local Communists that such action had been taken. (The chargé d'affaires had left for Moscow, leaving only a Second Secretary who could provide little information on the Soviet position.) On the other hand, while seeking friendly relations with the Soviet Union, the Bagryanov government was making every effort to eradicate the Communist partisan movement; in Soviet eyes this branded Bagryanov a hypocrite and a fascist.[45]

Negotiations with the Fatherland Front

Bagryanov's attitude toward the Communists changed rapidly following Rumania's surrender. On August 23, he met Dimo Kazasov, a former leader of Zveno who had once been connected with Tsankov but was now in the Fatherland Front. According to Kazasov, Bagryanov was in obvious panic and wanted to arrange a meeting at once with the Fatherland Front.[46] Bagryanov had met with Front members soon after he came to power in May 1944 and had seemed willing to compromise on a number of issues. He had even admitted that the partisan movement had been necessary as the only way of opposing the Germans. More concretely, he had promised a full amnesty and the opening of the concentration camps, and had requested that the Communists recommend someone acceptable to them as director of police. As we have seen, Bagryanov also had tried to induce members of both the democratic opposition and the Communist-dominated Front to accept portfolios in his new cabinet. But on orders from Moscow, the Front had refused to cooperate with him. Bagryanov also failed to keep his promises. The new director of police was not someone acceptable to the Communists, but Colonel Kutsarov, a fanatical fascist. The Minister of the Interior, Alexander Stanishev, was ardently pro-German and had given orders to crush the partisans. Under Bagryanov's regime the concentration camps were fuller than before.

Thus there was a great deal of mistrust and ill feeling when Bagryanov met again with the representatives of the Front on August 24. The Front told him that Bulgaria could only be saved by turning over the government to "the true representatives of the people." Bagryanov replied that a decision was impossible without the approval of the Regents, and he invited the Front to seek a meeting with Filov, Mihov, and Prince Kiril. The Front representatives refused, saying that it was the prime minister's duty to speak with the Regents on this matter. Bagryanov then left for a short time and returned to say that the Regents had refused to grant any audience because there was no cabinet crisis.* The Zvenoist Petko Stainov proposed that the Front should support Bagryanov if he would agree to implement its program, but since this was totally unacceptable to the other Front representatives present, the meeting adjourned without results.[47]

This failure and the discouraging news from Rumania resulted in a redoubled Bulgarian effort to reach agreement with the Allies by the end of August. Bagryanov's difficulty, however, lay in the fact that he was no more willing to make concessions to the Allies than to the Fatherland Front. On August 27, the Regents changed their position and invited the leading members of the opposition—ranging from the Communists to the Tsankovists—to a meeting. Since polit-

---

* Bagryanov claimed to have replied "Then we will create one," but this is implausible. Interview, Bulgaria.

ical parties had officially been abolished in 1934, these men had been invited as individuals and not as spokesmen for the different parties and factions. This was the cause—or the pretext—for the withdrawal of Ivan Pashov, Nikola Petkov, and Grigor Chesmedzhiev from the meeting, for they demanded to be recognized as representatives of the Fatherland Front.*

The other opposition leaders were not anxious to cooperate with the regime, because they believed that it had been largely discredited and because they expected to be called to power within a few days. Filov's continued unwillingness to make any concessions was based upon the assumptions that the USSR would respect Bulgaria's neutrality and that an armistice with the West was imminent. The Fatherland Front, on the other hand, was already planning a coup and was awaiting the appearance of Soviet troops on Bulgaria's northern border. They did not have long to wait: on August 31, Soviet troops entered Bucharest and headed south.

---

* Kimon Georgiev, who had just been released from internal exile in Burgas, had not had time to consult colleagues in the Front and did not walk out with them. The Fatherland Front had by this time approximately 3,600 members, organized in 670 cells (an average of five-and-a-half persons per cell), of which 57 cells were in Sofia. The National Committee had been increased to fifteen members in August; five were Communists, three were Agrarians (Pladne), two were Social Democrats, and five had other affiliations. Oren, "Bulgarian Communist Party," pp. 335–36; Valev, p. 67; *Rabotnicheski delo*, 8.ix.49; interviews, Bulgaria.

CHAPTER 16

The Partisans

I N A CONVERSATION with the Vrabcha Agrarian leader, Dimiter Gichev, Bagryanov argued, "Well, at least I have bought three months for Bulgaria." But Gichev's rejoinder was more realistic: "You have lost three valuable months for Bulgaria!"[1] Among the beneficiaries of Bagryanov's miscalculations were the Communists, whose ranks swelled with opportunists as the Red army approached the border. Before recounting the climactic events of September 1–9, 1944, a review of the Party's history will help clarify its role in the war's final phase.

The Failure of the Resistance Movement in 1941

The Communist armed resistance movement in Bulgaria was generally poorly organized, poorly armed, and poorly led. On June 24, 1941, two days after the German invasion of the Soviet Union, the Bulgarian Communist Party formed a Central Military Commission (TsVK) and called for an armed struggle against the "German oppressors and their Bulgarian lackeys."[2] But the Party rank and file were by no means enthusiastic about their new role, especially as they saw scores of their leaders quickly captured by the Bulgarian police. Those few leaders who remained were soon forced to conclude that the resistance was costing the Party far more than the results justified. According to one, Traicho Kostov, by trying to conduct a campaign of violence, the BKP was risking "isolation from the masses and the possibility of having to bear the burdens of the fight all alone."[3] Others argued that a better policy would be to wait until conditions became more favorable to partisan activity, and even the TsVK admitted that armed resistance at this time only served to bleed the Party white.[4]

Statistics vary widely on the number of partisan attacks during 1941, but a reasonable estimate would be two in July, about two dozen in August, and about one dozen in September. More than half of these attacks were in the "new lands"—the territories recently annexed to Bulgaria—and were therefore not attributable to the regular Bulgarian Communist organization. Calculations are difficult, but the total of all violent anti-government incidents during 1941 probably did not exceed 85, most of which were quite minor. Of these, 22 were against agricultural targets, 12 against factories, 11 against warehouses, and 10 against railroads and transports. About 40 percent were in the Sofia district, the most significant action there being the burning of a small fur company in the city.[5] Only two incidents during 1941 are worthy of particular mention. One was the attempt to liberate inmates of the Gonda Voda concentration camp: of two assaults made on the camp, the first, by 70 partisans on August 15, failed completely and the second, on August 31, was intercepted before the force ever reached the camp.[6] The second case involved an individual act of sabotage by Leon Tadzher, a Jewish Communist, who set fire to a large quantity of oil and gasoline at a depot in Ruse and killed an unarmed German soldier. After his execution for sabotage, he became a major hero of the resistance.[7] Tightened government security and the "temporary successes of the fascist armies on the Eastern Front," however, discouraged any imitators. By the end of 1941, most partisan bands had either been destroyed or reduced to a handful of fighters.[8]

The Russians tried to assist the Bulgarian partisans by sending Bulgarian émigré agents into the country by submarine and parachute in August and September 1941, but they had no more success than the local Communists; the country was simply not ready for revolution.[9] A major handicap for the partisans was that Bulgaria was not an occupied country. Armed attacks and sabotage had to be directed not against the Germans but against fellow Bulgarians. With the Bulgarian government and army intact, there was no disintegration of authority or availability of large supplies of weapons from a defeated army, as was the case in Poland, France, and Yugoslavia. Bulgaria was an island of peace in a sea of war; even those who were opposed to the Axis and unimpressed by the territorial gains could not deny that the Tsar's foreign policy had enjoyed considerable success. Thus, during the early part of the war, the partisans were unable to gain much popular support. "They fought an isolated war, alone in a countryside riddled with informers, surrounded on every side by enemy troops, many hundreds of miles from their nearest allies, who had neither the resources nor the intent to give them aid. Only a handful of those who took up arms in 1942 survived to see the liberation of Bulgaria."[10]

The 1943 Partisan Revival

The Russian victory at Stalingrad in January 1943 revived the demoralized Bulgarian Communists and led to renewed partisan activity. Such inspiration was desperately needed. The already decimated Party leadership had suffered a serious setback in the spring of 1942 when the police arrested Traicho Kostov, Anton Ivanov, the "submariner" Tsvyatko Radoinov, and other leaders during the "Zaimov Affair"—the abortive conspiracy of General Vladimir Zaimov (see Chapter 7).[11] Armed attacks on German soldiers in Sofia in December 1942 had only led to a police blockade of the capital and further setbacks.[12]

Even after Stalingrad, the struggling Bulgarian resistance movement did not suddenly blossom into a full-scale partisan campaign. Whatever the situation on the Eastern Front, the Tsarist government was very much in control within Bulgaria. The Communist Party remained plagued by a "capitulation attitude" so serious that a number of comrades released from the concentration camps chose to return to the camps rather than become partisans. Many BKP members continued to believe that the Party should conserve its forces rather than engage in activity that could endanger its cadres. The prevailing attitude among the rank and file was to "wait and see," to neither resist nor collaborate.[13]

Resistance consequently took the form not of partisan warfare—as in Yugoslavia or Greece where large bands roamed the countryside—but of urban terrorism and sabotage conducted by small groups of three to six men and women. Members of these "fighting groups" (*boini grupi*), unlike partisans, usually had jobs and legal residences in the cities. On February 13, 1943, the extreme nationalist leader General Hristo Lukov was shot dead by a fighting group allegedly led by a 19-year-old girl, Violeta Yankova. (As mentioned in Chapter 9, the identity of the assassins was a matter of much speculation at the time.) An unsuccessful attempt was made on Lukov's secretary on April 6; and on April 15, 1943, a fighting group killed Sotir Yanev, the chairman of the Narodno Subranie's Foreign Affairs Committee. Two weeks later, on May 3, the Yankova team killed Colonel Pantev, the head of the Sofia Military Tribunal.[14] The Party leadership had always harbored serious misgivings about the program of political assassinations and even after the war was reluctant to claim credit for the murders of Lukov and others. After the spring incidents of 1943, the increased police activity and the Communist losses discouraged the Party from further efforts at urban terrorism. "After these actions, the position of the fighting groups in Sofia became more difficult. Only in Sofia did individual fighters remain."[15]

In dissolving these units, the Party relinquished a valuable weapon that required little effort to operate but was extremely difficult to counter. The partisan units in the countryside had much less impact and, at least during 1943, were little more than an irritation. Other assassinations did occur, most notably that of the Deputy Governor of Plovdiv in July 1943, but in general thereafter the only officials in danger were those in remote areas. The urban terrorist campaign and the resulting setbacks contributed to the growth of the partisan movement by forcing many Communists to flee to the mountains. They were joined there by others, inspired by Stalingrad. Their number was not large, but their growth rate was impressive: the police estimate of 180 partisans in January 1943 doubled by March and doubled again by June.[16] Accomplishments were less impressive. Although the number of "partisan" attacks during this period rose from 12 in

January to 58 in March to 145 in June, most of these were of slight significance, and the majority were minor acts of sabotage rather than attacks by partisan bands.[17]

An average band (*cheta*, pl. *cheti*) numbered about a dozen members, who, during this period at least, were necessarily much more concerned with their own survival than with partisan operations. In the Turnovo region, for example, the total accomplishment of the four partisan bands during 1943 was the killing of a policeman and a village mayor, and the seizure of two dozen rifles and some food.[18] In the Burgas zone, one of the twelve Insurrection Operation Zones (VOZ) into which the Communists divided the country in March 1943, only five partisan units (*otryadi*, which were larger than *cheti*) were active during 1943. Otryad No. 1 repeatedly suffered heavy losses and by the end of 1943 had practically disappeared. Otryad No. 2 had greater success—it raided a coal mine in August and in September briefly occupied the town Golyamo Shivachevo and executed its mayor—but reverses in December weakened the unit for several months. The other three units were of virtually no significance in 1943.[19] Then during the winter of 1943–44, the partisans suffered heavy losses. In particular, the famous partisan unit "Anton Ivanov" was destroyed in the Rhodope Mountains in March 1944; 135 of its 153 members were killed in action or captured and beheaded by the gendarmerie.[20] With the return of the warm weather, however, partisan ranks were swelled by volunteers from the cities. Most members of the BKP and the Communist youth organization RMS—Rabotnicheski Mladezhki Suyuz (Union of Young Workers)—had hitherto not answered the Party's call to arms; now, as prospects brightened for an Allied victory, they flocked to the mountains.

The Bulgarian partisans created the first two brigades in Bulgaria proper in April 1944, followed by two others in May. Although Filov noted in his diary in March that the growing Communist forces still posed no threat, by late April he and his co-regent General Mihov had become concerned at the number and scope of partisan successes. Both Mihov and the German advisers in Sofia described much of the Bulgarian military planning as "hidebound, detailed, and bookish," and the Germans criticized the army's inadequate reconnaissance and poor radio discipline (*Klartextfunken*).[21]

The partisans themselves were not fully effective, owing to a lack of arms and adequate training. Thus they remained only a potential threat rather than an actual danger. This was demonstrated by their most dramatic raid during the month of June 1944—the raid on the Kazanluk-Plovdiv train. The train was halted by the partisans at a small village on the edge of the Sredna Gora, the range of mountains where guerrilla forces were most concentrated. The passengers and crew were ordered out of the train to be searched. Among the passengers, but apparently unrecognized, was the Vice President of the National Assembly, Peter Kioseivanov, the brother of the former premier. Before the partisans discovered him, they were interrupted and put to flight by the arrival of an army rescue force from a nearby town. The rescue force consisted of a lieutenant and four soldiers.[22]

British Assistance to the Partisans

The British government sought to aid the Bulgarian partisans with arms and advisers but had little success. As early as the summer of 1943, the Special Operations Executive (SOE) tried to establish contact with the partisans. A team under Major Mostyn Davies parachuted into Serbia in August 1943 and laboriously made its way to the Bulgarian border, where it was joined in January 1944 by Captain Frank Thompson, a Communist sympathizer who spoke fluent Bulgarian. This team set up a liaison with Vlado Trichkov of the partisan general staff and prepared for other advisory teams to follow. Disaster overtook the mission in March 1944, however, and Mostyn Davies was killed. Thompson escaped, but in May he and most of the other members of the Second Sofia Partisan Brigade were killed by Bulgarian troops. Undaunted, the SOE sent John Harrington into Thrace (Belomorie) with the "Jampuff" mission, followed by Ian Macpherson's "Mizzen" team and "Triatic" under Donald Riddle. These teams did not join up until August 1944 and consequently had little effect on events in Bulgaria before the country left the war.[23]

The British also promised the partisans large-scale air drops of arms and supplies. But because of the shortage of aircraft, bad weather, inaccurate supply drops, and faulty communications, the deliveries were much smaller than expected. During one period, only three of the fifteen promised drops were made. The partisans were already highly suspicious of British motives and attributed these failures to a deliberate policy of curbing Communist strength. This was not British policy, but the Communist suspicions were heightened in June 1944 when Ivan Bagryanov's assumption of the premiership coincided with a diversion of Allied transports and bombers to support the Normandy invasion. The aircraft remaining in the Balkans gave priority to Yugoslavia, where the partisan effort was most effective. The Bulgarians were told that the already infrequent supply drops would come even less frequently, which seemed to confirm all the partisans' suspicions.[24]

The government's policy toward the Communists and other troublemakers was strangely inconsistent. On the one hand, the police acted with exceeding brutality against captured partisans and freely used terror and torture against villages suspected of being sympathetic to the insurgents. On the other hand, a significant number of apprehended Communists were released at various times throughout the war, especially in 1942. Lazar Popov protested in the Narodno Subranie in August 1944 that there seemed to be no rational policy: "One time we forgive them, another time we persecute them, yet another time we persecute even those suspected of aiding them."[25]

The deputies to the Assembly were themselves part of the problem, for even some of the staunchest anti-Communists would occasionally intercede for incarcerated constituents. Filov complained in July 1944 that when the leader of one band was wounded and captured by the police, a cabinet minister, Vasilev, persuaded the authorities to release him.* In 1942, the Tsar himself had interceded for the First Secretary of the BKP Central Committee, Traicho Kostov, commuting his death sentence to life imprisonment—an act that ironically was used

---

* There were two Vasilevs in the Bagryanov cabinet; it is not clear to which Filov was referring. Filov, *Dnevnik*, 7.vii.44.

against Kostov in the 1949 Communist purge but that was apparently the result solely of personal, not political, reasons.*

A German intelligence report of July 1, 1944, estimated that partisan forces had grown to 12,000, half of whom operated in the occupied territories. These forces, the report stated, still posed "no serious danger" to the regime but were growing rapidly in strength.[26] This strength was not necessarily reflected in action by individual partisan units. The "Georgi Dimitrov" Brigade, for example, was blockaded in the mountains by large army units from May to September and accomplished very little. The "Vasil Levsky" band in the Varna area was one of the most active partisan units—the authorities estimated its strength at 3,000, although it actually had only 150 members—but its total reported accomplishments during July and August were the killing of five men and the seizure of two dozen rifles. The band's losses were far more severe. In the last half of August it was repeatedly attacked by strong army units, food ran short, and deserters thinned the ranks. One turncoat led a police attack on the guerrillas during a political meeting, and in the ensuing battle the band was decimated.[27] The partisans alone, therefore, were not in a position to topple the government without assistance from either the Soviet or the Bulgarian army.

Prime Minister Bagryanov felt that the partisan movement had to be defused one way or another—either assimilated or destroyed—before the Red army came much closer to Bulgaria; characteristically, he chose both alternatives. He offered an amnesty to the partisans at the beginning of August, and at the same time launched a massive effort ("Operation Bogdan") to destroy the partisan bands in the Sredna Gora. Both efforts failed.[28] Encouraged by the Russian advance into the Balkans, the partisan movement continued its rapid growth. The total number of partisans climbed from an estimated 4,000 in

---

* According to Oren, Kostov was a close friend of the son of A. Balan, a distinguished philologist and adviser to the Tsar. Balan argued that Kostov was a bright young man whose life should be spared, and, after much hesitation, Boris agreed. Interview with Nissan Oren in Jerusalem, Israel; *The Trial of Traicho Kostov and His Group*, pp. 68–71.

early summer 1944 to approximately 10,000 by late summer.* Compared with the partisan forces in Yugoslavia and Greece, however, they were an almost insignificant force. A German intelligence report on the Balkans in mid-August 1944 listed the strength and location of each major partisan unit in Yugoslavia and Greece, and identified two partisan units in Bulgarian-occupied Vardar Macedonia. No units at all, however, were shown for Bulgaria proper.[29]

The Bulgarian partisans, even at their peak strength, were too weak to seize control of the state by themselves. Yet they felt that it would be humiliating for a party that so prided itself on its revolutionary tradition to wait passively for liberation by the Red army. They also believed that they must act immediately to ensure their position in the postwar government. Therefore, the Communists sought the support of the Bulgarian army, which had long persecuted the partisans but was now paralyzed by fear of the Russian advance.

---

* Present-day Bulgarian statistics vary widely on the estimated number of partisans, ranging from approximately eight thousand estimated by the historian Voin Bozhinov to thirty thousand suggested by a former Deputy Minister of Defense, Diko Dikov (Bozhinov, p. 117; *Rabotnichesko delo*, 22.ix.58). These and other estimates are fully discussed in Oren, "Bulgarian Communist Party," pp. 271–84. The estimates given in the text above are based on a detailed examination of the available records, both published and unpublished, of the various partisan units and the reports of partisan activity in each of the twelve VOZs. This analysis also indicated that the individual units were often much less active than the total figures on partisan actions would suggest. Archives of the Museum of the Revolutionary Movement, Sofia.

CHAPTER 17

The Last Phase

※☆※

ON AUGUST 30, 1944, the USSR announced that it refused to accept Bulgaria's August 17 declaration of neutrality. Even as
Moshanov and Colonel Zheleskov were flying to Cairo for negotiations with the Western Allies, the underlying assumption propping
up the Bagryanov regime—that the Soviets would respect Bulgaria's
neutrality—was destroyed. On the 31st, with reports reaching Sofia
that Soviet troops were streaming south from Bucharest, Foreign Minister Draganov played his last card: he informed the Russians that
German ships in Varna and Burgas had been disarmed and that all
German troops would be out of Bulgaria by midnight. This was not
quite true, but the Germans were leaving without offering any resistance.[1] The next day, as the situation continued to deteriorate,
Bagryanov and his cabinet resigned. In Cairo, negotiations with the
Allies were broken off until Moshanov could receive new credentials
from Bagryanov's successor. The Red army was approaching the Danube; there could be no question of selecting another prime minister
who was closely associated with the previous regimes. The pro-Allied
democratic opposition must at last be brought to power in order to
secure an armistice and save Bulgaria from a Soviet occupation.

The Formation of a New Government

The most obvious choices to head the new government were Dimiter Gichev, Nikola Mushanov, Konstantin Muraviev, and (a distant
fourth) Georgi Kioseivanov. Gichev was intelligent, honest, ambi-

tious, and strongly pro-Allied; he had been a theology student before becoming an Agrarian politician, and his firm principles sometimes hampered his effectiveness as a political leader. Despite his attitude toward the Fatherland Front, Gichev was not against cooperating with the Communists; throughout the war, he and Nikola Mushanov had been the only Bulgarian politicians who dared have regular and open contacts with the Soviet diplomats. Mushanov, the leader of the small Democratic Party, was 62 years old and the senior statesman of the democratic opposition. He had been in the Narodno Subranie since 1902 and had served as prime minister from 1931 to 1934. Thus far during the war, he and Petko Stainov had been the backbone of the weak opposition group in the Assembly. Konstantin Muraviev was the nephew of Stambolisky, who had named him minister of war when only 29. Muraviev's incompetence and his neglect in 1923 of reports that a coup was imminent were partially responsible for Stambolisky's downfall. Muraviev held cabinet posts again in the Agrarian coalition government (1931–34), and had matured into an intelligent and capable politician, although he still tended to be lazy and careless.

The Regents' selection of Muraviev for prime minister was a surprise to almost everyone, especially to Gichev, who had expected to be chosen. Muraviev's acceptance of the premiership and the opposition's decision to form a government under Filov's Regency required a substantial compromise of principles; in September 1943, only a year before, Muraviev along with the other opposition leaders had denounced the formation of the Regency as illegal because no Great National Assembly had been convoked and the Constitution had been disregarded. However, they now realistically decided that they could be of more service to the country by taking office than by adhering to a narrow legalistic position that would virtually preclude the formation of a non-Communist government acceptable to the Allies. Weighing heavily on the minds of the opposition was the fear that otherwise the Regents might suicidally invite a pro-German government to take power.[2]

On the eve of his coming to power, Muraviev drew up two lists for his cabinet: the first included members of the Fatherland Front, the second did not. For the sake of national unity, Muraviev felt it essential for all the opposition groups (excepting, of course, Tsankov's pro-German supporters) to participate in the new government; hence, when the Regents called on him to be prime minister, he tried to form a cabinet from his first list. Petko Stainov, a Russophile leader of Zveno with ties to the Fatherland Front, was asked to become foreign minister and agreed, but a number of other opposition leaders were unexpectedly reluctant to take positions in the new government. Although Hristo Pastuhov, the Social Democrat leader, accepted readily enough, others conditioned their acceptance upon the participation of the Communist Party and Fatherland Front in the government.

The Front, however, was unwilling to take part in a cabinet it did not dominate. Although Muraviev and his supporters genuinely wanted peace and the establishment of a democratic society, the Front immediately initiated a campaign against them. In fact, the first indication of the Front's unwillingness to cooperate with a new government came in a broadcast from the "Hristo Botev" radio station in the USSR on August 30, even before Bagryanov resigned. This broadcast warned the Front against joining any coalition that did not accept the Front's program or that would weaken its influence.

When Stainov was informed that the Front did not wish him to participate in the Muraviev government, he immediately withdrew, whereupon the Agrarian Nedelko Atanasov and others also declined to serve. Pastuhov wanted to participate despite the disapproval of the Fatherland Front, but the executive committee of his Social Democratic Party forced him to withdraw. This was a heavy blow to the plan for a truly representative national government. The Communists believed that Muraviev was trying "to isolate the Communist Party from its allies, break up the Fatherland Front by discrediting the Agrarians working with it, and make Vrabcha the sole representative of the Agrarian party."[8] Despite this major obstacle, Muraviev formed a government from his second list that had a reasonable chance of securing an armistice. Gichev, Mushanov, and Atanas Burov were made ministers without portfolio. Vergil Dimov, Gichev's brother-in-law, became interior minister; and the distinguished old Democratic politician and historian Alexander Girginov was named minister of finance. The other posts were held by men who were relatively unknown, although mention should be made of the Minister of War, General Ivan Marinov, who was secretly conspiring with the Communists. The ministries of trade, of railroads, and of education were left unoccupied so that they could be filled by members of the Fatherland Front if the opportunity arose. Muraviev himself held the position of foreign minister but was prepared to relinquish it if the Front could be persuaded to accept it. Two other cabinet ministers were also prepared to resign if their places were needed for a broader coalition.

It quickly became clear that the coalition was in difficulty. On the very day that Muraviev formally took office, the BKP issued a statement strongly attacking the new government for not having taken a firm stand against Germany:

> Bulgaria has a new government headed by K. Muraviev. But be on the alert! This government has not come by the will and wishes of the Bulgarian people but by the favor of the Bagryanovites! It does not represent the organized forces of the Fatherland Front.
>
> Patriots! The government of Muraviev does not give any guarantee that it will take to heart the destinies of Bulgaria and the Bulgarian people. Because of this, do not believe his words, but judge by his actions! Why has the Muraviev government not broken immediately and decisively with the Germans?[4]

Muraviev's Initial Actions

On September 3, the government issued an executive order halting the execution of political prisoners. On the following day, it announced a twelve-point political program that included the following provisions: a constitutional administration was promised, all fascist institutions were abolished, a complete amnesty was offered to all who had opposed dictatorship, the Narodno Subranie would be dissolved, Bulgarian troops would continue to withdraw from Serbia, and negotiations for an armistice with the Allies would be given priority. Muraviev repeated Bagryanov's mistake, however, in insisting on a policy of neutrality toward all the belligerent countries, including Germany, unless they took hostile actions. He particularly sought to avoid a clash with the retreating Germans that might push Bulgaria into the war and bring the "support" of nearby Russian troops, who would occupy the country. This procrastination, however, enabled his opponents to question the sincerity of his desire to abandon the Axis.[5]

As mentioned earlier, the negotiations in Cairo had been suspended following the resignation of Bagryanov. Moshanov had told Bagryanov in mid-August that he would arrange an armistice if the latter would form a new cabinet. Since no new cabinet was forthcoming, though, Moshanov decided to conclude an armistice without waiting for the change. Unfortunately, he only made the decision on September 1, just before he learned of Bagryanov's resignation. When he took power, Muraviev cabled Moshanov to continue the negotiations, but Moshanov noted that the new cabinet did not include certain opposition groups who were "apparently hanging back so that Muraviev can bear the odium of accepting possibly severe terms, after which the Left will oust his government." The Allies offered no hope of softer peace terms merely because a pro-Allied government was now in power in Bulgaria, and as a politician Moshanov was reluctant to associate himself with such a harsh and unpopular settlement. Therefore, the British requested that he be allowed to return to Turkey and be replaced, if possible, by Balabanov.*

The Soviet attitude toward Bulgaria continued to be somewhat ambiguous. By September 3, the Red army had reached the Bulgarian-Rumanian border in the Dobruja and along the Danube. However, it had been ordered not to advance without further instructions; not even standard reconnaissance missions were permitted—whether on the ground or in the air—because they would violate Bulgarian bor-

---

* The Allies are sometimes blamed for this delay because supposedly they refused to deal further with Moshanov until he had obtained a new set of credentials. Authorization did have to be obtained from the incoming government, but this problem was less important than the attitude of Moshanov. Chargé to the Greek government-in-exile, Shantz to Hull, Cairo, 1.ix.44, 4.ix.44, FRUS 1944, 3: 388–94. See also Turkish criticism of the British for delays in the negotiations with Bulgaria in Steinhardt, Ankara, 2.ix.44, FRUS 1944, 3: 392–93.

ders. As a result, the Commander of the Third Ukranian Front, General (later Marshal) Sergei Biryuzov, had little information on the situation in Bulgaria and had to be satisfied with radio interceptions and the reports of a few partisan leaders.[6] The Soviet Union had requested permission to enter Bulgarian territory on September 1, but Bagryanov's resignation had delayed an official reply and Muraviev had taken no action on the request.* The Russians hoped to enter the country once again as liberators, rather than as invaders. It was presumably for this reason that they postponed their attack for several days, although this allowed the escape of many small German units.[7]

Clashes with the Germans

A number of German units had not yet left the country. The official Bulgarian position was that the Nazis should be encouraged to leave as quickly as possible and that no obstacles should be placed in their way. However, control of the situation was slipping from the hands of the government. On September 3, a German force of about 400 men was halted at the railroad station in Ihtiman, a town on the Sofia-Plovdiv line about 30 miles southeast of Sofia. The German soldiers offered no resistance and allowed themselves to be interned in a nearby schoolhouse, although many retained their weapons. On the 6th, another German unit of about 200 men arrived in the town and tried to free the soldiers in the school, but after a brief battle they too surrendered.† The Muraviev government took no action.[8]

German passivity during the withdrawal suggested that there was, in fact, little danger of a Nazi attack on Bulgaria, but the threat persisted. On September 4, German troops in Macedonia captured and disarmed many of the units in the Bulgarian occupation corps, but fighting broke out when two Bulgarian regiments at Byala Palanka refused to disarm. This provocation gave Bulgaria justification for satisfying Allied demands for stronger action against Germany, but Muraviev failed to seize the opportunity. Nonetheless, on the morning of September 5, Muraviev decided to break off relations with Ger-

---

* The Allies believed that the Soviet request had been the cause of Bagryanov's resignation, but this is not absolutely certain: see Berry, Istanbul, 1.ix.44, FRUS 1944, 3: 387.
† The Bulgarians turned these men over to the Russians on September 14.

many and was seriously considering a declaration of war. However, the Minister of War, General Marinov, recommended that the declaration be postponed 72 hours in order to allow the remaining Bulgarian forces in Macedonia to withdraw and avoid capture by the Germans.[9] This advice had great significance: Marinov was secretly in contact with the Communists, who were planning a coup d'état.* If Muraviev had declared war on Germany, the Communists would have found it more difficult to convince others that his government was fascist. The planned coup might have had to be canceled or else it would have seemed absurd.[10]

The Soviet Declaration of War

At three o'clock on the afternoon of September 5, the Regents and the cabinet met to discuss the severing of diplomatic relations with Germany. Such a move seemed a political and military necessity, but it was hotly debated in a session that lasted until midnight. Filov was strongly opposed to breaking off relations and threatened to resign; General Mihov still hoped for a German victory. The Minister of Justice, Boris Pavlov, later said that the decision to break relations was made at four or five o'clock in the afternoon; Mihov, on the other hand, stated that it was made only at midnight. The timing is of some importance, for at 9 P.M. came the startling news that the Soviet Union had declared war on Bulgaria. Just two hours earlier, Molotov had informed the Bulgarian Ambassador in Moscow that the Soviet government had been patient thus far because it realized that a small country like Bulgaria was not in a position to oppose a powerful nation like Germany. For this reason the Soviets had also tolerated the fact that Bulgaria was being used as a base for German military operations against the Soviet Union. However, Molotov had continued, now that Germany was facing disaster on every side and had ceased

---

* Marinov was the only member of the cabinet not indicted by the People's Court in December 1944, after the Communists came to power; instead, he was appointed Army Chief of Staff. He was Ambassador to France during 1946 and 1947, held a minor post in the Ministry of Foreign Affairs from 1948 to 1950, and taught in the Rakovsky Military Academy from 1950 to 1953. In 1953, at the age of 57, he was retired and transferred to the Army Reserve.

to be a major threat, there was no excuse for Bulgaria's failure to declare war on Germany. Therefore, the Soviet government was forced to declare war on Bulgaria.

The Allied diplomats in Moscow learned of this declaration only shortly before the Bulgarians did, and were not at all certain that it was warranted by the situation. Sir Archibald Clark Kerr was instructed to inform the Russians of the British government's astonishment that the USSR had declared war on Bulgaria "without previous consultation and at a time when Bulgaria appeared to be anxious to make peace with the Allies."[11] Muraviev first heard of the declaration when it was broadcast by the Russians at nine o'clock. Upon receiving the news, he immediately sent two high-ranking officials from the Foreign Ministry to contact the Soviet chargé d'affaires, Yakovlev, and tell him that Bulgaria had already decided to break off relations with Germany and was on the verge of declaring war on the Axis. Yakovlev was surprised by the Bulgarian request for an armistice because he had not been informed that his government was planning to declare war.

The Bulgarian government almost immediately issued a communiqué stating that owing to events in Macedonia, the cabinet had decided to take "firm measures against the provocative action of the German units"; the implication was that war would be declared on Germany that very evening. The meeting finally adjourned, however, after it had been decided to sever relations with Germany but not to declare war. The Communists charged that even this decision had been taken only after the announcement of Russia's declaration of war on Bulgaria, and they criticized Muraviev for acting on the basis of the recent incident in Macedonia rather than on a general opposition to fascism.[12]

The Soviet Union may have declared war for the reason given by Molotov, but it is more likely that other considerations were involved. The West believed at the time that Russia declared war in order to have an equal voice in the peace negotiations with Bulgaria. It now seems that the real motive was to enable the Red army to enter Bulgaria and assist in the creation of a Communist state. The USSR realized that if the members of the Muraviev government were not discredited as fascist but were able to conclude a peace treaty with the Allies, they would be in a strong position vis-à-vis the Fatherland Front. Nevertheless, this does not excuse the Bulgarian cabinet's failure to take an action that was so clearly a political necessity. A strong leader would have pushed aside any objections to a declaration of war on Germany and would have welcomed the resignation of all those opposed to the change in policy. Muraviev was not such a man.

Communist Strikes and Demonstrations

Communist strikes and demonstrations heightened the political tension within Bulgaria. The first demonstration occurred in Sofia on September 4 in front of the Ministry of Justice. From there the demonstrators marched to the Soviet Embassy, where they sang and also shouted slogans such as "Muraviev is a Hitlerite agent." The crowd was dispersed by the police and a number of the demonstrators were arrested, but not before part of the crowd had attacked the German Embassy. The demonstration, composed largely of pro-Communist students, was only partially successful, for it attracted few of the townspeople.

On the evening of September 5, following the Soviet declaration of war, the leaders of the Communist Party organization in the Sofia district, including the future premier Todor Zhivkov, decided that the long-discussed coup would be carried out in the early hours of September 9. In the meantime, all efforts would be made to dislocate the political and economic system by partisan attacks, strikes, and political demonstrations. The next evening, they gathered to protest the continued presence of German soldiers in Bulgaria. A crowd massed in front of a Sofia hotel where German officers were staying and was reportedly fired upon by the officers there. The police arrested over 300 of the demonstrators.[18]

September 6, 1944, also marked the beginning of a series of military uprisings that shook the government's faith in the army's loyalty. Military police in Dedeagach had uncovered a Communist cell among the occupation troops there and had arrested its twelve members; but as the prisoners were being taken through the center of the town they were freed by a large group of sailors. During the same period desertions greatly increased and several small military units defected to the partisans.[14] Also on September 6, a strike of streetcar operators and factory workers began in Sofia and continued into the following day despite energetic police activity. On September 7, the miners at Pernik began a serious strike, which erupted into violence when the police intervened; six strikers were killed in the clash and 23 were wounded. The purpose of this strike, according to one historian, was to divert the government's attention in order to facilitate the coup in Sofia.[15] Strikes also erupted on the 7th in other cities. The tobacco workers in Plovdiv, who had been responsible for the country's last major strike in June 1940, were joined by railroad employees and other workers in Pleven, Silistra, and Varna. The strikers in these cities stormed the prisons and released political prisoners. In Sofia a large demonstration took place in front of the main railroad station. When the police tried to break up the crowd, armed partisans who had slipped into the city opened fire. A number of policemen and demonstrators were killed in this brief skirmish.[16]

The Coup of September 9, 1944

The Muraviev government was still in control of the country, but its future was dismal. Beginning on September 6, it made a frantic effort to repeal the laws and change the administrative personnel that connected it with the previous government. The anti-Jewish laws, the 1934 law abolishing political parties, and other repressive statutes were formally repealed.* The prefects of six of the provinces were replaced, as were a number of officials in the Foreign Ministry. General Lukash (the Chief of Staff), General Trifonov (the Commander of the Fifth Army), General Stoyanov, and several other high-ranking military officers either resigned or were removed.

War Minister Marinov informed the commander of the German Military Mission on the evening of September 6 that all German

---

* The laws against the Jews had been declared null and void by Bagryanov, but they had not been officially repealed.

troops, without exception, must be gone from Bulgaria by the morning of the 7th. The Germans acknowledged this warning but made no promises.[17] The Bulgarians also requested the Germans to pass through Sofia only at night in order not to provoke a resumption of Allied bombing on the capital.* The Soviet Union was unimpressed by these efforts and not unjustly criticized the Muraviev government for being evasive. The prime minister had informed the Soviet chargé d'affaires on the night of September 5 that Bulgaria was breaking relations with Germany; the next day, however, he announced that he had asked the USSR for an armistice but made no mention of relations with Germany. A Soviet communiqué commented: "Such a contradictory situation cannot but arouse in the Soviet Government mistrust of the position of the Bulgarian Government. In view of this, the Soviet Government was unable to consider the request of the Bulgarian Government for an armistice." General Tolbukhin, the commander of the Soviet forces massing on Bulgaria's border, issued a proclamation on September 7:

The Red Army has no intention of fighting with the Bulgarian people and its Army, because it considers the Bulgarian people as a brother people. The Red Army has one task—to defeat the Germans and bring a general peace as soon as possible.

For this it is necessary that the Bulgarian Government cease to serve the German cause, that it break all relations with the Germans immediately, and go over to the side of the coalition of democratic countries.[18]

Despite the frequent Soviet references to Bulgaria's relations with Germany, it is doubtful that they were the deciding factor behind Soviet actions. Vasil Kolarov, a leading Bulgarian Communist who was to become prime minister in 1949, gave a lecture in Moscow at this time on Soviet policy toward the Muraviev government. He sharply denounced Muraviev for his supposed refusal to include rep-

---

* The Allied air forces were heavily attacking the routes used by the Germans in evacuating Bulgaria: Nish was repeatedly hit, and a total of 1,373 heavy bomber sorties were made on the retreating Germans during the first week of September. TsDIA, f. 284, op. 1, a.e. 8735, 8737, 8740; People's Court, Sustav I, 4: 1510–11; Ilcho Dimitrov, "Poslednoto pravitelstvo," pp. 16–17; *Zarya* (Sofia), 6.ix.44; *Dnevnik* (Sofia), 7.ix.44; TsDIA, f. 370, op. 1, a.e. 1572.

resentatives of the Fatherland Front in his government (by which Kolarov meant that Muraviev would not allow the Front to dominate the government), but he made no mention whatsoever of Bulgaria's delay in breaking relations with Germany.[19]

Bulgaria finally severed diplomatic ties with Germany on September 7, 1944. On the morning of the 8th, the cabinet met to decide on a declaration of war on Germany. But Muraviev had delayed too long; shortly after the cabinet meeting began, Russian troops crossed the border into Bulgaria. The Bulgarian soldiers had been instructed to offer no resistance, but it is unlikely that they would have fought even under orders from the government. As a result, there was nothing to stop the Red army's drive on Varna, Burgas, and Shumen. In these circumstances, with the German danger gone and in the face of the long-feared Russian occupation, the government might have been expected at last to take prompt and decisive action. Yet the decision to declare war on Germany was not made until two o'clock that afternoon. Filov resigned rather than approve the declaration, which was to go into effect at six o'clock that evening, September 8, 1944. Bulgaria was now at war with Germany, Great Britain, the United States, and the Soviet Union.[20]

The military garrison at Burgas openly rebelled against the government and arrested its own officers; the 4th Border Regiment in Varna went over en masse to the partisans; the 24th Infantry Regiment revolted; and the occupation forces in Thrace were no longer reliable. On September 8, the National Committee of the Fatherland Front urged the Bulgarians to welcome the Russians as liberators and claimed: "in Moscow and in other capitals of the Allies it has been declared that only a government of the Fatherland Front can have the confidence of the Powers, in whose hands the fate of Bulgaria lies."[21] With Communist forces on the verge of a takeover in Bulgaria and with the Muraviev government almost completely discredited, the Soviet Union surprisingly agreed to a cease-fire. "In view of the fact that the Bulgarian Government has broken relations with Germany and has turned to the Soviet Union with a request for an armistice, Soviet troops will cease military activity in Bulgaria from ten o'clock in the evening of 9 September." The reason for this action is not clear. Was Russia mainly interested in facilitating the advance of the Red army, or was the cease-fire agreed to with the knowledge that Muraviev would be overthrown before it came into effect? The most likely explanation is that the Russians assumed that the Fatherland Front was too weak to overthrow the government, since it had not already done so. General Tolbukhin, who accepted by radio the Bulgarian request for an armistice, apparently knew nothing of the plans for a coup; representatives of the Fatherland Front had merely assured him that the Red army would be enthusiastically welcomed by the Bulgarian people. Russian forces would soon be in Sofia, so a coup seemed unnecessary.[22]

For internal political reasons, however, it was important for the Fatherland Front itself to seize power from Muraviev. The Bulgarian army was demoralized and the government no longer enjoyed the confidence of the people. Much of the Sofia garrison had been dispersed to outlying villages as a result of Allied air attacks. Thus the government was extremely vulnerable to a coup. At two o'clock on the morning of September 9, 1944, a heterogeneous force of rebellious soldiers, cadets from the Sofia Military Academy, and partisans occupied strategic positions in the capital. With the help of General Marinov, the minister of war, the rebels arrested Muraviev, Gichev, and other government leaders. Within an hour the operation was completed.* At six o'clock that morning, Georgiev announced on the radio that the old government had been overthrown and that he had been named prime minister. "A new government was immediately formed by the Fatherland Front under the leadership of Kimon Georgiev, in which there were four Communists. The real power, however, was in the hands of the Bulgarian Communist Party."[23]

---

* The coup was organized by Kimon Georgiev and Damian Velchev, who had also led the coup of 1934 and who had participated in the coup of 1923. *Deveti Septemvri: Spomeni* (Sofia: 1957).

Epilogue

ENGEANCE descended almost indiscriminately after the coup of
September 9, 1944. People's Courts were established before the
end of the year, and the three regents, the members of every wartime
cabinet (including the recent Bagryanov and Muraviev cabinets),
130 of the 160 deputies of the Narodno Subranie, and numerous court
advisers and bureaucrats were brought to trial. On February 2, 1945,
Filov, General Mihov, and Prince Kiril were executed; they were
followed by former premiers Bozhilov and Bagryanov, 68 Narodno
Subranie deputies, two dozen former cabinet ministers (among them
interior ministers Peter Gabrovsky and Docho Hristov), and several
royal advisers, including Yordan Sevov. Muraviev, the last premier
before the September coup, received a life sentence; Dimiter Gichev,
the Vrabcha Agrarian leader, was sentenced to a one-year term but
actually spent most of his remaining two decades in prison. Ironically,
the pro-German leaders often fared well: Alexander Tsankov fled
first to Germany, then to Argentina; and Legionnaire leader Ivan
Dochev escaped to Canada. Stoyan Kosturkov, the leader of the small
Radical Party that had been confident of a German victory, was now
welcomed into the Fatherland Front; his son became mayor of Sofia.

People's tribunals were also established at the provincial and village
level throughout the country, and thousands of old scores were settled.
The percentage of the population executed in Bulgaria probably ex-
ceeded that in any other Axis country, although the number of actual
"war crimes" was comparatively low. The army was initially spared

the full extent of the purges because the Russians wanted to use it against the Germans. By this tactic, the Soviets secured the services of an unenthusiastic but disciplined force for the advance through Yugoslavia. The political commissars who maintained Communist control over the army allegedly equated high casualties with political devotion; yet the sacrifice of 30,000 troops did not earn Bulgaria the right to retain its wartime acquisitions in Greece or Yugoslavia. Only in the Southern Dobruja was Bulgaria's largely undisputed rule maintained.

The Communists' political strategy for attaining complete domination over the country involved several stages. The first was the execution or imprisonment of the leaders of the former regime and, where possible, the opposition. Second, the BKP undermined the power of the remaining opposition leaders by covertly aiding the minority factions within their parties. Next, the leaders of these minority factions were in turn ousted by cliques even more dependent on Communist support. Finally, the Communists purged their own ranks of both opportunists and the most ambitious. A good example of this strategy involved the Agrarian Party. The imprisonment of Gichev and his followers eliminated the Vrabcha wing of the party. The Pladne Agrarian leader G. M. Dimitrov ("Gemeto") returned in late September 1944 from his wartime exile in the Middle East to resume leadership over his wing. However, he was ordered by Soviet viceroy General Biryuzov to resign his party post in January 1945, and he was soon forced to flee the country again. His successor, Nikola Petkov, soon became disillusioned with collaboration and was replaced by Alexander Obbov, who in turn was followed by Kosta Traikov. When Petkov refused to stop criticizing the new regime, he was charged with conspiracy against the government and executed in September 1947 after an outrageously biased trial.

Similarly, the Social Democratic leader Hristu Pastuhov was displaced and jailed in favor of Grigor Chesmedzhiev, who had been an early supporter of the Fatherland Front and a minister in the Front's first government. But Chesmedzhiev himself proved too independent, and in May 1945 he was replaced by Dimiter Neikov. Even Zveno was ultimately not spared, although the pattern was somewhat different. After the German defeat, Interior Minister Anton Yugov (BKP) began purging the army of both suspected fascists and Zveno supporters. War Minister Damian Velchev (Zveno) was accused in the press of various crimes, and his private secretary—like Nikola Petkov's—died under torture designed to extract a confession implicating Velchev and Premier Georgiev. When this plan miscarried, Velchev was sent instead as Bulgarian diplomatic representative to Switzerland, where he remained until his death in 1954. Georgiev was demoted from premier, first to foreign minister and then to minister of electrification, a position in which he showed his genius for survival by remaining from 1947 to 1959.

The Communists were also not immune. Traicho Kostov, the First Secretary of the BKP Central Committee and the leading Communist in Bulgaria until the return of Georgi Dimitrov from Moscow in late 1945, was executed for treason in December 1949 and only posthumously rehabilitated. The brutal Anton Yugov was more fortunate: he was ousted from influence along with Kostov but survived to re-emerge as deputy premier several years later. Georgi Dimitrov and Vasil Kolarov were leading Bulgarian-born Communists who had lived in the Soviet Union for many years and had taken Soviet citizenship. They remained in the Soviet Union after the September coup, although Dimitrov assumed the chairmanship of the BKP's Central Committee. Why they did not return to Bulgaria at once remains unknown; one theory holds that Moscow believed the fiction of the Fatherland Front as a coalition government could better be maintained if the former Secretary General of the Comintern (Dimitrov) stayed abroad. This was thought necessary to secure Allied recognition and legitimize the new government. The Allied conference at Yalta in February 1945 promised free elections for Bulgaria, but the Communists so obviously rigged the electoral process and terrorized the populace that Western protests secured the postponement of the August 1945 elections on the very day for which they were scheduled. This setback to Communist morale led both to Dimitrov's return from Moscow on November 7, 1945, and to a tougher BKP attitude toward the opposition. Nine days after his return, Dimitrov renounced his Soviet citizenship and became a Bulgarian again for the elections of November 18, 1945. The opposition boycotted these elections, which this time were not postponed. The BKP consequently scored a sweeping electoral victory, and Kolarov, who had returned to Bulgaria in September 1945, became president of the Communist-dominated Narodno Subranie. Dimitrov, although he now dominated the political life of the nation, did not assume the premiership for another year.

During this period, the young Tsar Simeon remained the nominal ruler of Bulgaria through a new Regency Council established after the 1944 coup. Part of the Communists' strategy involved eliminating the monarchy, and in this aim they were aided by the general lack of popular enthusiasm for the Saxe-Coburg dynasty after two disastrous world wars. A plebiscite on the future of the dynasty was held on September 8, 1946, and the government claimed that 93 percent of the voters favored the abolition of the monarchy. Within a matter of days, Simeon and his mother, Queen Ioanna, left Bulgaria. They traveled first to join her father, the former King Victor Emmanuel III of Italy, in Egyptian exile, and later went to Spain. The brief reign of the Third Bulgarian Empire was at an end.

Reference Matter

Notes

꙰

Complete authors' names, titles, and publication data are given in the Bibliography. Personal interviews in Bulgaria, Germany, Israel, and the United States helped me to fill in some missing details and provided unique pictures of the wartime situation. In Bulgarian archival citations in the Notes, I have abbreviated *papka, opis,* and *poreden* pap., op., and por., respectively. In addition, I have used the following abbreviations throughout the Notes.

AMVnshR   Arhiv na Ministerstvoto na Vunshnite Raboti (Archives of the Bulgarian Foreign Ministry)

AMVtrR   Arhiv na Ministerstvoto na Vutreshnite Raboti (Archives of the Bulgarian Interior Ministry)

BIN   *Bulletin of International News*

DAI   Deutsches Ausland-Institut, German Federal Archives, Coblenz. DAI-808 is entitled "Bulgarien 1940"; DAI-879 is "Bulgarien 1941." Both contain collections of clippings about Bulgaria from various newspapers.

DBA   Deutsches Bundesarchiv (German Federal Archives), Coblenz

DBFP   *Documents on British Foreign Policy*

DDI   *I Documenti Diplomatici Italiani*

DGFP   *Documents on German Foreign Policy*

DNB   Deutsche Nachtrichtenbüro (the official German news agency)

DOS   Department of State, United States

FO   Foreign Office, Great Britain

FRUS   *Foreign Relations of the United States*

IMT   International Military Tribunal

KTB   Kriegstagebücher (war diaries)

OKH   Oberkommando des Heeres (German Army High Command)

OKW   Oberkommando der Wehrmacht (Armed Forces High Command)
RGMA   Reports of the German Military Advisers in Bulgaria
RSHA   Reichssicherheitshauptamt (State Security Agency)
SD-Ber.   Sicherheitsdienst Berichte (State Security Service Intelligence Reports)
SSF   Staatssekretär Files of the German Foreign Office
TsDIA   Tsentralen durzhaven istoricheski arhiv (Central State Historical Archives, Bulgaria)
XXV-NS   Stenografski dnevnitsi na XXV-to Obiknoveno narodno subranie (stenographic reports of the 25th Narodno Subranie, Bulgaria)

Historical Introduction

1. Todorov, *Balkan Firebrand*, p. 306; two variants are given in Studnitz, p. 73.
2. Trevor-Roper, *Hitler's Table Talk*, p. 379.

Chapter One

1. Report by Eric Phipps, 26.viii.39, FO R6822.790.7.
2. See Rendel, Sofia, 11.v.39, FO R3971.790.7; and 1.viii.39, FO R6825.1118.7. Rendel served as British Ambassador to Bulgaria from June 1938 until March 1941.
3. Reported by Palairet, Athens, 9.ix.39, FO R7370.790.7; XXV-NS, 1st reg. sess., 27th sitting; see also G. Stefanov, "Bulgarie: La politique extérieure," p. 2.
4. George VI to Boris, 15.ix.39, FO R7477.790.7.
5. Rendel, p. 166; see also the secret document "Anglo-French Liaison: Military Policy in the Balkans," 20.i.40, FO R1033.5.67.
6. Churchill to Halifax, 24.ix.39, FO R7979.790.7.
7. Butler, p. 66; Reile, p. 323; Germany, Foreign Office, *Geheimakten*; Weygand, *Mémoires*, 3: 28–39.
8. Toynbee, *Eve*, p. 129.
9. Gafencu, p. 260.
10. Von Papen, p. 456.
11. *Ibid.*, pp. 455–56; Talamo, Sofia, 25.xi.39, DDI, 2: 274.
12. Report of Weizsäcker-Draganov discussions, Berlin, 1939, in DGFP, 8: 277.
13. *Istoriya na Bulgaria*, p. 357.
14. Woermann report, Berlin, 18.ix.39, DGFP, 8: 93.
15. Richthofen, Sofia, 4.xii.39, DGFP, 8: 84–85.
16. Weizsäcker report, Berlin, 15.xii.39, DGFP, 8: 533–34.

17. Boris to King Victor Emmanuel of Italy, 10.xii.39, DDI, 2: 418–19.
18. Reported by U.S. Ambassador Lane in Belgrade, 12.i.40, FRUS 1940, 1: 454.
19. Rendel, Sofia, 27.i.40, confidential, FO R1570.4.7, p. 32.
20. Blücher, German Ambassador to Finland, quoted in D. Clark, p. 89; see also Rendel, Sofia, 30.xii.39, FO R249.249.7; *The Times* (London), 6.i.40.
21. *Rabotnichesko delo* (Sofia), 8.ix.39.
22. Pavlov, *Protiv*.
23. *Materiali*, p. 142; *Nelegalni*, pp. 229–31.
24. Kazasov, *Burni godini*, p. 644.
25. *Materiali*, p. 142; *Nelegalni*, pp. 230–31. Kioseivanov's policy was described as "the only correct stand at the moment" (Pavlov, *Protiv*). The democratic opposition did not advocate joining the Allies but opposed joining the Axis (interviews, Bulgaria).
26. *Rabotnichesko delo*, issue of May 1940, cited in *Rabotnichesko delo: Izbrani*, pp. 346–47.
27. Tsanev, *Purvomaiskite*.
28. Penchev, *Nelegalnite*, p. 397; *Morgenblatt* (Agram [Zagreb]), 30.v.40, DAI-808.
29. Oren, *Bulgarian Communism*, p. 153.
30. Kodzheikov, pp. 258–60; Rendel, Sofia, 10.vii.40, FO R7044.38.7; *Istoriya Bolgarii*, pp. 246–49; Bochev, "Kum vuprosa"; TsDIA, f. 370, op. 1, arh. ed. 780; *Materiali*, pp. 144–45; *Istoriya na Bulgaria*, p. 369.
31. See XXV-NS, 1st reg. sess., p. 769; *Statisticheski*; Koen, "Ograbvaneto."
32. Lukacs, p. 359; Padev, *Escape*; *Pravda*, 12.viii.40; DAI-808.
33. Richthofen, Sofia, 20.vii.39, DGFP, 6: 944–45.
34. Todorov, *Balkan Firebrand*, p. 274. Kioseivanov was so described by Soviet Minister Raskolnikov.
35. Kazasov, *Burni godini*, p. 649.
36. Richthofen, Sofia, 17.i.39, DGFP, 5: 371–73; DBA, Reichskanzlei files, R4311.1428a, folio 1, 4.vii.39.
37. *La Parole Bulgare* (Sofia), 29.x.39.
38. BIN, 16.2: 1326; Kazasov, *Burni godini*, p. 648. The election dates were December 24, 1939, and January 14, 21, and 28, 1940.
39. Kazasov, *Burni godini*, pp. 650–51. See also *New York Times*, 16.ii.40 and 17.ii.40; *Der Bund* (Bern), 26.ii.40, in DAI-808.
40. Rendel, p. 164.
41. Knatchbull-Hugessen, pp. 157–58.
42. *Ibid.*
43. Rendel, Sofia, 15.v.40, 22.v.40, and 28.v.40, FO R6196.4.7.

44. Badoglio, p. 15. Italian Foreign Minister Ciano advised Bulgaria to follow "a moderate course" and thus "preserve peace in the Balkans." TsDIA, AMVnshR, pap. 80, op. 8, por. 532, p. 158; Talamo, Sofia, 13.ix.-39, DDI, 1: 120–21.

45. Rendel, pp. 170–71.

46. *Zora* (Sofia), 1.viii.40; *Völkischer Beobachter* (Vienna), 23.v.40; Heiber, ed., *Hitlers Lagebesprechungen*, pp. 120–21. In 1942 Germany gave General Zhekov an annual pension, which the Narodno Subranie made tax-free.

47. *Mir* (Sofia), 18.vi.40. An article in another Sofia newspaper stated: "Bulgaria received Pétain's words with double joy, for they signify that peace is near and that the troubles of 1919 have been torn asunder." *Slovo*, 18.vi.40.

Chapter Two

1. Schulenburg to Ribbentrop, Moscow, 23.vi.40, *Nazi-Soviet Relations*, p. 155.

2. Hitler revealed on June 22, 1941, that he had "advised acquiescence in the Soviet Russian demands—the cession of Bessarabia." Dallin, *Soviet Russia's Foreign Policy*, p. 237n; *Ciano's Diary*, 28.vi.40.

3. Reported by Schulenburg, Moscow, 26.vi.40, *Nazi-Soviet Relations*, p. 160.

4. Degras, p. 458; Macartney, *October Fifteenth*, 1: 404–5.

5. Ciano-Csaky discussions, Venice, 6.i.40 and 7.i.40, *Ciano's Diary*, p. 331. Draganov-Woermann discussions, Berlin, 27.vi.40, DGFP, 10: 37–38.

6. Helmreich, pp. 380–406; Zhebokritskii, pp. 226–50; *Anuarul Statistic al Romaniei 1939–40*, Bucharest, 1940; Roberts, p. 355.

7. Wolff, p. 192. Similar statements have been made by Seton-Watson (*Eastern Europe*, p. 401) and Waldeck (p. 133). For the contrary view, see Spector, p. 156.

8. *Ciano's Diary*, 28.vi.40. Italy's reply to Bulgaria's request for support was that the Italian government "was sympathetic toward Bulgaria's just claim and had requested her only to keep calm." Richthofen, Sofia, 29.vi.40, DGFP, 10: 55n; Magistrati, Sofia, 1.vii.40, DDI, 5: 138.

9. AMVnshR, 4.ix.39, pap. 141, op. 7, por. 789, p. 3; G. Stefanov, "Vunshnata politika," p. 424.

10. Toynbee, *Initial Triumph*, p. 324; Macartney, *October Fifteenth*, 1: 405.

11. Woermann memo of Boris-Richthofen discussions in Sofia, Berlin, 28.vi.40, DGFP, 10: 47.

12. Woermann memo, Berlin, 27.vi.40, DGFP, 10: 37–38.

13. Earle, Sofia, 17.vii.40, DOS Archives, 740.0011, Eur. War '39, 4709; BIN, 17.2: 911–12; Gunther, Bucharest, 2.vii.40, FRUS 1940, 1: 488. The American Minister to Bulgaria thought a Dobruja settlement was necessary; otherwise "the King and the Government might be forced by the army to take military steps." Earle, Sofia, 27.vi.40, FRUS 1940, 1: 482. See also Horthy, p. 133; Hillgruber, *Staatsmänner*, p. 164; *The Times* (London), 5.viii.40.

14. Hillgruber, *Hitler, König Carol*, pp. 70ff; Gheorge, pp. 50ff; BIN, 17.1: 691.

15. Waldeck, pp. 109–10. The Rumanian government's arrest of General Ion Antonescu at Predal on July 9, 1940, further chilled Rumanian-German relations.

16. Hitler to Carol, 15.vii.40, DGFP, 10: 217–20.

17. Ribbentrop, Fuschl, 16.vii.40, DGFP, 10: 173–74, 221–22; Hitler-Filov-Popov discussions, Obersalzburg, 27.vii.40, DGFP, 10: 244–45, 332–41; Earle, Sofia, 30.vii.40, FRUS 1940, 1: 496.

18. Magistrati, Sofia, 17.vii.40, DDI, 5: 246–47. Rumania and Hungary were unable to reach an agreement, however; on August 30 Germany and Italy imposed a settlement—the second Vienna Award—that gave Hungary most of Transylvania.

19. XXV-NS, 1st special sess., 1st sitting, 20.ix.40, p. 1.

20. *Slovo*, 4.x.40; DBA, Reichskanzlei files, R4311.14286.

21. XXV-NS, 1st reg. sess., 2d sitting, 21.ix.40, p. 36; 2d reg. sess., 13th sitting, 21.xi.40, p. 282; *Türkische Post* (Istanbul), 1.xii.40.

22. Ivan Georgiev, p. 436. Present-day Communist histories ignore Germany's role in the award: e.g., *Istoriya Bolgarii*, pp. 250–51; Kosev, *Kratka*, p. 265.

23. FO, *Bulgaria*, p. 9; see also Rendel, Sofia, 18.ix.40, FO R8150.38.7.

24. Rendel, p. 171; Rendel, Sofia, 10.ix.40, FO R7599.613.7, p. 266.

Chapter Three

1. Although Germany defended the exclusion by pointing to Russia's own unilateral action in the Baltic States, the result was—according to Ciano—that "the dream of an understanding with Russia had vanished forever in the rooms of the Belvedere at Vienna." *Ciano's Diary*, 19.ix.40, p. 291; Narkomindel to Ambassador Schulenburg, Moscow, 21.ix.40, *Nazi-Soviet Relations*, pp. 190–94; *Vneshnyaya politika SSSR*, pp. 35–41, 527; Gafencu, pp. 65–84; Ribbentrop to German Chargé in Moscow, Berlin, 25.ix.40, top secret, *Nazi-Soviet Relations*, p. 195. An editorial by a leading Bulgarian fascist, Todor Kozhuharov, in *Slovo*, 27.ix.40, ridiculed all rumors of a schism.

2. Boris to Hitler, 22.x.40, DGFP, 11: 364–65.

3. Earle, Sofia, 21.xi.40, conversation with Foreign Minister Popov, FRUS 1940, 1: 529–30; Halder, 5: 26 (November 1940); Greiner, p. 240; Papen, Sofia, 22.xi.40, conversation with Boris on 21.xi.40, DGFP, 11: 651–53; memo by Hewel (on Ribbentrop's staff), Berlin, 23.xi.40, Hitler-Draganov conversations, DGFP, 11: 672–78; Steinhardt, Moscow, 27.xi.40 and 29.xi.40, FRUS 1940, 1: 631–32; Dallin, *Soviet Russia's Foreign Policy*, p. 281; Beloff, p. 359.

4. DOS Records, Interrogation Mission, "Hermann Neubacher," 1946; see also Rendel, Sofia, 12.xi.40, very confidential, FO R8431.4.7.

5. Hitler-Draganov conversations, DGFP, 11: 672–78.

6. Richthofen, Sofia, 21.xi.40, DGFP, 11: 647; Papen and Richthofen, Sofia, 22.xi.40, DGFP, 11: 652; Woermann to German Embassy in Moscow, Berlin, 22.xi.40, DGFP, 11: 653–54.

7. Chichovska, *Sobolevata aktsiya*.

8. Richthofen, Sofia, 26.xi.40, top secret, DGFP, 11: 712–14.

9. Statement of Popov to Earle, 25.xii.41, Sofia, 27.xii.41, FRUS 1941, 1: 336; DOS Bulletin, 18.vii.48, p. 69; *Utro* (Sofia), 6.iv.43; enclosure to memo by Hewel on Hitler-Draganov talks, Berlin, 3.xii.40, DGFP, 11: 772–73.

10. Richthofen, Sofia, 28.xi.40 and 30.xi.40, DGFP, 11: 726, 757.

11. Valev, p. 14; Bochev, "Kum vuprosa," p. 49; *Materiali*, p. 148.

12. *The Times* (London), 11.xii.40.

13. Pundeff, "Bulgaria's Place," p. 319.

14. Report of Popov's discussions with Soviet Minister Lavrishchev, Richthofen, Sofia, 30.xi.40, top secret, DGFP, 11: 757; Rendel, Sofia, 30.xii.40, FO R32.32.7.

15. The Soviet notes of 6.xii.40 and 18.xii.40 kept the controversy alive. Richthofen, Sofia, 19.xii.40, DGFP, 11: 908.

16. Mussolini, *Memoirs*, p. 182.

17. Badoglio, p. 27.

18. *Ibid.*, p. 28.

19. Hohlfeld, p. 257; DGFP, 11: 638.

20. Colonel-General Alfred Jodl, Chief of Wehrmacht Operations, Staff of the OKW, questioned by Dr. Exner, 5.vi.46, IMT, 6: 342–43.

21. Halder, 4.xi.40 and 5.xi.40, 5: 6–8; Churchill, *Second World War*, 2: 474; Langer and Gleason, *Challenge*, p. 108; *IMT v. Jodl*, pt. II, p. 216; Greiner, pp. 238–41; the official British version of the Lemnos report is found in Butler, p. 369.

22. Trevor-Roper, *Hitler's War Directives*, "Directive No. 18." The directive that actually laid forth the plans for the invasion of Greece (Operation Marita) was No. 20, issued 13.xii.40 (*ibid.*, see pp. 46, 48).

23. Greiner, pp. 240, 248. The Tsar was described as taking a very hes-

itant attitude (*in merklicher Zurückhaltung*) toward the German operation. See "German Military Preparations in the Balkans," Führerhauptquartier, 21.xii.40, DGFP, 11: 940. Also, for over a year, three or four
German radio stations had been operating in Bulgaria. Hitler-Draganov
conversations, Berlin, 23.xi.40, DGFP, 11: 677; Steinhardt, Moscow,
30.xii.40, FRUS 1940, 1: 538; Ambassador Karl Ritter (on special assign-
ment) to Ribbentrop, Berlin, 23.xii.40, DGFP, 11: 937–38; Earle, Sofia,
8.x.40, DOS Archives, 762.74.54.

24. Hitler-Filov-Ribbentrop discussions, Obersalzburg, 4.i.41, DGFP,
11: 1018–27.

25. Conversation between Mussolini and German Ambassador Macken-
sen, Rome, 1.i.41, DGFP, 11: 997–98; *Ciano's Diary*, 13.i.41, p. 327.
Ciano himself had thought on January 2 that Filov's trip meant Bulgaria
was finally joining the Axis.

26. Nikolaev, p. 173.

27. XXV-NS, 2d reg. sess., 15th sitting, 22.xi.40, 1: 304–5.

28. *Ibid.*, 36th sitting, 28.xii.40, 3: 966. The original sentence read:
"The Bulgarian people have always been and today remain committed to
the idea of neutrality."

29. *Ibid.*, 37th sitting; BIN, 18.1: 31.

30. DNB, *Kraft durch Freude*, Sofia, 18.ix.40, in DAI-808; XXV-NS,
2d reg. sess., 25th–28th sittings, Vol. I, "Za organizirane na bulgarskata
mladezh."

31. *Deutsche Beobachter*, 26.xi.40, *Schwarzwälder Bote* (Württem-
berg), 16.viii.40, *Odenburger Zeitung*, 5.x.40, all in DAI-808.

32. SD-Ber., Berlin, 6.ii.41, T120 1305.485407; BIN, 18.1: 193, 227.

33. Filov, *Dnevnik*, 8.ii.41. The delegation was told that since all parties had been officially abolished the Tsar could not meet with men claiming to be party chiefs. This same excuse was used by Prime Minister Bagryanov in late summer 1944, with more serious results.

34. The first mention in a Bulgarian newspaper of German intervention appeared in *Mir* on January 6, 1941, based on an article in *Il Regime
Fascista* stating that because of the British threat in Greece, German troops
would soon join the fight there. SD-Ber., Berlin, 28.i.41, secret, T120
1305.485377.

35. Quoted in SD-Ber., Berlin, 30.i.41, secret, T120 1305.485377.

36. Lukacs (p. 770, n13) has pointed out the later advantage this was
to the BKP.

37. *Neue Züricher Zeitung*, 16.ix.40. See the speech by Peter Dumanov, XXV-NS, 2d reg. sess., 14th sitting, 21.xi.40, p. 285.

38. *Materiali*, p. 50.

39. TASS communiqué, 13.i.41, in Degras, p. 482.

40. Schulenburg, Moscow, 14.i.41, DGFP, 11: 1100–1101.
41. Weizsäcker, memo to Ribbentrop, Berlin, 17.i.41, DGFP, 11: 1122–23.
42. Ribbentrop to Weizsäcker, Fuschl, 21.i.41, DGFP, 11: 1155–56.
43. Memo by Weizsäcker, Berlin, 13.i.41, DGFP, 11: 1081.
44. The Bulgarian reaction, however, was that this was only a private opinion not based on official instructions from Moscow. *Ibid.*
45. Statement by the Undersecretary of State for Foreign Affairs in answer to a question in the House of Lords on September 5, 1940. George VI to Boris, 12.x.40, FO R8600.320.7. Yanev quoted in *Lavoro Fascista*, 1.xii.40.
46. FO, *Bulgaria*, p. 9.
47. Donovan later became head of the OSS (the forerunner of the CIA) and a major general. SD-Ber., Berlin, 21.i.41, T120 1305.485351; Earle, Sofia, 14.i.41, DOS Archives, 874.00.628; FRUS 1941, 1: 279; SD-Ber., Sofia, 25.i.41, T120 1305.485368, 1305.485371–72; SD-Ber., Berlin, 28.i.-41, T120 1305.485378.
48. Filov, *Dnevnik*, 21.i.41; Richthofen, Sofia, 22.i.41, DGFP, 11: 1160–61.
49. Donovan Papers, from Langer and Gleason, *Undeclared War*, pp. 397–98. During the discussion Boris told Donovan: "I must avoid a head-on collision with a stronger nation; I must not run the risk of having my country overrun without first attempting to reduce the shock." Ford, p. 100.
50. Langer and Gleason, *Undeclared War*, p. 398; Ford, p. 102; Earle, Sofia, 21.i.41, DOS Archives, 740.001, Eur. War '39, 7729; FRUS 1941, 1: 282.
51. Earle, Sofia, 23.i.41, DOS Archives, 740.0018, Eur. War '39, 71.
52. Rendel, p. 171; *Ciano's Diary*, 19.x.40, p. 299.
53. Churchill, *Second World War*, 2: 4–84; see also Langer and Gleason, *Undeclared War*, p. 393; Lukacs, p. 349.
54. Richthofen, Sofia, 26.xi.40, DGFP, 11: 712–14.
55. Hitler to Mussolini, Vienna, 20.xi.40, DGFP, 11: 641; Ribbentrop to Richthofen, 28.xi.40, DGFP, 11: 725; Richthofen, Sofia, 1.xii.40, DGFP, 11: 759–60; Weizsäcker, Berlin, 13.xii.40, SSF, T120 265.172536; Richthofen, Sofia, 12.xii.40, SSF, T120 585.242817–18; Richthofen, Sofia, 30.xi.40, SSF, T120 585.242788–89.
56. Foreign Minister Popov, XXV-NS, 2d reg. sess., 20th sitting, 3.xii.-40, 1: 416; *Völkischer Beobachter* (Vienna), 22.xii.40. The Bulgarian press suggested that all Turkish family names should be changed as well.
57. *Yeni Sabah*, 5.ii.41, cited in BIN, 18.1: 194.
58. Rendel, p. 172.

59. *Ibid.*

60. FRUS 1941, 1: 289.

Chapter Four

1. BIN, 18.1: 293–94; Earle, Sofia, 6.iii.41, DOS Archives, 740.0018, Eur. War '39, 8831.

2. Ribbentrop to Filov, Vienna, 1.iii.41, DGFP, 12: 203.

3. Filov, *Dnevnik*, 2.iii.41; Kazasov, *Burni godini*; Earle, Sofia, 2.iii.-41, FRUS 1941, 1: 294.

4. Trevor-Roper, *Hitler's Table Talk*, 31.iii.42, p. 179.

5. Interviews, Bulgaria; see also Reile, pp. 333–34; Busch-Zanter, p. 217.

6. Hassell, p. 187.

7. SD-Ber., Berlin, 11.iii.41, T120 1305.485447. A contrary view was given by Earle: "The peasants and workers sullenly resent the arrival of German troops, especially since it brings the war so close to them." Sofia, 4.iii.41, DOS Archives, 740.001, Eur. War '39, 8762; FRUS 1941, 1: 295–96.

8. Filov, *Bulgariens Weg*, speech of 19.xi.41, p. 18.

9. Interviews, Bulgaria; see also Rendel, p. 162.

10. Filov, *Dnevnik*, 1.iii.41.

11. Schulenburg, Moscow, 1.iii.41, *Nazi-Soviet Relations*, pp. 278–79.

12. *Pravda*, 3.iii.41; in DOS Archives, 740.0011, Eur. War '39, 8733.

13. Reported by Steinhardt, Moscow, 4.iii.41, FRUS 1941, 1: 296; *Izvestiia*, 4.iii.41.

14. Dallin, *Soviet Russia's Foreign Policy*, p. 285; Halder, 3.iii.41, 6: 13; Sohl, "Die Kriegsvorbereitungen," p. 106; interview, Bulgaria.

15. *Materiali*, pp. 151–52.

16. SD-Ber., 5.iii.41, T120 1305.485439; Richthofen, Sofia, 11.iii.41, Bulgarian note enclosed, DGFP, 12: 274–75.

17. Hassell, 23.iii.41, p. 192; Rendel, Sofia, 8.iii.41, FO R2191.86.7.

18. Earle, Sofia, 11.ii.41, DOS Archives, 121.67.1576; and 24.ii.41, DOS Archives, 740.0018, Eur. War '39, 8578. BIN, 18.1: 227–28; FO, *Bulgaria*, p. 10; Sweet-Escott, *Baker Street*, p. 56.

19. G. Stefanov, "Vunshnata politika"; FO, *Bulgaria*, p. 10.

20. Filov, *Dnevnik*, 3.iii.41.

21. *Ibid.*, 5.iii.41; BIN, 18.1: 357.

22. Rendel, Sofia, 26.iii.41, FO R3269.36.7; Woodward, p. 134n.

23. *Ibid.*; see also Filov, *Dnevnik*, 3.iii.41 and 6.iii.41; G. Stefanov, "Vunshnata politika."

24. Sweet-Escott, *Baker Street*, p. 56; see also Busch-Zantner, p. 218.

25. Churchill, *Second World War*, 3: 90–91. The respected military critic B. H. Liddell Hart wrote in March 1941 that Great Britain was mak-

ing a serious mistake in getting bogged down in Greece, inviting another Dunkirk at a time when victories in Africa could arouse flagging spirits. *Daily Mail* (London), 21.iii.41. See also Papagos, p. 309; Playfair, 1: 384; Greece, Genikon Epiteleion Stratou, *Agones*; Butler, p. 444.

26. This also was the opinion, for example, of the German counterespionage chief in Bulgaria, Colonel Wagner; Reile, pp. 326–27.

27. Halder, 8.iii.41, 6: 19. On March 6, 1941, the Yugoslav cabinet voted unanimously in favor of acceding to the Tripartite Pact but took no immediate action.

28. Statement of the Tsar's Chief Chancellor, Svetoslav Pomenov, before the People's Court in December 1944, AMVtrR, II Naroden sud-12, p. 188; Charova, "Die deutsche Aggression," p. 541; see also AMVtrR, II Naroden sud-14, p. 276.

29. Daskalov statement, AMVtrR, II Naroden sud-14, p. 8.

30. Germany, Foreign Office, *Dokumente*, pp. 128–29.

31. Ribbentrop, p. 225.   32. Filov, *Dnevnik*, 25.iii.41.

33. Hassell, 25.iii.41, p. 193.   34. *Ibid.*

35. IMT, case against Jodl, 7.xii.45, PS-2765, exhibit GB-124, 2: 220.

36. Hoptner, p. 275; see also Ristich; Chulinovich, *Dvadeset sedmi mart*; Milovanovich; Trago; Stojadinovich; Pavelich.

37. Churchill, *Speeches*, 27.iii.41, 1: 373, 375.

38. Macartney and Palmer, *Independent*, pp. 441–42; Auty, *Tito*, pp. 158–61; Frauendienst.

39. Directive No. 25, 27.iii.41, in Trevor-Roper, *Hitler's War Directives*, p. 61; Greiner, p. 273; Hillgruber, *Hitlers Strategie*, pp. 464–65; IMT, 28: 22–23.

40. Telegram from Bulgarian Ambassador Draganov in Berlin; Filov, *Dnevnik*, 28.iii.41.

Chapter Five

1. Schmidt-Richberg; Schramm von Thadden; KTB, "Der Balkan Feldzug 1941," OKH, H 10–317; interviews, Munich; Churchill, *Second World War*, 3: 203–4; BIN, 18.1: 516; Cervi, pp. 275ff.

2. Playfair, 2: 86; Earle, Sofia, 7.iv.41, DOS Archives, 740.0011, Eur. War '39, 9769.

3. BIN, 18.1: 558; Earle, Sofia, 14.iv.41, DOS Archives, 740.0011, Eur. War '39, 9959. Earle visited the scene and protested to Britain about the bombing of the open city; SD-Ber., 24.iv.41, T120 1305.485466.

4. Lukacs (p. 374) described the Sofia night bombing as a "strategic operation which had some psychological effects but did no harm at all to the Germans."

5. SD-Ber., 22.iv.41, T120 1305.485462.

6. Earle, Sofia, 22.iv.41, DOS Archives, 740.0011, Eur. War '39, 10202; and 9.v.41, DOS Archives, 740.001, Eur. War '39, 10781.

7. SD-Ber., 21.iv.41, T120 1305.485457.

8. SD-Ber., 2.v.41, T120 1305.485469.

9. SD-Ber., Berlin, 24.iv.41, T120 1305.485466.

10. *Ibid.*

11. Menemenchoglu, Sofia, 10.iv.41, DGFP, 13: 503.

12. Filov, *Dnevnik*, 11.iv.41.

13. BIN, 18.1: 511. The Bulgarian occupation of Macedonia is discussed in Chapter 11.

14. BIN, 18.1: p. 586.

15. Filov, *Dnevnik*, 17.iv.41.

16. Telegram from Popov to Bulgarian Legation in Ankara, 17.iv.41, printed in *Naroden sud*, 18.xii.44, p. 16.

17. Earle, Sofia, 11.iv.41, FRUS 1941, 1: 304.

18. American Chargé d'Affaires Morris, Berlin, 16.iv.41, FRUS, 1: 306; DOS Bulletin, 26.iv.41, p. 495.

19. Memo by Welles, Washington, 26.iv.41, FRUS 1941, 1: 307–8.

20. Earle, Sofia, 27.iv.41, FRUS 1941, 1: 308–9.

21. Morris, Berlin, 25.iv.41, FRUS 1941, 1: 306–7; Filov, *Dnevnik*, 18.iv.41 to 20.iv.41; Greiner, p. 286.

22. The city of Sofia donated 100,000 leva, but the Macedonian Bank contributed 500,000 and the Union of Exporters gave over 2,500,000. *Wochenschau* (Sofia), 15.iv.41, DAI-879.

23. XXV-NS, 3d reg. sess., 12th sitting, 14.xi.41, 1: 162.

24. Quoted in Bretholz, p. 46.

Chapter Six

1. Earle, Sofia, 23.vi.41, FRUS 1941, 1: 316–17.

2. Filov, *Dnevnik*, 22.vi.41.

3. *Stuttgart N.S.-Kurier*, 25.vi.41, DAI-879.

4. Ribbentrop to Beckerle, Berlin, 14.iv.41, DGFP, 12: 372.

5. Toynbee, *Hitler's Europe*, 1: 70.

6. Hillgruber, *Hitlers Strategie*, p. 536n.

7. *Slovo* (Sofia), 9.x.41.

8. Filov, *Dnevnik*, 8.viii.41.

9. Hassell, 20.ix.41, p. 231.

10. XXV-NS, 3d reg. sess., 11th sitting, 13.xi.41, 1: 145–46.

11. *Ibid.*, 12th sitting, 14.xi.41, 1: 160.

12. *Ibid.*, pp. 148–49.

13. *Vneshnyaya politika SSSR*, 1: 119–20; "KTB des Wehrwirtschaftsoffiziers in Sofia," 27.vii.41, Vol. 1, DBA.

14. Steinhardt, Moscow, 16.viii.41, FRUS 1941, 1: 324–25; Carlyle, 2: 326.

15. General of Bulgarian Army to Wehrmachtbefehlshaber Südost, Sofia, monthly report, September 1941, top secret, RGMA, T501 292.229; "KTB des Wehrwirtschaftsoffiziers in Sofia," 30.ix.41, Vol. 3, DBA; *Struggle*, p. 51; Thompson, p. 175; for the Bulgarian protest, see *Vneshnyaya politika SSSR*, 1: 143.

16. TsDIA, Sofia, f. 370, op. 1, a.e. 1, l. 303; *Istoriya na Bulgaria*, p. 302.

17. Earle, Sofia, 4.vii.41, FRUS 1941, 1: 321.

18. *Struggle*, p. 37; see also *Le Canada* (Bern), 23.ix.41; Pozolotin, p. 24. For an account of life in the Gonda Voda camp, see Stoyan Stoimenov, "Telenite mrezhi i visokite zidove ne slomiha duha na boitsite," in *Pobeda, 1941–1944* (Sofia, 1969), pp. 201–92.

19. Papen, p. 474.

20. Ribbentrop to Beckerle, 20.ix.41, DGFP, 13: 537.

21. Beckerle, Sofia, 25.ix.41, DGFP, 13: 537.

22. Earle, Sofia, 2.xii.41, FRUS 1941, 1: 355.

23. Ganevich, p. 53.

24. Monthly report to Wehrmachtbefehlshaber Südost, 28.viii.41, RGMA, T501 292.247.

25. TsDIA, Sofia, f. 370, op. 1, a.e. 1677, l. 1–29.

26. Note of 10.ix.41; *Vneshnyaya politika Sovetskovo Soyuza*, 1: 140–43.

27. Decree of the Council of Ministers, 22.ix.41; XXV-NS, 5th reg. sess., 33d sitting, 26.i.44 [*sic*], p. 467; TsDIA, Sofia, f. 456, op. 1, a.e. 6, l. 113–14.

28. Earle, Sofia, 15.x.41, FRUS 1941, 1: 333.

29. Heeresleitung in Bulgaria to OKW, monthly report, December 1941, RGMA, T501 292.180.

30. *Ibid*.

31. See *Istoriya na Bulgaria*, p. 375.

32. Papen, Ankara, 5.viii.41, cited in *Documents Secrets*, p. 36.

33. Hitler-Popov talks, Führerhauptquartier, 27.xi.41, DGFP, 13: 858–59.

34. Ribbentrop to Papen, Fuschl, 17.v.41, DGFP, 12: 836.

35. Directive No. 32, 11.vi.41, in Trevor-Roper, *Hitler's War Directives*, p. 80; see also Hillgruber, *Hitlers Strategie*, p. 545n.

36. See Hassell, 30.viii.41, p. 223, for Hitler's view of this project.

37. Earle, Sofia, 26.vi.41, FRUS 1941, 1: 319.

38. Signed by Ivan Popov and Beckerle, Sofia, 22.xi.41, DGFP, 13: 811.

39. XXV-NS, 3d reg. sess., 21st sitting, 13.xii.41, p. 353.

40. Testimony of tsarist adviser Yordan Sevov, People's Court, 27.xii.44.

41. Mihov, *Dnevnik*, 19.iv.44.

42. *Struggle*, p. 34; interviews, Bulgaria.

43. Earle, Sofia, via Istanbul, 27.xii.41, DOS Archives, 740.0011, Eur. War '39, 17921.

44. Editorial in *Slovo* (Sofia), 15.xii.41.

45. Hull, 2: 1175–76.

46. *Ibid.*, p. 1114.

Chapter Seven

1. Barker, *Truce*, p. 43; see also "KTB des Wehrwirtschaftsoffiziers in Sofia," Lagebericht No. 1, 3.viii.41, Vol. 3, DBA, Wi/IC5.16.

2. Testimony of tsarist adviser Lyubomir Lulchev, People's Court, 25.xii.44.

3. Testimony of tsarist adviser Peter Morfov, People's Court, 22.xii.44.

4. Filov, *Dnevnik*, 16.ii.42.

5. Quoted from *The Times* (London), 16.iii.42, in Toynbee, *Hitler's Europe*, pp. 611–12.

6. Filov, *Dnevnik*, 21.iii.42—on the eve of the Tsar's departure for Germany.

7. Beckerle, Sofia, 11.ii.42, SSF, T120 237.179016.

8. Killinger, Bucharest, 6.iii.42, SSF, T120 237.181887–89.

9. Filov, *Dnevnik*, 20.iii.42.

10. "Die Lage in Bulgarien," unsigned memo, Berlin, 28.iii.42, DBA, Reichskanzlei files, R4311.1428b.

11. Ribbentrop memo, 26.iii.42, SSF, T120 244.181903–4. When German intelligence was using a "turned around" Communist radio station in Belgium, they tested to see if the Russians had become suspicious by requesting additional funds. Soon there arrived from Bulgaria a can of beans containing £100 in notes. Dallin, *Soviet Espionage*, p. 175.

12. Hassell, Sofia, 13.iv.42, p. 263.

13. Filov, *Dnevnik*, 19.i.42.

14. *Ibid.*, 25.ii.42.

15. *Ibid.*, 5.iii.42.

16. SD-Ber., Berlin, 17.ii.42, T120 1305.485522.23.

17. Letter from Beckerle to author, 17.xi.66.

18. See SD-Ber., Berlin, January 1941, T120 1305.485349 and .485361.63.

19. For example, SD-Ber., 17.ii.42, T120 1305.485520.

20. Ribbentrop, 25.iii.42, p. 3, SSF, T120 244.181905; Beckerle, Sofia, 26.iii.42, p. 3, T120 1305.485550.

21. Schellenberg to Luther, Sofia, 5.iv.42, T120 1305.485558; and 6.iv.42, .485561. See also Ribbentrop, 25.iii.42, top secret, SSF, T120 244.191905; and Sofia, 26.iii.42, T120 1305.485550.

22. Trevor-Roper, *Hitler's Table Talk*, 31.iii.42, p. 379.

23. SD-Ber., Bülow to Ribbentrop, Berlin, 5.iii.42, T120 1305.485532–33.

24. Trevor-Roper, *Hitler's Table Talk*, 4.iv.42, p. 396.

25. Goebbels, *Diaries*, 25.i.42, pp. 61–62.

26. *Ibid.*, 28.iii.42, pp. 179–80.

27. Filov, *Dnevnik*, 20.vi.41.

28. It is interesting to note that British Ambassador Rendel made a similar argument to Tsar Boris in 1940. Rendel, Sofia, 4.iv.40, FO R4462.4.7, p. 185.

29. See generally Runciman.

30. See *Naroden sud* (Sofia), 4.ii.45, p. 5; Valev, p. 22; interview, Bulgaria; interview with Professor Georg Statmüller, University of Munich. For an account of an analogous case of German propaganda concerning Greece, based on the Fallmerayer theory of 1830, see Mylonas, pp. 169–82.

31. Trevor-Roper, *Hitler's Table Talk*, 31.iii.41, pp. 378–79.

32. G. L. Lewis believes that the German victories encouraged Turkey to adopt legislation on the Nazi model, and that in particular the Turkish *varlik vergisi* (property tax) and other discriminatory measures were inspired by the Nazi racial laws. Lewis, pp. 117–21.

33. Papen, Ankara, 6.iv.42, SSF, T120 244.181937–38; Lewis, pp. 117–21.

34. Papen, p. 474; for further details of this long dispute, see SSF, T120 237.179081, et seq.

35. *Mir* (Sofia), 2.i.43.

36. Testimony of tsarist adviser Yordan Sevov, People's Court, 26.xii.-44.

37. Trevor-Roper, *Hitler's Table Talk*, 8.viii.42, p. 621.

38. Beckerle, Sofia, 14.iv.42, SSF, T120 244.181954; see also Danailov and Zaimov; Poptsvyatkov.

39. Filov, *Dnevnik*, 8.iv.42.

40. Beckerle, Sofia, 15.iv.42, SSF, T120 244.181956.

41. Beckerle, 12.iv.42, SSF, T120 244.181952–53; Filov, *Dnevnik*, 15.iv.42.

Chapter Eight

1. Hull, 2: 1176; Beckerle, Sofia, 9.iv.42, SSF, T120 244.181945–46.

2. Interviews, Bulgaria.

3. Filov, *Dnevnik*, 27.ii.42; SD-Ber., Berlin, 7.iii.42, T120 1305.485539.

4. SD-Ber., Berlin, 7.iii.42, T120 1305.485539.

5. Filov, *Dnevnik*, 23.vii.42.

6. Beckerle, Sofia, 5.viii.42, 11.viii.42, and 15.viii.42, SSF, T120 244.182026, .182030–31, .182036.

7. Beckerle, Sofia, 15.viii.42, SSF, T120 244.182036.

8. Filov, *Dnevnik*, 23.vii.42; Ribbentrop, 25.iii.42, SSF, T120 244.-181904; Beckerle, Sofia, 19.viii.42, SSF, T120 244.182053 and .182055; 21.viii.42, .182060.

9. Conversation with Boris, Berlin, 21.ix.42, SSF, T120 244.182106 and .182104–5.

10. Sofia, 17.x.42 and 31.x.42, SSF T120 244.182131 and .182144. Germany attempted to assist the negotiations but to no avail; there were at least four different official versions of the original map (*Mutterkarte*) of the demarcation line agreed on at Vienna. Sofia, 16.x.42, SSF, T120 244.182130.

11. Filov, *Dnevnik*, 4.vi.42; *Durzhaven vestnik*, No. 125, ukase of 6.vi.42; Beckerle, Sofia, 12.vi.42, SSF, T120 244.182001.

12. Filov, *Dnevnik*, 10.vii.42.

13. *Ibid.*

14. *Ibid.*, 30.viii.42.

15. Trevor-Roper, *Hitler's Table Talk*, 16.viii.42, p. 630.

16. Filov, *Dnevnik*, 16.ix.42.

17. Beckerle, Sofia, 17.ix.42, SSF, T120 244.182095; memo, Berlin, SSF, T120 244.182117.

18. TsDIA, Sofia, f. 456, op. 1, a.e. 8, l. 101; Filov, *Dnevnik*, 16.ix.42; *Istoriya na Bulgaria.*

19. Testimony of Yordan Sevov, People's Court, 27.xii.44; Filov, *Dnevnik*, 26.ix.42.

20. XXV-NS, 4th reg. sess., p. 252; Mohrmann memo, Sofia, 9.x.42, SSF, T120 244.182126–27; Beckerle, Sofia, 27.x.42, SSF, T120 244.182-143; Filov, *Dnevnik*, 27.ix.42 and 7.x.42.

21. Mohrmann, Berlin, 21.ix.42, SSF, T120 244.182107.

22. SD-Ber., Berlin, 5.xi.42, T120 1305.485627–28.

23. *Ibid.*, 11.xi.42, T120 1305.485631–32.

24. Beckerle, Sofia, 11.xii.42, SSF, T120 244.182179.

25. Conversation with Boris, Berlin, 21.ix.42, SSF, T120 244.182106.

26. SD-Ber., 25.xi.42 and 23.xii.42, T120 1305.485636 and .485645.

27. Interview, Bulgaria; monthly report, November 1942, Heeresleitung in Bulgaria to OKH, RGMA, T501 292.–56.

28. Heeresleitung in Bulgaria to OKH, 13.xi.42, top secret, RGMA, T501 292.–59.

29. Woermann, Berlin, 22.x.42, SSF, T120 244.182140–41.

30. Paul Schmidt, discussion with Filov, 19.x.42, SSF, T120 244.182-134 and .182137.

31. Filov, *Dnevnik*, 9.xii.42; Hitler's conversation with Boris, Berlin, 21.ix.42, SSF, T120 244.182104.

32. Erdmannsdorff to SS-Obergruppenführer Wolff, Staff of the Reichsführer SS, 23.xii.42, IMT document NG-3665; Ribbentrop to Beckerle, 14.xii.42, SSF, T120 244.182181; Beckerle to Ribbentrop, Sofia, 15.xii.42, SSF, T120 244.182184–86.

33. Filov, *Dnevnik*, 11.vii.42.

34. *Ibid.*, 1.ix.42; testimony of Lyubomir Lulchev and statements of public prosecutor, People's Court, 26.xii.44.

35. Filov, *Dnevnik*, 1.ix.42.

36. Schmidt to Ribbentrop, Berlin, 19.x.42, SSF, T120 244.182139.

37. Mohrmann, Berlin, 21.ix.42, SSF, T120 244.182106.

38. Filov, *Dnevnik*, 9.xii.42.

39. *Ibid.*, 30.viii.42.

40. Kazasov, *Burni godini*, p. 696.

41. XXV-NS, 4th reg. sess., 29th sitting, 29.xii.42, 2: 646–47.

42. Kazasov, *Burni godini*, p. 696.

43. Filov, *Dnevnik*, 20.ix.42.

44. XXV-NS, 4th reg. sess., 9th sitting, 11.xi.42, 1: 200.

Chapter Nine

1. Weidemann, p. 112; *Mir* (Sofia), 24.ii.41; *Völkischer Beobachter* (Vienna), 18.x.40; *Bulgarische Presseauszüge* (Vienna), 8.iii.41; *Bucharester Tageblatt*, 10.xi.40; XXV-NS, 11th extra. sess., 3d sitting, 11.-vii.41, Serafim Georgiev and Nikola Mushanov, 1: 58; 2d reg. sess., 11th sitting, 19.xi.40, Dimiter Andreev, 1: 212.

2. O'Neill, p. 98.

3. "Wirtschaftlicher Überblick," Report of 1936, DBA, Reichskanzlei files R4311.1428a, folder 1, p. 4; "Die Lage in Bulgarien," Berlin, 28.iii.42, DBA, Reichskanzlei files; Stefen Kensuloff, Sofia, 21.x.42, T120 1305.-486259.

4. *Archiv der Gegenwart*, 1939, 9.ii.39, 3935A.

5. Jan Munzer, "Jews-Bulgaria," in Roucek, pp. 542–43.

6. Kazasov, *Burni godini*, p. 660.

7. Hilberg, p. 476.

8. XXV-NS, 2d reg. sess., 31st sitting, 20.xii.40, 2: 701–20.

9. Hilberg, p. 476.

10. *Ibid.*, pp. 476–77; Matkovski, "The Destruction"; XXV-NS, 2d reg. sess., 11th sitting and subsequent sittings, 15.xi.40, pp. 204ff.

11. Copies in the Archive of the Sofia Synagogue; also in *Evrei zaginali,* pp. 357–62.

12. *Evrei zaginali,* p. 356.

13. Letter from Exarch Stefan to Jewish Consistory, 17.i.50, in the Archive of the Sofia Synagogue, folder 90.

14. SD-Ber., January 1941, T120 1305.485360.

15. *Byuletin,* Central Consistory of the Jews of Bulgaria, 30.v.41, p. 3.

16. XXV-NS, 4th extra. sess., 4th sitting, 25.vi.42, 1: 66–68.

17. *Ibid.,* 5th sitting, 26.vi.42, 1: 86.

18. *Ibid.,* 4th sitting, 25.vi.42, 1: 66ff; 7th sitting, 28.vi.42, 1: 219; *Durzhaven vestnik,* 9.vii.42; Archive of the Sofia Synagogue, folder 3.

19. SD-Ber., Schellenberg to Luther, Berlin, 9.xi.42, T120 1305.486224–26; Arendt, p. 168.

20. SD-Ber., Schellenberg to Luther, Berlin, 9.xi.42, T120 1305.486224–26.

21. *Ibid.,* T120 1305.486224.

22. *Ibid.*

23. *Ibid.,* T120 1305.486224–26; XXV-NS, 4th reg. sess., 10th sitting, 12.xi.42, p. 230.

24. Beckerle, Sofia, 28.ix.42, 9.x.42, 19.xi.42, 14.xii.42, T120 1305.-486230, .486236, .486239, .486274–76.

25. *U.S. Military Tribunal,* case 11, judgment, pp. 28, 303–4; Grinberg, *Dokumenti,* p. 7.

26. *Donauzeitung* (Belgrade), 11.vi.42, mentioned in Hilberg, p. 482.

27. Hilberg, p. 290.

28. Beckerle, Sofia, 6.vii.42 and 10.iii.43, T120 1305.486302; Luther to Ribbentrop, Berlin, 4.xii.41, *U.S. Military Tribunal v. Weizsäcker,* IMT, NG-4667, 13: 195–96. Note that Popov, the Bulgarian Foreign Minister, was the one who first suggested that the European countries should agree on a uniform treatment of the Jews.

29. Beckerle, Sofia, 15.x.42, 2.xi.42, 16.xi.42, T120 1305.486262–63, .486237, .486261; 9.xi.42, T120 1305.486254. The justice minister was said to have told Belev that the Jews should not be deported and that no deadlines should be set.

30. Ribbentrop to Beckerle, Berlin, 4.vi.43, top secret, Archive of the Sofia Synagogue, folder 56.

31. *Ibid.*

32. Dannecker-Belev agreement, original draft, Sofia, 22.ii.43, Archive of the Sofia Synagogue, folder 38; Grinberg, *Dokumenti,* pp. 8–11; testimony of L. N. Panitsa, People's Court, Sustav VII, p. 349.

33. Matkovski, "The Destruction," p. 227.

34. Grinberg, *Dokumenti*, pp. 30–31.
35. Interviews, Bulgaria and Israel. For a somewhat different view, see Chary, *The Bulgarian Jews.*
36. Bulgaria, Jewish Cultural Society of Sofia, "Ekspozitsiya."
37. Filov, *Dnevnik*, 19.iii.43 and 24.iii.43.
38. *Istoriya na Bulgaria*; Beckerle, Sofia, 26.iii.43, T120 1305.173863–64.

39. Grinberg, *Dokumenti*, pp. 17, 51–55; Matkovski, *Tragedijata*; letter of Vasil Gerasimov to Jewish Antifascist Committee in Sofia, Moscow, 10.ix.45, Archive of the Sofia Synagogue, folder 148; Beckerle, Sofia, 5.iv.43, to RSHA, T120 1305.486316–19 (IMT, NG-4144); Wagner, Berlin, 3.iv.43, T120 1305.486329 (IMT, NG-4180); *Bulgarian Atrocities*, p. 15. A large literature exists on the subject of the deportation of Jews from Bulgarian-occupied territories.
40. Testimony of tsarist adviser Lyubomir Lulchev, People's Court, 25.xii.44.
41. Beckerle, Sofia, 5.iv.43, to RSHA, IMT, NG-4144.
42. Ribbentrop to Beckerle, 4.iv.43, top secret, SSF, T120 255.173891.
43. SD-Ber., Berlin, 17.v.43, T120 1305.486342–43.
44. Filov, *Dnevnik*, 17.ii.43; Bergman, Berlin, 13.ii.43, Archive of the Sofia Synagogue, folder 56; protest by the Grand Mufti of Jerusalem, SD-Ber., May 1943, T120 1305.486337.
45. Filov, *Dnevnik*, 17.ii.43; Woermann, Berlin, 22.ii.43, SSF, T120 255.173825–26; Beckerle, Sofia, 24.ii.43, SSF, T120 255.173829–30; Hilberg, p. 500; Bergmann, Berlin, 13.ii.43, and to Eichmann, 10.iii.43, Archive of the Sofia Synagogue, folder 56; SD-Ber., Berlin, 3.iv.43, T120 1305.486323; SD-Ber., Pausch, Berlin, 7.iv.43, T120 1305.486332; SD-Ber., Wagner, 8.v.43, T120 1305.486308; Beckerle, Sofia, 5.iv.43, IMT, NG-4144.
46. Beckerle, Sofia, 7.vi.43, T120 1305.486353–54; Mohrmann, Sofia, 25.v.43, T120 1305.486346; unpublished memoirs of Moshe P. Farhi, Archive of the Sofia Synagogue, folder 98, case 7; Kazasov, *Burni godini*, p. 721; *Evrei zaginali*. There was also a roundup in Plovdiv in February 1943; see *Struggle*, p. 43. A description of the demonstration is given in *Materiali*, pp. 202–3. Filov (*Dnevnik*, 26.v.43) says that the Tsar "approved fully the measures against the Jews," but does not say if this meant only the expulsions from the cities or also deportation.
47. Hilberg, p. 474.
48. Dr. Chapuisat to Eli Echkenazi, Geneva, 8.vi.48, Archive of the Sofia Synagogue, folder 56; Hoffmann and Beckerle, Sofia, 24.vi.43, IMT, NG-096, and T120 1305.173955–56.

49. Letter from Beckerle to author, 3.ix.66.

50. See Arendt, p. 169. The value of her judgment here is reduced, however, because of her reliance on a questionable analogy with France. Reitlinger, p. 383.

51. Hoffmann, Sofia, 7.vi.43, IMT, NG-2357.

52. SD-Ber., Berlin, 17.v.43, T120 1305.486341; Wagner to Kaltenbrunner, Berlin, 31.viii.43, IMT, NG-3302.

53. Beckerle, Berlin, 7.vi.43, T120 1305.486353–54.

54. Wagner to Kaltenbrunner, Berlin, 31.viii.43, IMT, NG-3302.

55. Unpublished memoirs of Dr. Albert Adroki on Samobit camp, in the Archive of the Sofia Synagogue, folder 31; unpublished memoirs of Rahamin Alkalai, also in the Archive of the Sofia Synagogue, folder 93, case 5; interviews, Bulgaria.

Chapter Ten

1. Filov, *Dnevnik*, 26.i.43.

2. *Ibid.*, 10.ii.43.

3. Studnitz, 1.ii.43, p. 7.

4. Kleist was made a field marshal for this overrated exploit. Beckerle, Sofia, 26.ii.43, SSF, T120 255.173837–38.

5. Filov, *Dnevnik*, 1.ii.43.

6. *Ibid.*, 29.iii.43.

7. *Ibid.*, 12.i.43 and 15.i.43; Beckerle, Sofia, 28.xii.42 and 30.xii.42, T120 244.182212–13 and .182215; testimony of Yordan Sevov, People's Court, 26.xii.44. For the Turkish view of political developments during this period, see Weisband, *Turkish Foreign Policy*.

8. Hassell, p. 302.

9. Ambassador Steinhardt, Ankara, 2.ii.43, FRUS 1943, 4: 1060–65; Beckerle-Filov conversation, Sofia, 1.ii.43, SSF, T120 255.173801.

10. Filov, *Dnevnik*, 12.i.43 and 15.i.43.

11. Ribbentrop to Beckerle, report of Hitler-Boris conversations, Fuschl, 4.iv.43, SSF, T120 255.173891; Filov, *Dnevnik*, 5.vi.43.

12. Boberach, 5.iv.43, p. 379; Filov, *Dnevnik*, 27.iv.43.

13. Woermann, Berlin, 5.ii.43, SSF, T120 255.173798; Weizsäcker, Berlin, 8.ii.43, SSF, T120 255.173806–9; Woermann, Berlin, 22.ii.43, SSF, T120 255.173825–26; Beckerle, Sofia, 24.ii.43, SSF, T120 255.-173833–34; Beckerle, conversations with the Tsar and Mihov, Sofia, 26.ii.43, SSF, T120 255.173837–38.

14. Testimony of Yordan Sevov, People's Court, 26.xii.44; the details of the rumor, which included an offer by Kuyumdzhiisky to change the plans for air attacks on Sofia if concessions were made to the Jews, were

given by tsarist adviser Pavel Gruev, People's Court, 20.xii.44, but Gruev said he doubted the story. In his later testimony before the People's Court, Sevov described the trip in detail but did not even mention this point.

15. Milev to Sofia, Geneva, 27.iii.43, AMVnshR, polit. direk. II/1/11, pap. no. 1, dokladi 43–44, pp. 4–5, in Bozhinov, p. 43.

16. Feis, pp. 110–11.

17. Hull, in Washington, D.C., to Steinhardt, in Ankara, 13.iii.43, FRUS 1943, 1: 484–85.

18. British Embassy in Washington to U.S. Dept. of State, Aide-Mémoire, 6.iv.43, FRUS 1943, 1: 489.

19. U.S. Dept. of State to British Embassy, Washington, D.C., 28.iv.43, Aide-Mémoire, 6.iv.43, FRUS 1943, 1: 492–93.

20. Letter from Beckerle to author, 17.xi.66.

21. Filov, *Dnevnik*, 13.vii.43.

22. *Ibid.*, 4.viii.43.

23. *Ibid.*

24. DOS Archives, 741.74.12; FRUS 1943, 1: 495–97.

25. *Ibid.*

26. Filov, *Dnevnik*, 16.viii.43.

27. *Ibid.*, 9.viii.42.

28. Montague, p. 127; Deakin, *Brutal Friendship*, pp. 383–86.

29. Filov, *Dnevnik*, 5.vi.43 and 10.vi.43.

30. Lukacs, 11.vi.43, p. 498.

31. Filov, *Dnevnik*, 13.vii.43.

32. *Ibid.*, 25.vii.43, 26.vii.43, 28.vii.43.

33. *Ibid.*, 28.vii.43, 29.vii.43, 2.viii.43.

34. This account of the Lukov incident is based chiefly on the following sources: Stoinov, "Boinite grupi," pp. 145–46; *Struggle*, pp. 66–67; *Materiali*, p. 199; FO, *Bulgaria*, pp. 12, 30; Beckerle, Sofia, 14.ii.43, 18.ii.43, 20.ii.43, and 4.v.43, SSF, T120 255.173815–16, .173818–19, .173824, and .173904–5; FO R9209.470.7, 21.ix.43.

35. FO, *Bulgaria*, pp. 12, 30.

36. Stoinov, "Boinite grupi," p. 146.

37. Filov, *Dnevnik*, 17.ii.43.

38. Stoinov, "Boinite grupi," p. 146.

39. See Stoimenov, "Antifashistkata demonstratsiya," pp. 81–86.

40. Beckerle, Sofia, 23.i.43, SSF, T120 244.182233.

41. Filov, *Dnevnik*, 17.ii.43.

42. XXV-NS, 4th reg. sess., 33d sitting, 14.i.43, 2: 723–24.

43. Interviews, Bulgaria; *Naroden sud* (Sofia), November and December 1944; Georgieff and Spiru, p. 263.

Chapter Eleven

1. Busch-Zanter, p. 219; Kofos, p. 102; Wolff, p. 206.

2. DNB, Sofia, 19.iv.41, in DAI-879; interviews, Macedonia and Bulgaria.

3. Seton-Watson, *Eastern Europe*, p. 315.

4. Interview, Macedonia; the British vice-consul in Skopie, however, had reported in 1940 that the majority of Macedonians were for autonomy rather than for union with Bulgaria. British Foreign Office Research Department, "Macedonia," RR IX.40.i, 8.i.44.

5. Seton-Watson, *East European*, p. 123.

6. SD-Ber., 29.x.42, secret, T120 1305.485618; interviews, Bulgaria and Macedonia.

7. XXV-NS, 4th extra. sess., 3d sitting, 24.vi.42, p. 35.

8. Kofos, p. 109; interview, Macedonia.

9. Burks, p. 97; Wolff, p. 206; Darby, p. 138.

10. Filov, 20.ix.41, quoted in Terzioski, "Nekoi," p. 3.

11. Terzioski, "Nekoi," p. 46.

12. XXV-NS, 2d extra. sess., 2d sitting, 10.vii.41, 1: 14–15. This bill is just one of many examples. Stavrianos, *The Balkans*, p. 768; *Zora* (Sofia), 21.xii.43; Lukacs, p. 529; Kazasov, *Burni godini*, p. 736.

13. Terzioski, "Nekoi," p. 57.

14. *Krakauer Zeitung*, 5.v.41, DAI-879. Terzioski ("Nekoi") states that three, not four, eparchies were created; perhaps he excludes Aegean Macedonia.

15. Terzioski, "Bugarskata," pp. 47–76.

16. *Durzhaven vestnik*, 10.vi.42, No. 124, Article 8; Kofos, pp. 100–101; Decision No. 2012 of Bulgarian Council of Ministers, in Lemkin, p. 264; and Decision No. 3121, 1.viii.41, Lemkin, pp. 633–35.

17. For Macedonian background, see Swire; Barker, *Macedonia*; Wilkinson; and Ivan Mihailov, *Spomeni*.

18. Mihail Apostolskii [Mihajlo Apostolski], et al., "Polozhenie okkupirovannoi Makedonii vo vremya Vtoroi mirovoi voiny," in *Les Systèmes d'occupation en Yougoslavie*, p. 313; Greek Foreign Ministry Archives, secret, A.24317.2.1949, in Kofos, p. 108; Barker, *Macedonia*, p. 43; FO, *Bulgaria*, pp. 11–12.

19. SD-Ber., Berlin, 29.x.42, secret, T120 1305.485621–22; *Makedonska Tribuna* (Indianapolis, Indiana), 22.ii.51.

20. Rothschild, p. 192, note 3.

21. Stavrianos, *The Balkans*, p. 768; Kofos, p. 101.

22. *Bulgarian Atrocities*, pp. 13–14, 21–22, 22–23.

23. Lemkin, p. 189; Xydis, p. 19; Christopoulos, *Bulgarian Occupation*, pp. 1–4; Vranchev, p. 423; interviews with several Bulgarians who had been garrisoned in Aegean Macedonia during this period confirmed the harshness of the occupation.

24. Christopoulos, pp. 115–16; Kedros, pp. 95–96; *Istoriya na Bulgaria*, p. 391; Shterev; *Slovo* (Sofia), 4.x.41; SD-Ber., Berlin, 22.x.41, T120 1305.485491; SD-Ber., Ribbentrop-Popov talks, Berlin, 26.xi.41, T120 1305.416180–81; BIN, 30.v.42, 19: 498; Lemkin, p. 189; Vranchev, pp. 444–45; *Bulgarian Occupation*, p. 5.

25. Kedros, pp. 95–96; see also Woodhouse, p. 123; Christopoulos, pp. 115–16.

26. Kedros, pp. 94–95; Shterev, p. 58. See also Lefaki, pp. 64–67.

27. *Bulgarian Occupation*, pp. 5–6.

28. *Bulgarian Atrocities*, p. 21; Christopoulos, p. 116; S. Mitev and H. Kovachev, *Partizanskata voina*, p. 123.

29. The chief Greek partisan groups in Macedonia were the Communist EAM/ELAS guerrillas and the non-Communists under "Andon Tsaous" (Andonios Fosteridhis). The supposed agreement between the Bulgarian government and the Greek Communists (EAM/ELAS), reputedly signed on Mt. Kaimaxillar in January 1944, is probably a forgery. Condit, p. 41; Barker, *Macedonia*, p. 82; Woodhouse, p. 297.

30. Report, 30.vii.42, Greek Foreign Ministry document E.474.I.1.1942, in Kofos, p. 102.

31. *Zora* (Sofia), 3.ix.42, 22.xi.43, 30.i.44; *Govori*, 1: 158; Wolff, p. 248; Seton-Watson, *East European*, p. 134.

32. Ribbentrop in Berlin to German Embassy in Sofia, 14.iv.41, DGFP, 12: 372.

33. Toskowa, pp. 539–63.

34. Clodius and Richthofen, Sofia, 24.iv.41, DGFP, 12: 623–24; *Berliner Zeitung*, 11.ix.41; *Revue d'Histoire de la Deuxième Guerre Mondiale*, no. 72, "Sur la Bulgarie en Guerre," pp. 55–56; Wiskemann, p. 318.

35. Ribbentrop to Richthofen, 17.iv.41; Ritter to Richthofen, 26.iv.41; Ritelen to Ritter, 26.iv.41; all DGFP, 12: 577.

36. Kofos, p. 103; Bramos, pp. 102–3; Barker, *Macedonia*, p. 81.

37. Woermann, Berlin, 22.x.42, SSF, T120 244.182140–41.

38. Bozhinov, pp. 28, 31; Kofos, p. 107; testimony of Yordan Sevov, People's Court, December 1944.

39. Condit, p. 234.

40. Mojsov, *Bugarska*, pp. 60–62.

41. Oren, *Bulgarian Communism*, p. 191.

42. Shoup, pp. 52–54; Auty, *Tito*, p. 169; Mojsov, *Bugarska*, pp. 60–62.

43. Yugoslavia, Vojno-istorijski Institut, *Zbornik dokumenata*, 9.2: 154–57; Mojsov, *Bugarska*, pp. 108–9; Shoup, pp. 82–83.

44. Mojsov, *Bugarska*, pp. 71–72, 95–96; Oren, *Bulgarian Communism*, pp. 191–95; *Rabotnichesko delo*, 20.ix.44; Darby, p. 220.

45. Memoirs of Svetozar Vukmanovich (Tempo), serialized in the Belgrade daily *Politika*, 8.ii.71 (see also his published memoirs *Revolutsija koja teche*); Peter Bogdanov, speech to the 5th Congress of the BKP, December 1948, in *Peti kongres na BKP*, 1: 567–77.

46. Barker, *Macedonia*, p. 90; Wolff, p. 215, puts the date in late 1942, which is much too late; Oren, *Bulgarian Communism*, p. 195, accepts the earlier date.

47. Yugoslavia, Vojno-istorijski Institut, *Hronologija*; *Les Systèmes*, p. 11.

48. Vukmanovich memoirs, *Politika*, 8.ii.71.

49. Peter II to Roosevelt, Washington, 22.vii.42, FRUS 1942, 3: 805.

50. "KTB des Wehrwirtschaftsoffiziers in Sofia," 20.i.43, Vol. V, DBA. The successful Soviet defense at Stalingrad probably contributed to this partisan resurgence.

51. Mihov, *Dnevnik*, 20.ix.43.

52. Yugoslavia, Vojno-istorijski Institut, *Hronologija*, p. 428; Barker, *Macedonia*, p. 91; *Istorijski arhiv KPJ*, pp. 229–45; Yugoslavia, Vojno-istorijski Institut, *Zbornik dokumentata*, 2.10: 143–62, 232; Clissold, pp. 135–46.

53. Palmer and King, pp. 76–93.

54. Neubacher, p. 67.

55. Barker, *Macedonia*, p. 83.

Chapter Twelve

1. A. Clark, p. 363.

2. V. L. Izraelyan, p. 114; see also Ivanov, p. 37; *Istoriya Bolgarii*, p. 294.

3. Rendel, p. 180.

4. Interviews, Bulgaria.

5. Beckerle, Sofia, 4.viii.43, 11.viii.43, 16.viii.43, SSF, T120 255.-174008–9, .174019, .174029; Jagow, Budapest, 5.viii.43, 11.viii.43, SSF, T120 255.174010, .174016.

6. SD-Ber., SS-Obergruppenführer Kaltenbrunner to Himmler, Berlin, 16.viii.43, T120 1305.485662–63.

7. Hristu Pastuhov, speech printed in *Narod* (Sofia), 4.xi.44.

8. Interview, Bulgaria.

9. Rendel, pp. 180–81; see also Ivanov, p. 37.

10. The following account is based largely on Heiber, "Der Tod"; Filov, *Dnevnik*, 27.viii.43 and 28.viii.43; *Mir* (Sofia), 27.viii.43 and 28.viii.43; Bretholz, p. 48; and Constant Schaufelberger, "Boris III, L'Homme et le Roi," in Nikolaev, pp. 88–90. Schaufelberger was the private tutor of young Prince Simeon. See also Queen Ioanna of Bulgaria, "Memorie," serialized in the Italian magazine *Oggi*, 1961, part 10; Beckerle, Sofia, 24.viii.43 to 28.viii.43, SSF, T120 255.174042 to .174148.

11. Kazasov, *Burni godini*, p. 728.

12. Papen, Ankara, 28.viii.43, SSF, T120 255.174079; Kazasov, *Burni godini*, p. 728; *New York Times*, 28.viii.43; *Neue Züricher Zeitung*, 29.viii.43; Yust, 1: 381; Queen Ioanna, "Memorie," part 10; *Mir* (Sofia), 30.viii.43.

13. Beckerle, Sofia, 29.viii.43, SSF, T120 255.174095.

14. The following discussion of the autopsy issue is based on Queen Ioanna, "Memorie"; Heiber, "Der Tod," pp. 400–401; Nikolaev, pp. 91–92; Beckerle, Sofia, 30.viii.43, SSF, T120 255.174105; Bretholz, p. 49; Toynbee, *Hitler's Europe*, p. 623; Papen, p. 502.

15. Papen, p. 502.

16. Nikolaev, pp. 91–92.

17. Beckerle, Sofia, 30.viii.43, SSF, T120 255.174105.

18. Queen Ioanna, "Memorie."

19. Bretholz, p. 49.

20. Interviews, Bulgaria.

21. Heiber, "Der Tod," pp. 393–94; Queen Ioanna, "Memorie."

22. Testimony of Pavel Gruev before the People's Court in December 1944.

23. Filov, *Dnevnik*, 15.viii.43; see also FO R8147.470.7, Stockholm, 24.viii.43.

24. The Queen has said in the *Oggi* article, however, that Boris had told Filov that he had not yielded on either a single point or a single soldier.

25. Prince Kiril, People's Court, December 1944.

26. Bretholz, p. 47; Nikolaev, p. 92; Heiber, "Der Tod," pp. 393–94; Queen Ioanna, "Memorie"; Bozhinov, p. 28; testimony of Prince Kiril and Pavel Gruev, People's Court, December 1944.

27. *Neue Züricher Zeitung*, 14.i.45 and 15.i.45; Heiber, "Der Tod," p. 392; Mourin, pp. 190–91; interviews, Bulgaria.

28. Baur, pp. 246ff.

29. See articles in *Le Figaro*, 14.xii.48 and 15.xii.48, written by an anonymous Bulgarian emigrant and supposedly based on a report by Baur found after the hurried evacuation of the German Embassy in Sofia in

1944; Papen, pp. 501–2; Heiber, "Der Tod," pp. 392–93; Nikolaev, p. 94; Rendel, p. 181; Queen Ioanna, "Memorie."

30. See Baur, p. 246.

31. See Queen Ioanna, "Memorie," for the airport incident.

32. Beckerle to author, 3.ix.66.

33. Steengracht memo, Berlin, 27.viii.43, SSF, T120 255.174059.

34. Papen, p. 501.

35. Semmler, 29.viii.43, p. 100.

36. "Goebbels-Tagebuch" in the Institut für Zeitgeschichte, Munich, 10.ix.43 and 11.ix.43, pp. 2663–64, 2703–4, 2710; Bretholz, p. 62; Papen, p. 502.

37. Heiber, "Der Tod," p. 402n; Mourin, p. 190, says Mafalda died on April 19, 1945; Neubacher, pp. 67–68.

38. SD-Ber., SS-Obergruppenführer Kaltenbrunner to Himmler, Berlin, 16.viii.43, T120 1305.485662–63; Beckerle to author, 3.ix.66 and 17.xi.66; interviews, Bulgaria and Munich.

39. Dr. Reinhard Gutschmidt, cited in Heiber, "Der Tod," p. 591.

40. Interviews, Bulgaria; FO R8377.470.7, Cairo, 4.ix.43.

41. Information on these troop movements comes from Queen Ioanna, "Memorie"; Heiber, "Der Tod," p. 394; Nikolaev.

Chapter Thirteen

1. Kazasov, *Vidyano*, pp. 610–11.

2. Article 29 of the Constitution; Black, *Establishment*, pp. 250–53, 315–19.

3. Filov, *Dnevnik*, 1.ix.43; Kazasov, *Vidyano*, p. 658.

4. Steengracht to Ribbentrop, Budapest, 6.ix.43, IMT, NG-118.

5. Heiber, "Der Tod," pp. 406–10; Haucke, *Bulgarien*, p. 53.

6. Filov, *Dnevnik*, 10.vii.43.

7. *Ibid.*, 6.ix.43.

8. XXV-NS, 6th extra. sess., 2d and 3d sittings, 8.ix.43 and 9.ix.43, pp. 1–17.

9. Testimony of Yordan Sevov, People's Court, 26.xii.44.

10. Filov, *Dnevnik*, 10.xi.43.

11. SD-Ber., Beckerle, Sofia, July 1942 and 27.viii.43, T120 1305.-485602–3 and IMT, NG-2609; Draganov, Madrid, 30.viii.43, SSF, T120 255 series; testimony of Pavel Gruev and Yordan Sevov, People's Court, 21.xii.44 and 26.xii.44. One should avoid the mistake of Charles and Barbara Jelavich (*The Balkans*, p. 105), who imply that Kiril was the only Regent and speak of his "increasingly pro-German actions."

12. Ribbentrop to Steengracht, IMT, NG-092.

13. Beckerle and Schönebeck, Sofia, 11.ix.43, SSF, T120 241.181108; Altenburg, Athens, 11.ix.43, SSF, T120 241 series.

14. SD-Ber., Berlin, 25.xi.42, T120 1305 series. However, the German historian Helmut Heiber insists that this new government "did not correspond to the German desires" and "was as much a slap [*Bruskierung*] at Germany as was possible in a country where the Wehrmacht was much in evidence": see Heiber, "Der Tod," p. 413.

15. Heiber, "Der Tod," p. 413.

16. "Goebbels-Tagebuch," 15.ix.43, pp. 2667f; SD-Ber., Beckerle, Sofia, 14.ix.43, T120 1305.241.

17. Feis, pp. 75, 127, 152; Churchill, *Second World War*, 5: 133–37, 6: 66; Sherwood, p. 780.

18. FRUS, *Cairo and Tehran Conferences*, p. 210; Roosevelt, pp. 134–44.

19. Buckley, *Five Ventures*, pp. 225–27.

20. *Ibid.*, pp. 229–42; *Zora* (Sofia), 10.xi.43 and 20.xi.43; see also Churchill's speech in the House of Commons, 22.ii.44, *Hansard's*, Vol. 397, col. 707.

21. Filov, *Dnevnik*, 23.x.43. Filov's growing pessimism was also shared by the leader of the Fascist-inclined "Otets Paisii" organization, Professor Georgi Genov. Sofia, 15.ix.43, SSF, T120 241.18128–29.

22. Filov, *Dnevnik*, 23.x.43; Schmidt, pp. 266–68; Pundeff, "Bulgaria's Place," p. 456.

23. Deakin, *Brutal Friendship*, Vol. 2, *The Last Days of Mussolini*; Skorzeny; Foley, pp. 28–49.

24. Filov, *Dnevnik*, 27.ix.43; Macartney, *October Fifteenth*, 2: 194–95.

25. Lukacs, pp. 520, 537.

26. Pundeff, "Bulgaria's Place," p. 455.

27. Schmidt, pp. 266–68.

28. Feis, p. 279.

29. Churchill, *Second World War*, 5: 286; Papen, p. 516; Filov, *Dnevnik*, 10.xi.43 and 23.xii.43.

30. Kazasov, *Burni godini*, pp. 727–28; interview, Bulgaria.

31. Interviews, Bulgaria.

32. Mushanov memoirs, "Spomeni," No. 1839, pp. 27–46, in Central Party Archive, Sofia, cited in an article by N. Gornenski in *Istoricheski pregled*, 1964, No. 4, p. 48; Kazasov, *Burni godini*, p. 725; *Istoriya na Bulgaria*, p. 396.

33. *Istoriya na Bulgaria*, p. 396; interview, Bulgaria.

34. Barker, *Truce*, p. 42.

35. Kazasov, *Burni godini*, pp. 727–28; Barker, *Truce*, p. 42; interview, Bulgaria.

Chapter Fourteen

1. Dugan and Stewart.

2. Combined Chiefs of Staff to Eisenhower, 23.x.43, in Craven and Cate, 2: 584.

3. Sweet-Escott, *Baker Street*, p. 201; Kazasov, *Burni godini*, p. 736; interviews, Bulgaria.

4. For details, see Sexton to McCarthy, 15.xi.43, Air Ministry Weekly Intelligence Summary, pp. 221–22, in Craven and Cate, 2: 584; Kazasov, *Burni godini*, p. 736; speech of Bozhilov, XXV-NS, 5th reg. sess., 13th sitting, 24.xi.43, p. 121; Moyzisch, p. 140.

5. Filov, *Dnevnik*, 19.i.44.

6. *Ibid.*

7. *Nelegalni*, p. 283; Gornenski, *Vuoruzhenata borba*, pp. 401, 408.

8. Filov, *Dnevnik*, 30.i.44.

9. *Ibid.*, 31.i.44.

10. Testimony of Pavel Gruev, People's Court, 21.xii.44; Mihov, *Dnevnik*, 25.iii.44; Kazasov, *Burni godini*, p. 746.

11. Filov, *Dnevnik*, 30.iii.44 and 31.iii.44; Mihov, *Dnevnik*, 29.iii.44 and 1.iv.44; speech of Todor Kozhuharov, XXV-NS, 5th reg. sess., 37th sitting, 24.iii.44, p. 620.

12. KTB der Heeresleitung in Bulgarien, Sofia, 17.iv.44, 18.iv.44, 21.vi.44, T501 293.297, .300, .498; Mihov, *Dnevnik*, 18.iv.44.

13. Mihov, *Dnevnik*, 21.iv.44. The attitude of Sofia toward Filov was reflected in a cartoon published shortly after his downfall. The former archeology professor is shown standing amid the ruins of Sofia saying, "I brought Sofia to this condition not from sycophancy or servility but from a love of excavation!" *Narod* (Sofia), 19.x.44.

14. Slessor, p. 596.

15. AMVnshR, Sofia, II, 1/11, p. 4; Bozhinov, pp. 45–46.

16. Stettinius to Harriman in Moscow, Washington, 10.ii.44, FRUS 1944, p. 300 (see other reports on pp. 300–304); AMVnshR, Ankara, 1944, Vol. I, No. 91, in Bozhinov, p. 48.

17. Berry, Istanbul, 3.iii.44, FRUS 1944, pp. 306–7.

18. *Ibid.*, p. 307.

19. Filov, *Dnevnik*, 26.ii.44 and 13.iii.44.

20. Mihov, *Dnevnik*, 16.iii.44.

21. XXV-NS, 5th reg. sess., 35th sitting, 23.iii.44, p. 595.

22. Filov, *Dnevnik*, 16.iii.44 and 17.iii.44.

23. *Hansard's*, Vol. 398, col. 832.

24. Lukacs, p. 578; XXV-NS, 5th reg. sess., 33d sitting, 26.i.44, p. 480.

25. *Mir* (Sofia), March 1944 issues; Mihov, *Dnevnik*, 23.iii.44 and 11.iv.44.

26. Berry, Istanbul, 25.iii.44, FRUS 1944, pp. 317–19.

27. Squires, Istanbul, 16.v.44, and Steinhardt, Ankara, 16.v.44, FRUS 1944, pp. 328–29.

Chapter Fifteen

1. SD-Ber., 10.ii.44, 3.iii.44, and 7.iii.44, T120 1305.485424, .485430, .485433; Padev, *Dimitrov*, p. 33; interviews, Bulgaria.

2. Lukacs, p. 578.

3. Interviews, Bulgaria.

4. Interviews, Bulgaria; Kazasov, *Burni godini*, pp. 748–49; *Istoriya na Bulgaria*, p. 414; KTB der Heeresleitung in Bulgarien, Sofia, 21.vi.44, T501 293.496; Todorov, *Balkan Firebrand*, p. 269.

5. Kazasov, *Burni godini*, pp. 750ff; testimony of Petko Stainov at the trial of Pastuhov, People's Court, 11.vi.46; Oren, "Bulgarian Communist Party," p. 333. This idea of a Fatherland Front government headed by Bagryanov was revived briefly at the end of August 1944, but was then totally unacceptable to the Bulgarian Communists.

6. *Govori radiostantsiya "Hristo Botev,"* Vol. VI, 2.vi.44 and 5.vi.44; see also *Materiali*, p. 221.

7. Pospelov et al., 4: 299; interview, Bulgaria.

8. Vasilev, p. 480; see also KTB der Heeresleitung in Bulgarien, Sofia, 21.vi.44, T501 293.496.

9. *Zarya* (Sofia), 4.vi.44.

10. *Neues Wiener Tageblatt*, 5.vi.44.

11. *Zarya*, 18.vi.44.

12. Finance Minister Dimiter Savov announced many of the measures on Radio Sofia, 19.vi.44, and they were printed in the newspapers the next day; see *Zarya*, 20.vi.44 and 30.vi.44; Padev, *Dimitrov*, pp. 33–34.

13. Filov, *Dnevnik*, 18.vi.44; see also Berry, Istanbul, 21.vii.44, FRUS 1944, 3: 348–49.

14. Draganov to Zagorov in Moscow, Sofia, 18.vi.44, in Bozhinov, pp. 79–80.

15. KTB der Heeresleitung in Bulgarien, Sofia, 21.vi.44, T501 293.496.

16. *Ibid.*, T501 293.497.

17. AMVnshR, Sofia, polit. direk., 11.15.221, op. 4, por. no. 38, dok. 1, in Bozhinov, p. 102.

18. "Proposed Terms for the Surrender of Bulgaria," 17.vi.44, FRUS 1944, 3: 341–44. Bretholz, p. 53, says that Sevov went to Ankara in June 1944 on the pretext of inspecting the plans for the construction of the

Bulgarian Embassy there; the Allies reportedly refused to deal with him because they had lost confidence in Bagryanov.

19. Berry, Istanbul, 21.vii.44, FRUS 1944, 3: 348–49.

20. AMVnshR, Sofia, polit. direk., 11.15.216, ruski konsulat, dok. 50, in Bozhinov, pp. 80–82.

21. *Vneshnyaya politika SSSR*, 2: 198.

22. *Zarya* (Sofia), 3.iii.44, 16.vii.44, 21.vii.44, 30.vii.44, 1.viii.44, and 2.viii.44. Filov, *Dnevnik*, 1.viii.44; note of Gen. Popov–Gen. Gade meeting, 5.v.44, T501 293.397; Bozhinov, p. 83.

23. *Hansard's*, Vol. 402, 2.viii.44, cols. 1483–84.

24. XXV-NS, 7th extra. sess., 4th sitting, 20.viii.44, p. 76.

25. XXV-NS, 7th extra. sess., 2d sitting, 18.viii.44, p. 29.

26. Milev to Draganov, Geneva, 16.viii.44, AMVnshR, Sofia, polit. direk., 11.15.219, op. 1, p. 4, por. no. 40 and dok. 3, p. 2, in Bozhinov, p. 102.

27. *Zarya*, 15.viii.44.

28. Filov, *Dnevnik*, 16.viii.44; instructions to Draganov, 17.viii.44, and text presented to Sarachoglu on 21.viii.44, Bozhinov, pp. 85–86.

29. A. Clark, p. 405.

30. *Ibid.*; Guderian, pp. 366–67; KTB of Army Group F, "Die Grosse Absetzbewegung in Südosten," DBA, H 11–16.

31. XXV-NS, 7th extra. sess., 1st sitting, 17.viii.44, p. 9; *Zarya, Mir, Zora*, and others, 18.viii.44. The headline of *Zarya* on that day was "Bulgarian People Never Desired to Become Involved."

32. Pundeff, "Bulgaria's Place," pp. 466–67; Kazasov, *Burni godini*, p. 753; FRUS 1944, 3: 358.

33. XXV-NS, 7th extra. sess., 2d, 3d, and 6th sittings, 18.viii.44, 19.viii.44, and 22.viii.44.

34. Kazasov, *Burni godini*, pp. 754–55; Pundeff, "Bulgaria's Place," pp. 466–67.

35. British Embassy in Washington, D.C., to U.S. Dept. of State, Aide-Mémoire, 20.viii.44, FRUS 1944, 3: 358–60.

36. *Ibid.*, pp. 360–61.

37. Berry, Istanbul, 23.viii.44 and 24.viii.44, FRUS 1944, 3: 363–64.

38. This brief account is based on a large number of sources, including Kissel; Matsulenko; Friessner, pp. 1–100; A. Clark, pp. 404–5; Hillgruber, *Hitler, König Carol*, pp. 209–31; KTB of Army Group F, August 1944, DBA, H 11–16.1.

39. Pospelov et al., 4: 299; *Materiali*, p. 234; Padev, *Dimitrov*, p. 35; Harriman, Moscow, 25.viii.44, FRUS 1944, 3: 376–77; Woodward, p. 295.

40. FRUS 1944, 3: 370.

41. Ambassador Wint in Great Britain, London, 25.viii.44 and 27.-viii.44, FRUS 1944, 3: 367–70, 374–76.

42. Steinhardt, Ankara, 28.viii.44 and 29.viii.44; and Berry, Istanbul, 30.viii.44, FRUS 1940, 3: 376–80.

43. Memo by the Division of Southern European Affairs for U.S. Under Secretary of State Edward R. Stettinius, Washington, D.C., March 1944, FRUS 1944, 3: 304–5.

44. Harriman, Moscow, 19.iii.44, FRUS 1944, 3: 316–17.

45. Berry, Istanbul, 25.iii.44, 22.vi.44, 21.vii.44, and 30.viii.44, FRUS 1944, 3: 318, 340, 350, 381–82.

46. Kazasov, *Burni godini*, pp. 750ff.

47. *Ibid.*; testimony of Petko Stainov at the trial of Pastuhov, People's Court, 11.vi.46; Oren, *Bulgarian Communism*, p. 333; BKP Central Party Archive, Sofia, f. 65, op. 1, a.e. 8-v; "Appeal of the National Committee of the Fatherland Front to the Bulgarian People," 25.viii.44; interview, Bulgaria.

Chapter Sixteen

1. Interview, Bulgaria.

2. G. Dimitrov, *Suchineniya*, 2: 196; *Materiali,* pp. 165–68. The meeting place at 48 Aksakov Street in Sofia is now a shrine.

3. Kostov, pp. 5–8.

4. Vukmanovich, "Memoirs," *Politika*, 8.ii.71; article by Anton Yugov in *Novo Vreme* (September 1953), pp. 59–75; Oren, *Bulgarian Communism*, pp. 88–89.

5. TsDIA, f. 370, op. 1, arh. ed. 1088; Boris Stoinov, "Kum vuprosa," p. 19; Boris Stoinov, "Boinite grupi," p. 138.

6. Gornenski, *Vuoruzhenata borba*, p. 34; *Narodna armiya* (Sofia), 4.ix.54.

7. Police report on Leon Tadzher, Archive of the Sofia Synagogue, folder 59; German military attaché Bruckmann to Lt. Col. Kostov in Bulgarian Ministry of War, Sofia, 6.xi.41, in Archive of the Museum of the Revolutionary Movement, Sofia; monthly report to German Wehrmachtbefehlshaber Südost, September 1941, RGMA T501 292.230; Stoimenov and Georgiev, p. 40; *Evrei zaginali*—date incorrectly given as September 28 rather than October 28.

8. Bochev, "Kum vuprosa," p. 91; Pozolotin, p. 24; Gornenski, *Vuoruzhenata borba*, pp. 67–69; Kühnrich, p. 120; Borachev, pp. 4–5; Valev, pp. 55–56.

9. *Istoriya na BKP* (1970 edition), pp. 451–52; Vidinski; Vinarov, pp. 557–72; Gornenski, *Vuoruzhenata borba*, pp. 86–87.

10. Thompson, pp. 175–76.

11. TsDIA, f. 370, op. 1, a.e. 1097, p. 50; Gornenski, *Vuoruzhenata borba*, pp. 71, 122–24; *Istoriya na BKP*, p. 454; Boris Stoinov, *Nespokoen til*, pp. 21–23; Stoimenov and Georgiev, pp. 44–74. Zaimov's story is related in Poptsvyatkov; Radoinov's experiences are given in Dragolyubov.

12. "KTB des Wehrwirtschaftsoffiziers," Lageberichte, 31.xii.42, Vol. IV, p. 1, DBA; Beckerle to Ribbentrop, in Reile, pp. 327–29; exchange between Interior Minister Gabrovsky and Representative Petko Stainov, XXV-NS, 4th reg. sess., 43d sitting, 23.ii.43, 2: 858–59; Borachev, pp. 12–13.

13. Borachev, pp. 12–13; Iribadzhakov, p. 273.

14. Violeta Yankova was captured and executed in 1944. Boris Stoinov, "Boinite grupi," pp. 145–46; *Materiali*, p. 199; Beckerle, Sofia, 14.ii.43, 18.ii.43, 20.ii.43, 4.v.43, SSF, T120 255.173815–16, .173818–19, .173824, .173904–5; Filov, *Dnevnik*, 3.v.43, 5.v.43; testimony of Yordan Sevov, People's Court, 27.xii.44.

15. Filov, *Dnevnik*, 3.v.43, 5.v.43; Kazasov, *Burni godini*; SD-Ber., Beckerle, Sofia, 3.v.43, T120 1305.485655; testimony of Yordan Sevov, People's Court, 27.xii.44; Boris Stoinov, "Boinite grupi," pp. 145–46; testimony of Pavel Gruev, People's Court, 21.xii.44.

16. Gornenski, *Vuoruzhenata borba*, p. 137.

17. TsDIA, f. 370, op. 1, a.e. 1303, p. 36; Ganevich, *Bor'ba*, p. 140; Kühnrich, p. 424; "KTB des Wehrwirtschaftsoffiziers," Lageberichte, 28.ii.43, Vol. V, p. 1, DBA.

18. Iribadzhakov, pp. 262ff.

19. Bogdan Atanasov, pp. 84–134.

20. Koev; Serkedzhiev. For every partisan head, the government paid the substantial bounty of 50,000 leva.

21. See Oren, *Bulgarian Communism*; Filov, *Dnevnik*, 9.iii.44, 27.-iii.44; Mihov, *Dnevnik*, 27.iii.44, 27.iv.44, 23.iv.44; KTB der Heeresleitung in Bulgarien, Sofia, 18.iv.44, T501 29.369.

22. Report by German police attaché Hoffman, Sofia, 11.viii.44, TsDIA, f. 370, a.e. 1578, pp. 257–64; "KTB des Wehrwirtschaftsoffiziers," Sofia, i.vii.44, Vol. XI, DBA.

23. Thompson, pp. 176–80; Sweet-Escott, *Baker Street*, pp. 188–219; Vasilev, pp. 564–73; Ganevich, p. 237; *Struggle*, p. 79; Doinov and Draev, *Za svobodata*, pp. 268–80; Oren, *Bulgarian Communism*, pp. 253–63.

24. Sweet-Escott, *Baker Street*, pp. 213–15; Ganevich, pp. 238–39; Valev, p. 30; Slavka Petrova, "Neuspehut," p. 9, n4; *Rabotnichesko delo*, 7.ix.47; Wolfgramm, 8: 513; Maclean, pp. 402–3; Shterev, pp. 97–104; Georgi Dimitrov, *Spasitelniyat*, p. 61; Lambrev, pp. 253–70, describes the assistance by the partisans to downed Allied airmen.

25. XXV-NS, 7th extra. sess., 2d sitting, 18.viii.44, p. 37.

26. "KTB des Wehrwirtschaftsoffiziers," Sofia, 1.vii.44, Vol. XI, DBA.

27. Borachev, pp. 26–32.

28. Slavka Petrova, "Neuspehut," pp. 20–39. The Regents strongly opposed the amnesty on the grounds that it would impair the antipartisan campaign.

29. KTB of Army Group F, DBA, H 11–16.1.

Chapter Seventeen

1. Berry, Istanbul, 30.viii.44, FRUS 1944, 3: 381; SD-Ber., Schellenberg, 27.viii.44, T120 1305.485684; _Zarya_ (Sofia), 22.viii.44; IMT, NG-3912; AMVnshR, Sofia, 11.15.220, dok. 9; Bozhinov, p. 99; Pundeff, "Bulgaria's Place," p. 469.

2. See manuscript of Muraviev entitled "Events and People," People's Court transcripts, Sustav I, 4: 1579–80, 1608 (see also 5: 1623–24); Ilcho Dimitrov, "Poslednoto pravitelstvo," pp. 8–13; Dellin, p. 117; _Dnevnik_ (Sofia newspaper), 1.ix.44; _Slovo_ (Sofia), 2.ix.44; TsDIA, f. 370, op. 1, a.e. 1572, p. 147.

3. TsDIA, f. 456, op. 1, a.e. 12, pp. 97–109; Ilcho Dimitrov, "Poslednoto pravitelstvo," pp. 10–11. See also Kunyu Kozhuharov, "60 godini," _Istoricheski pregled_, 1960, No. 1, p. 35; this article, commemorating the 60th anniversary of the Agrarian Party, refers to the "Muraviev-Gichev clique, which headed the last fascist government."

4. Appeal of 2.ix.44, in Gornenski, _Vuoruzhenata borba_, pp. 644–45; see also Padev, _Dimitrov Wastes No Bullets_, p. 27, for comments.

5. Two somewhat different versions are given in Ilcho Dimitrov, "Poslednoto pravitelstvo," pp. 15–16; and Berry, Istanbul, 5.ix.44, FRUS 1944, 3: 396–97.

6. Biryuzov, p. 172.

7. _Ibid._, pp. 171–202.

8. Petkov, pp. 92–96.

9. Marinov has related his account in "Pet dni v pravitelstvo na K. Muraviev," _Istoricheski pregled_, 1968, No. 3, pp. 81–102.

10. Ilcho Dimitrov, "Poslednoto pravitelstvo," pp. 23–24; People's Court, Sustav I, 4: 1468, 5: 1615; Dellin, pp. 118, 121; _Naroden sud_ (Sofia), 18.xii.44; _Kratka Bulgarska Entsiklopediya_, "Marinov," 3: 347; commentary of Jacobson and Hillgruber in Telpuchowski, p. 391: The delay, according to Telpuchowski, served "to give the Soviets the opportunity to declare war on Bulgaria—a motivation that represented the ultimate in hypocrisy" [translation mine].

11. People's Court, Sustav I, 4: 1516; TsDIA, Sofia, f. 370, op. 1, a.e.

1572; Ilcho Dimitrov, "Poslednoto pravitelstvo," pp. 24–25; Woodward, p. 295; Kazasov, *Burni godini*, p. 764; *Vneshnyaya politika SSSR*, 2: 181–83; Harriman, Moscow, 7.ix.44, FRUS 1944, 3: 401.

12. People's Court, Sustav I, 5: 2015–16; Ilcho Dimitrov, "Poslednoto pravitelstvo," p. 24; TsDIA, f. 284, op. 1, a.e. 3736, p. 1; *Zarya* (Sofia), 6.ix.44, and Steinhardt, Ankara, 6.ix.44, FRUS 1944, 3: 397–99. The Sofia newspapers the next morning quoted a broadcast by Radio Sofia that shortly before midnight predicted war would be declared. The headlines of September 6 gave prominence to the German action against the occupation corps in Macedonia and placed in smaller type the heading "The Soviet Union considers itself in a state of war with Bulgaria."

13. *Materiali*, pp. 236–38; Radulov, p. 85; Ilcho Dimitrov, "Poslednoto pravitelstvo," p. 27; Georgieff and Spiru, pp. 372–74.

14. Gornenski, *Vuoruzhenata borba*, pp. 668–70; *Otechestvenata voina*, 1: 156.

15. Bozhinov, p. 127.

16. *Materiali*, p. 238; *Istoriya Bolgarskoi kommunisticheskoi partii*, p. 381; Gornenski, *Vuoruzhenata borba*, p. 688; Ilcho Dimitrov, "Poslednoto pravitelstvo," p. 27; Bozhinov, p. 127; Gornenski, "Materiali i publikatsii," *Istoricheski pregled*, 1950, No. 1, p. 93.

17. Craven and Cate, pp. 473–74; KTB der Heeresleitung in Bulgarien, 6.ix.44, T501 294.–71.

18. Gornenski, *Vuoruzhenata borba*, p. 673; *Zarya*, 9.ix.44; Soviet Foreign Ministry communiqué, 9.ix.44, quoted in FRUS 1944, 3: 406–7.

19. Details of Kolarov's lecture are given in Harriman to Hull, Moscow, 9.ix.44, FRUS 1944, 3: 408; see Matsulenko, p. 101.

20. *Zarya*, 9.ix.44; Kazasov, *Burni godini*, p. 766; Biryuzov, p. 177n.

21. Georgieff and Spiru, pp. 374–75.

22. Biryuzov, pp. 172, 179; Gornenski, "Materiali i publikatsii," p. 93; *Zarya*, 9.ix.44; Barker, *Truce*, pp. 45–46; TASS statement, 9.ix.44, *Vneshnyaya politika SSSR*, 2: 201–2; Bulgarian historians seldom admit that the Muraviev government declared war on Germany and almost never mention the fact that Russia accepted Muraviev's appeal for an armistice; an exception is Ilcho Dimitrov, "Poslednoto pravitelstvo," p. 29.

23. Vrachev, "Vuoruzhenata borba," p. 29; Petkov, p. 92; *Prinosut*, p. 61.

Bibliography

I have listed only the most important of the many articles on Bulgaria during the Second World War to be found in the following periodicals: *Istoricheski pregled, Izvestiya na instituta za bulgarska istoriya, Voenno-istoricheski sbornik,* and *Cahiers internationaux de la résistance* (Vienna).

Aleksoski, V. K., ed. NOV Makedonije. Skopje, 1964.

Alfieri, Dino. Due dittatori di fronte. Milan, 1948. Translated into English as Dictators Face to Face. New York, 1955.

Allen, Harold B. Come over into Macedonia. New Brunswick, N.J., 1943.

Allen, W. E. D., and Paul Muratoff. The Russian Campaigns of 1944–1945. London, 1946.

American Bulgarian League. Bulgaria's True Record. Oak Park, Ill., 1945.

Anastasoff, Christ. The Tragic Peninsula: A History of the Macedonian Movement for Independence Since 1878. St. Louis, Mo., 1938.

Anfuso, Filippo. Roma, Berlino, Salò, 1936–1945. Milan, 1950.

Antonov, Dimitur. Ot monarhiya kum Bulgarska narodna republika. Sofia, 1946.

Apostolski, Mihajlo. Zavrshne operatsije za oslobodenje Makedonije. Belgrade, 1953.

Arditti, Benjamin. Rolyata na Tsar Boris III pri izselvaneto na evreite ot Bulgaria. Tel Aviv, 1952.

———. Yehuday Bulgaria beshnot hamishtar Hanatsi 1940–1944. Tel Giborim, Israel, 1962.

Arendt, Hannah. Eichmann in Jerusalem. New York, 1963.

Atanasov, Bogdan. Vuoruzhenata borba v shesta Vustanicheska operativna zona. Sofia, 1968.

Atanasov, Shteriu. Pod znameto na partiyata. Sofia, 1962.

———, et al. Bulgarskoto voenno izkustvo prez kapitalizma. Sofia, 1959.

———. Kratka istoriya na Otechestvenata voina. Sofia, 1958.

Atanasov, V. B. Geroi na antifashistkata borba, 1923–1944. Sofia, 1966.

Auty, Phyllis. Tito. New York, 1970.

———. Yugoslavia. London, 1965.

Avakumovich, Ivan. History of the Communist Party of Yugoslavia. Vol. I. Aberdeen, Scotland, 1964.

Avramov, Mois. Po stupkite na suprotivata. Sofia, 1969.

Badoglio, Marshal Pietro. Italy in the Second World War: Memoirs and Documents. London, 1948.

Barker, Elizabeth. Macedonia: Its Place in Balkan Power Politics. London, 1950.

———. Truce in the Balkans. London, 1948.

Barros, James. The League of Nations and the Great Powers: the Greek-Bulgarian Incident, 1925. Oxford, 1970.

Basdevant, Denise. Against Tide and Tempest: The Story of Rumania. New York, 1966.

Batakliev, Ivan. Stopanskoto znachenie na Belomorieto. Sofia, 1943.

Bathe, Rolf, and Erich Glodschey. Der Kampf um den Balkan. Berlin, 1942.

Baur, Hans. Ich flog Mächtige der Erde. Kempten, Germany, 1956.

Beamish, Tufton. Must Night Fall? London, 1950.

Beloff, Max. The Foreign Policy of Soviet Russia. Vol. II. London, 1949.

Betts, Reginald Robert, ed. Central and South East Europe, 1945–1948. London, 1950.

Bibliografiya na nelegalniya antifashistki perioditchen pechat, 1923–1944. Sofia, 1948.

Biryuzov, Sergei S. Sovetskii soldat na Balkanakh. Moscow, 1963.

Bitola, 11 Mart 1943. Skopje, 1958.

Black, C. E. Challenge in Eastern Europe. New Brunswick, N.J., 1954.

———. The Establishment of Constitutional Government in Bulgaria. Princeton, N.J., 1943.

Boberach, Heinz, ed. Meldungen aus dem Reich: Auswahl aus dem geheimen Lageberichten des Sicherheitsdiensts der SS. Berlin, 1965.

Bochev, Iliya Petrov. "Kum vuprosa za nazryavneto i razvitieto na politicheskata kriza v Bulgariya v usloviyata na Vtorata svetovna voina 1941–1944." Unpublished dissertation for the degree of Candidate of Historical Science. Sofia, 1961.

———. Revolyutsionniyat protses v Bulgaria, 1940–1944. Sofia, 1969.

Bodenstadt, Adolf. Der Sonderbericht der deutschen Wochenschau vom Überfall auf Jugoslawien und Griechenland am 6. April 1941. Hamburg, 1958.

Boev, B., et al. Slavna epopeya, 1941–1944. Sofia, 1965.

Bogdanov, Ts. Tsarskite manevri. Sofia, 1937.

Bolitho, Hector. Rumania Under King Carol. London, 1939.

Borachev, Maj. Gen. Demir. "Varnenskata okruzhna partiina organizatsiya i grad Varna (Stalin) v purvite reditsi na vuoruzhenata osvoboditelna borba," *Voenno-istoricheski sbornik*, 1954, No. 4.

Borkenau, Franz. The New German Empire. New York, 1939.

Bosil'chich, Slobodan. Istochna Srbija. Belgrade, 1963.

Botev, Nikola. Silistrentsi v Otechestvenata voina 1944–1945. Sofia, 1957.

Bozhinov, Voin. Politicheskata kriza v Bulgariya prez 1943–44. Sofia, 1957.

Bozhkov, Liuben [Lyuben Boshkov]. La Bulgarie et la mer Egée. Sofia, 1946.

Brailsford, H. N. Macedonia: Its Races and Future. London, 1906.

Brajovich, Petar, et al., eds. Les Systèmes d'occupation en Yougoslavie, 1941–1945. Belgrade, 1963.

Bramos, Kostas. Slavokommounisti kai Organoseis en Makedonia: Propaganda kai Epanastatiki Dhrasis. Salonika, 1954.

Bretholz, Wolfgang. Ich sah sie stürzen. Vienna, 1955.

Brown, J. F. Bulgaria Under Communist Rule. New York, 1970.

Bruns, Viktor. Politische Verträge. Vol. III. Berlin, 1941.

Brusasca, Giuseppe. Il Ministero degli Affari Esteri. Rome, 1948.

Buchheit, Gert. Der deutsche Geheimdienst: Geschichte der militärischen Abwehr. Munich, 1966.

Buchner, Alexander. Der deutsche Griechenland-Feldzug Operationen der 12. Armee, 1941. Heidelberg, 1957.

Buckley, Christopher. Five Ventures. London, 1954.

———. Greece and Crete, 1941. London, 1952.

Bulgaria. Archive of the Sofia Synagogue, Institute for Balkanistics. Sofia.

———. Arhiv na muzeyata na revolyutsionnoto dvizhenie v Bulgaria [Archive of the Museum of the Revolutionary Movement in Bulgaria]. Sofia.

———. Jewish Cultural Society of Sofia. "Ekspozitsiya na postoyannata izlozhba na tema: 'Spasenieto na bulgarskite evrei.' " Sofia, 1966. Typewritten documents concerning the wartime Jewish question collected for an exhibition in December 1966.

———. Narodno Subranie. Stenografski dnevnitsi na XXIV-to Obiknoveno narodno subranie. Sofia, 1938 and 1939.

———, ———. Stenografski dnevnitsi na XXV-to Obiknoveno narodno subranie. Sofia, 1940–44.

———. People's Court [Naroden sud]. Transcripts of the Trials of the Former Government Leaders, 1944–45. Sustav [Series] I: Trials of the regents, premiers, cabinet ministers, and royal advisers; Sustav VII: Trials of those who persecuted the Jews during the war. Sofia.

———. Tsentralen durzhaven istoricheski arhiv [Central State Historical Archives]. Sofia. Document series 173, 190, 284, 370, and 456.

Bulgarian Academy of Science [Bulgarska akademiya naykite]. Ustanovyavane i ukrepvane na narodnodemokratichnata vlast, sept. 1944–mai 1945. Sofia, 1969.

Bulgarian Atrocities in Greek Macedonia and Thrace. Athens, 1945.

Bulgarian Occupation in Thrace and Eastern Macedonia. Sofia, 1945.

Bulgarskata komunisticheska partiya v rezolyutsii i resheniya na kongresite, konferentsiite i plenumite na TsK, 1923–1944. Vol. III. Sofia, 1954.

Burks, R. V. The Dynamics of Communism in Eastern Europe. Princeton, N.J., 1961.

Burmov, A. K., and P. H. Petrov, eds. Hristomatiya po istoriya na Bulgaria. Sofia, 1964.

Busch-Zantner, Richard. Bulgarien. Leipzig, 1943.

Butler, J. R. M. Grand Strategy. Vol. II. London, 1957.

Byrnes, James F. Speaking Frankly. New York, 1947.

Byrnes, Robert F. Yugoslavia. New York, 1957.

Carlyle, Margaret, ed. Documents on International Affairs: Hitler's Europe. London, 1954.

Cervi, Mario. The Hollow Legions: Mussolini's Blunder in Greece 1940–1941. Garden City, N.Y., 1971.

Charova, Krumpka. "Die deutsche Aggression auf dem Balkan und die Rolle Bulgarien (April–Mai 1941)," in Vitka Toskowa, ed., *Etudes Historiques*, Vol. V. Sofia, 1970.

Chary, Frederick B. Bulgaria and the Jews: "The Final Solution," 1940 to 1944. Ph.D. dissertation, University of Pittsburgh, Penn., 1968.

———. The Bulgarian Jews and the Final Solution, 1940–1944. Pittsburgh, Penn., 1972.

Chashule, Vanga. BKP i Makedonskoto prashanye, 1944–1968. Skopje, 1968.

Chichovska, Vesela. Sobolevata aktsiya. Sofia, 1972.

Christopoulis, Georgios. Bulgaria's Record. Chicago, 1944.

Christowe, Stoyan. Heroes and Assassins. London, 1935.

Chulinovich, Ferdo. Dvadeset sedmi mart. Zagreb, 1965.

———. Jugoslavija izmedju dva rata. Zagreb, 1961. 2 vols.

Churchill, Winston S. The Second World War. London, 1950. 6 vols.

———. The War Speeches of the Rt. Hon. Winston S. Churchill. Comp. Charles Eade. London, 1951.

Ciano, Galeazzo. Ciano's Diary, 1939–1943. London, 1947.

———. Ciano's Diplomatic Papers. London, 1948.

Clark, Alan. Barbarossa: The Russian-German Conflict, 1941–1945. New York, 1965.

Clark, Douglas. Three Days to Catastrophe: Britain and the Russo-Finnish War. London, 1966.

Clissold, Stephen. Whirlwind. New York, 1949.

Collier, Richard. Duce: A Biography of Benito Mussolini. New York, 1971.

Condit, D. M. Case Study in Guerrilla War: Greece During World War II. Washington, D.C., 1961.

Confino, Baruch. Aliya "B" mehupei Bulgaria 1938–1940. Jerusalem, 1965.

Craven, W. F., and J. L. Cate. The Army Air Force in World War II. New York, 1949.

Dakin, Douglas. The Greek Struggle in Macedonia, 1897–1913. Salonika, 1966.

Dallin, David J. Soviet Espionage. New Haven, Conn., 1955.

———. Soviet Russia's Foreign Policy, 1939–1942. New Haven, Conn., 1942.

Dami, Aldo. Fatalités bulgares. Geneva, 1946.

Danailov, L., and S. Zaimov. General Vladimir Zaimov. Sofia, 1957.

Danov, Andrei. Prez Nish startsin Drava mur. Sofia, 1965.

Danubian Group of Economic Experts. Chronology of Political and Economic Events in the Danube Basin, 1918–1936: Bulgaria. Paris, 1938.

Darby, H. C., et al. A Short History of Yugoslavia. Cambridge, Eng., 1966.

Davidson, Basil. Partisan Picture. Bedford, Eng., 1946.

Deakin, F. W. D. The Brutal Friendship: Mussolini, Hitler and the Fall of Italian Fascism. London, 1962.

———. The Embattled Mountain. London, 1971.

Dedijer, Vladimir. Tito Speaks. London, 1953.

Degras, Jane, ed. Soviet Documents on Foreign Policy. Vol. III. London, 1953.

Dellin, L. A. D., ed. Bulgaria. New York, 1957.

Dendias, Michael. La Thrace grecque et le débouché bulgare sur la mer Egée. Paris, 1946.

Deutsch-Bulgarischen Gesellschaft. Bulgarien: Jahrbuch der Gesellschaft. Berlin, 1938 et seq.

Deutsches Auslandswissenschaftliches Institut. Bulgarien. Leipzig, 1942.

Deveti Septemvri: Spomeni. Sofia, 1957.

Dimitrov, Georgi. Rechi, dokladi, statii, 1942–1947. Vol. 3. Sofia, 1947.

———. Spasitelniyat put za Bulgaria. Sofia, 1945.

———. Suchineniya. Sofia, 1951–1955. 14 vols.

Dimitrov, Ilcho. Burzhoaznata opozitsiya v Bulgaria 1939–1944. Sofia, 1969.

———. "Poslednoto pravitelstvo na burzhoazna Bulgaria," *Istoricheski pregled*, 1964, No. 5.

Dimitrov, Mihail. Poyava, razvite i ideologiya na fashizma v Bulgariya. Sofia, 1947.

Dinerstein, Herbert Samuel. Fifty Years of Soviet Foreign Policy. Baltimore, Md., 1968.

Dinev, Angel. Politichkite ubistva vo Bulgarija. Skopje, 1951.

Djilas, Milovan. Conversations with Stalin. London, 1962.

Djoumalieff, Stancho. Le Droit de la Bulgarie sur la Thrace occidentale. Sofia, 1946.

Documents on British Foreign Policy, 1919–1939. Eds. E. L. Woodward and Rohan Butler. 3d ser., Vol. V. London, n.d.

Documents on German Foreign Policy. Series D. Washington, D.C., 1953–62.

Documents Secrets du Ministère des Affaires Etrangères d'Allemagne: Turquie. Paris, 1946.

Doinov, D., and I. Draev, eds. Bulgari boitsi za svobodata na drugi narodi. Sofia, 1963.

———. Za svobodata na bulgarskiya narod. Sofia, 1967.

Dokumenti od sozdavanyeto i razvitokot na N. R. Makedonija, 1944–1946. Skopje, 1949.

Dollman, Eugen. Dolmetscher den Diktatorian. Bayreuth, 1963.

Domarus, Max, comp. Hitler: Reden und Proklamationen 1932–1945. Vol. II. Munich, 1965.

Dragolyubov, P. General-maior Tsvyatko Radoinov. Sofia, 1960.

Dramaliev, Kiril. Istoriya na Otechestveniya front. Sofia, 1947.

Dugan, James, and Carroll Stewart. Ploesti: the Great Ground-Air Battle of August 1943. New York, 1962.

Duichev, Ivan. Makedoniya v bulgarska istoriya. Sofia, 1941.

Dummert, Rudolf. Deutschlands Nachbarn in Südosten. Leipzig, 1938.

Dyakovich, V. Bulgarite v Besarabiya. Sofia, 1930.

Dzelepy, Eleuthère N. Le Drame de la résistance grecque. Paris, 1946.

Erliiska, Mariya. Vuoruzhenata borba vuv vtorata Vustanicheska operativna zona 1941–1944. Sofia, 1965.

Evans, Stanley George. A Short History of Bulgaria. London, 1960.

Evrei zaginali v antifashistkata borba. Sofia, 1958.

Fabian Society. Hitler's Route to Bagdad. London, 1939.

Feis, Herbert. Churchill, Roosevelt, Stalin. Princeton, N.J., 1957.

Ferrario, Carlo Antonio. Storia dei bulgari. Milan, 1940.

Filov, Bogdan. Bulgariens Weg: Die Aussenpolitik der Bulgarischen Regierung. Sofia, 1942.

———. Dnevnik [Diary]. Though this diary has not been published in its entirety, it was presented as evidence at Filov's trial before the People's Court and extensive excerpts were printed in various Sofia newspapers.

————. Ideite i delata na dneshniya bezpartien rezhim. Sofia, 1942.

————. Putut na Bulgaria. Sofia, 1941.

Foley, Charles. Commando Extraordinary: The Remarkable Exploits of Otto Skorzeny. New York, 1957.

Ford, Corey. Donovan of OSS. Boston, 1970.

Foreign Relations of the United States. *See* United States, Department of State.

Fotich, Konstantin. The War We Lost: Yugoslavia's Tragedy and the Failure of the West. New York, 1948.

Fox, Annette Baker. The Power of Small States: Diplomacy in World War II. Chicago, 1959.

Frauendienst, Werner. Yugoslawiens Weg zum Abgrund. Berlin, 1941.

Frentagh-Loringhouen, Arel von. Deutschlands Aussenpolitik. Berlin, 1940.

Friessner, Hans. Verratene Schlachten: Die Tragödie der deutschen Wehrmacht in Rumänien und Ungarn. Hamburg, 1956.

Gafencu, Grigore. Prelude to the Russian Campaign. London, 1945.

Ganevich, I. V. Bor'ba bolgarskovo naroda pod rukovodstvom Komunisticheskoi Partii za Natsional'noe i Sotsialnoe Osvobozhdenie (1941–1944). Kiev, 1959.

Gellert, Johannes Fürchtegott. Mittelburgarien: das Kulturgeographische Bild. Berlin, 1937.

Genoff, G. P. Das Schicksal Bulgariens: Sein Kampf gegen das Friedensdiktat von Neuilly. Berlin, 1940.

Gentizon, Paul. Le Drame bulgare: du Ferdinand de Bulgarie à Stamboulisky. Paris, 1924.

Georgevitch, T. R. Macedonia. London, 1918.

Georgieff, Peter, and Basil Spiru. Bulgariens Volk im Widerstand, 1941–1944. East Berlin, 1962.

Georgiev, Georgi. 2194 dni: hronika na edna pobeda 1939–1945. Sofia, 1969.

Georgiev, Ivan. Dobrudzha v borbata za svobodna, 1913–1940. Sofia, 1962.

Georgiev, Velichko. Burzhoaznite i drebno burzhoaznite partii v Bulgaria 1934–1939. Sofia, 1971.

Georgov, Ivan. Die bulgarische Nation und der Weltkriege. Berlin, 1918.

Gerigk, Alfred. Spuk am Balkan: ein König, ein Oberst, ein General. Berlin, 1943.

Geroichno minalo: spomeni na partiini deitsi. Sofia, 1965.

Germany. Deutsches Bundesarchiv [German Federal Archives]. Koblenz.
———, ———. Deutsches Ausland-Institut.
———, ———. Economic Reports from the Wehrwirtschaftsoffizier in Sofia, and other special studies on Bulgaria.
———, ———. Military Reports from the Balkans and the war diaries [Kreigstagebücher] of various military units.
———, ———. Reichskanzlei files, 1939–1944.
———. Foreign Office. Staatssekretär Files. Diplomatic reports from the German Ambassador in Bulgaria to Berlin and replies, May 1939 to September 1944. Microfilm series T120; roll numbers 73, 225, 237, 238, 241, 244, 255, 265, 329, 585, and 688.
———, ———. Die Geheimakten des Französischen Generalstabes. No. 6, 1939/41. Berlin, 1941.
———, ———. Dokumente zum Konflikt mit Jugoslawien und Griechenland. No. 7, 1939/41.
———. Militärforschungsamt [Military Research Office]. Freiburg.
———, ———. Military Reports and Kriegstagebücher from Bulgaria.
———, ———. SD Intelligence Reports [SD-Berichte] from the Balkans, November 1943 to September 1944.
———, ———. Reports of the German High Command [OKW].
———. Goebbels-Tagebuch. Institut für Zeitgeschichte, Munich.
———. Reports of the German Military Advisers in Bulgaria. Microfilm series T501, rolls 292, 293, and 294.
———. Sicherheitsdienst (SD). Intelligence Reports, January 1941 to September 1943. Microfilm series T120, roll 1305.
Geshkoff, T. I. Balkan Union: A Road to Peace in Southeastern Europe. New York, 1940.
Gheorge, Ion. Rumäniens Weg zum Satelliten-Staat. Heidelberg, 1952.
Gilbert, Felix, ed. Hitler Directs His War: The Secret Records of His Daily Military Conferences. New York, 1950.
Ginchev, Ivan. Partizani. Sofia, 1969.
Gindev, Panaoit A. Kum vuprosa za haraktera na narodno-demokraticheskata revolyutsiya v Bulgaria. Sofia, 1956.
Girard, André. Les Minorités nationales, ethniques et religieuses en Bulgarie. Paris, 1933.
Girginov, Aleksander. Ispitaniyata v voinata. Sofia, 1936.
Goebbels, Paul Joseph. The Goebbels Diaries. New York, 1948.
Goebbels-Tagebücher aus den Jahren 1942–43. Zurich, 1948.
Gopchevich, Spiridion. Makedonien und Alt-Serbien. Vienna, 1889.
Gornenski, Nikifor. "Materiali i publikatsii: kratki danni za deistviyata na partizanskite chasti v navecherieto i po vremeto na devetoseptemvriiskoto vustanie," *Istoricheski pregled*, 1950, No. 1.

————. Vuoruzhenata borba na bulgarskiya narod, 1941–1944. Sofia, 1958.

Govori radiostantsiya "Hristo Botev." Sofia, 1950–52. 7 vols.

Great Britain. Admiralty. Handbook of Macedonia and Surrounding Territories. London, 1920.

————. Foreign Office. Exchange of notes between H.M. Government in the U.K. and Bulgarian Government regarding military, naval and air clauses of Treaty of Neuilly. London, 1939.

————, ————. Archives. Series 371, in the Public Record Office, London.

————, ————. Bulgaria: Basic Handbook. September 1943 [secret].

————. Naval Intelligence Office. Handbook of Bulgaria. London, 1920.

————, ————. Handbook of Macedonia. London, 1920.

Greece. Genikon Epiteleion Stratou. Agones eis tin Anatolikin Makedonian kai tin Dhytikin Thrakin 1941. Athens, 1956.

————. Royal Ministry for Foreign Affairs. Italy's Aggression Against Greece. Athens, 1940.

Greenfield, Kent Roberts, ed. Command Decisions. New York, 1959.

Gregorich, Danilo. So endete Jugoslawien. Leipzig, 1943.

Greiner, Helmuth. Die Oberste Wehrmachtführung 1939–1943. Wiesbaden, 1951.

Grigorov, K. I. Razvitie na burzhoaznata ikonomicheska misul v Bulgariya mezhdu dvete svetovni voini. Sofia, 1960.

Grinberg, Natan. Dokumenti. Sofia, 1945.

————. Hitleristkiyat natisk za unishtozhvane na evreite ot Bulgariya. Tel Aviv, 1961.

Gross, Feliks, ed. European Ideologies: A Survey of Twentieth Century Political Ideas. New York, 1948.

Gross, Hermann. Die Aussenhandelsverflechtung der Südoststaaten. Munich, 1960.

Grubcheva, Mitka. V imeto na naroda. Sofia, 1962.

Guderian, Heinz. Panzer Leader. New York, 1952.

Haider, Rudolf. Die Bulgarische Wiedergeburt. Berlin, 1941.

Halder, Franz. Diary. Vols. V and VI. Typewritten copies from the evidence submitted to the International Military Tribunal.

Hansard's Parliamentary Debates, Commons.

Hariev, Ivan. Nedovurshen razgovor: spomeni na partizanskiya lager. Sofia, 1969.

Hasluck, E. L. The Second World War. London, n.d.

Hassell, Ulrich von. Vom andern Deutschland. Zurich, 1946.

Hauch, Joseph. Tornado Across Eastern Europe. New York, 1942.

Haucke, Kurt. Bulgarien: Land, Volk, Geschichte, Kultur, Wirtschaft. Bayreuth, 1942.

————, ed. Bulgarien Jahrbuch 1940–41, and 1941–42. Berlin, 1941 and 1942.

Hedin, Sven Anders. Grosse Männer denen ich begegnete. Vol. II. Wiesbaden, 1952.

Heiber, Helmut. "Der Tod des Zaren Boris," *Vierteljahrshefte für Zeitgeschichte*. Vol. IX. Munich, 1961.

————, ed. Hitlers Lagebesprechungen: Die Protokollfragmente seiner militärischen Konferenzen 1942–1945. Stuttgart, 1962.

Helmreich, Ernst Christian. The Diplomacy of the Balkan Wars, 1912–1913. Cambridge, Mass., 1938.

Hilberg, Raul. The Destruction of the European Jews. London, 1961.

Hillgruber, Andreas. Hitler, König Carol, und Marschall Antonescu: Die Deutsch-Rumänischen Beziehungen 1938–1944. Wiesbaden, 1954.

————. Hitlers Strategie: Politik und Kriegführung 1940–1941. Frankfurt am Main, 1965.

————, ed. Probleme des zweiten Weltkrieges. Cologne, 1967.

————. Staatsmänner und Diplomaten bei Hitler. Frankfurt am Main, 1967.

Hinsley, F. H. Hitler's Strategy. Cambridge, Eng., 1951.

Hirschmann, Ira. Lifeline to a Promised Land. New York, 1946.

Hitler e Mussolini: Lettere e Documenti. Milan, 1946.

Hoffman, Walter. Südost-Europa: Bulgarien, Jugoslawien, Rumänien. Leipzig, 1932.

Hohlfeld, Klaus, ed. Dokumente der deutschen Politik und Geschichte. Vol. V. Berlin, 1951.

Hoptner, J. B. Yugoslavia in Crisis: 1934–1941. New York, 1962.

Horthy, Miklos. The Confidential Papers of Admiral Horthy. Budapest, 1965.

Hory, Ladislaus, and Martin Broszat. Der Kroatische Ustascha-Staat, 1941–1945. Stuttgart, 1964.

Höttl, Wilhelm. Die geheime Front. Zurich, 1950.

Hristov, Alexander, ed. Antifashistichko sobranie na narodnoto osluboduvanje na Makedonija: Zbornik na dokumenti. Skopje, 1964.

Hull, Cordell. Memoirs of Cordell Hull. London, 1948. 2 vols.

I Documenti Diplomatici Italiani. *See* Italy, Ministry of Foreign Affairs.

Ilyukhin, N. V. Bolgarskaya narodnaya armiya. Moscow, 1963.

International Military Tribunal [IMT]. Documents Prepared for the Trial of the Major War Criminals. Nuremberg, NG series.

————. The Trial of the Major War Criminals: Official Transcript. London, 1946.

Ioanna, Queen of Bulgaria. Memorie. Milan, 1964.

Ionescu, Ghita. Communism in Rumania, 1944–1962. London, 1964.

Iribadzhakov, Nikolai. Stranitsi ot vuoruzhenata borba protiv fashizma v Turnovski okrug. Sofia, 1957.
Istorijski arhiv KPJ: Makedonija; Narodnooslobodilachkom Ratu i Narodnoj Revoluciji 1941–1944. Ed. Jovan Marjanovich. Vol. VII. Belgrade, 1951.
Istoriya Bolgarii. Vol. II. Moscow, 1955.
Istoriya Bolgarskoi kommunisticheskoi partii. Moscow, 1960.
Istoriya na BKP. Sofia, 1969.
Istoriya na Bulgaria. Vol. III. Sofia, 1964.
Istoriya Yugoslavii. Moscow, 1963.
Italy. Ministry of Foreign Affairs. Documents relating to Bulgaria, jobs 11 and 301, reposited in the library of St. Antony's College, Oxford University. Unpublished.
———, ———. I Documenti Diplomatici Italiani. 9th ser. Rome, 1962– .
Ivanoff, J. Les Bulgares devant le Congrès de la Paix. Berne, 1919.
Ivanov, Lt. Col. Ivan T. "Myastoto na Balkanite v imperialisticheskite kroezhi prez Vtorata svetovna voina," Voenno-istoricheski sbornik, 1963, No. 1.
Iz buntovnoto Sredno goriya. Plovdiv, 1970.
Izraelyan, V. L. Diplomaticheskaya istoriya Velikoi otechestvennoi voiny. Moscow, 1959.
Jackson, George D. Comintern and Peasant in Eastern Europe, 1919–1930. New York, 1966.
Jacobson, Hans Adolf. 1939–1945: Der zweite Weltkrieg in Chronik und Dokumenten. Darmstadt, 1959.
Jelavich, Charles, and Barbara Jelavich, eds. The Balkans. Englewood Cliffs, N.J., 1965.
———. The Balkans in Transition. Berkeley, Calif., 1963.
Kállay, Nikolas. Hungarian Premier. London, 1954.
Karchev, Peter. Kabinetut Malinov i separativniyat mir. Sofia, 1919.
Kazasov, Dimo Totev. Burni godini: 1918–1944. Sofia, 1949.
———. Vidyano i prezhivyano, 1891–1944. Sofia, 1969.
———. Zveno bez grim. Sofia, 1936.
Kedros, André. La Résistance Grecque 1940–1944. Paris, 1966.
Kerner, Robert J., and Harry N. Howard. The Balkan Conferences and the Balkan Entente, 1930–1935. Berkeley, Calif., 1936.
Kiosev, D. G. Istoriya na makedonskoto natsionalno revolyutsionno dvizhenie. Sofia, 1954.
Kiranov, P. Natsionalen dohod na Bulgaria: 1939–1944–1945. Sofia, 1946.
Kirchev, I. V. Otechestvenata voina 1944–45. Sofia, 1946.
Kishales, Haim. Korot yehudei Bulgaria. Vol. III. Tel Aviv, 1969.
Kissel, Hans. Die Katastrophe in Rumänien, 1944. Darmstadt, 1964.

Knatchbull-Hugessen, Hughe. Diplomat in Peace and War. London, 1949.

Kodzheikov, Dragoi. Revolyutsionnoto profsuyuzno dvizhenie v Bulgariya. Sofia, 1957.

Koen, David B. Ograbvaneto i razoryavaneto na bulgarskoto stopanstvo ot germanskite imperialisti prez vtorata svetovna voina. Sofia, 1966.

———. "Ograbvaneto i razoryavaneto na bulgarskoto tutunevo stopanstvo," *Izvestiya na durzhavnite arhivi* (Sofia), 1960, No. 4.

Koev, Ivan. Bit na partizanskiya otryad "A. Ivanov." Sofia, 1962.

Kofos, Evangelos. Nationalism and Communism in Macedonia. Salonika, 1964.

Kolev, Stoiko. Borbata na BKP za naroden front, 1935–1939. Sofia, 1959.

Kolinkoev, I. K. Shest mesetsa na zatochenie v kontslagera pri selo Krusto pole. Svishtov, Bulgaria, 1945.

Kosev, Dino. Istoriya na Makedonski natsionalno revolyutsionno dvizhenie. Sofia, 1954.

———, et al. Kratka istoriya na Bulgariya. Sofia, 1962.

Kosev, K., and E. Statelova. Ikonomikata na Bulgaria. Vol. I. Sofia, 1969.

Kosier, Ljubomir S. Grossdeutschland und Jugoslawien. Berlin, 1939.

Kostoff, Boris. La Bulgarie et la Pacte Balkanique. Paris, 1938.

Kostov, Traicho. Politicheskoto polozhenie i zadachite na partiyata. Sofia, 1945.

Kousoulas, D. George. Revolution and Defeat: The Story of the Greek Communist Party. London, 1965.

Kovacs, Frederic W. L. The Untamed Balkans. London, 1942.

Kozhuharov, Kunyu. "60 godini borcheski put na bulgarskiya zemedelski naroden suyez (BZNS)," *Istoricheski pregled*, 1960, No. 1.

Krainikovski, A. I. La Question de Macédoine et la diplomatie européenne. Paris, 1938.

Kratka Bulgarska Entsiklopediya. Sofia. 5 vols.

Kratschunov, Kristo. Deutschland und Bulgarien: 1878–1942. Sofia, 1943.

Krecker, Lothar. Deutschland und die Türkei im zweiten Weltkrieg. Frankfurt am Main, 1964.

Kühnrich, Heinz. Der Partisanen Krieg in Europa 1939–1945. East Berlin, 1965.

Kuneva, M., and K. Bochevski, eds. Boiniyat put na Cherveno brezhkiya otryad "Georgi Benkovski" 1943–1944. Lovech, Bulgaria, 1969.

Kuznetsov, P. G. Marshal Tolbukhin. Moscow, 1966.

Laffan, R. Q. D. Survey of International Affairs: 1938. Vols. II and III. Oxford, 1951 and 1953.

Lalov, Ignat. Voinishkite komiteti i Bulgarskata narodna armiya prez septemvri 1944. Sofia, 1959.

Lambrev, Kosta. Srednogorski partizani. Sofia, 1952.

Lamouche, Léon. Les Bulgares en Macédoine dans les confins occidentaux et en Thrace. Paris, 1931.

Langer, William L., and S. Everett Gleason. The Challenge to Isolation, 1937–1940. New York, 1952.

——. The Undeclared War, 1940–1941. New York, 1953.

Lazov, Dimitur. Ekzarh Stefan: Zhivot, Apostolstvo i Tvorchestvo. Sofia, 1947.

Leahy, William D. I Was There. New York, 1950.

Lefaki, Georgiou N. Ai en Elladhi Voulgarika: Omotites. Athens, 1954.

Lemkin, Ralph. Axis Rule in Occupied Europe. Washington, D.C., 1944.

Lendvai, Paul. Eagles in Cobwebs. Garden City, N.Y., 1969.

Leverkühn, Paul. German Military Intelligence. London, 1954.

Lewis, G. L. Turkey. London, 1955.

Liddell Hart, B. H. The German Generals Talk. New York, 1948.

Lider, Julian. Armie Ludowe: Krótkie Zarysy Historyczne. Warsaw, 1965.

Logio, George Clinton. Bulgaria: Past and Present. Manchester, 1936.

Lowenthal, Zdenko, ed. The Crimes of the Fascist Occupants [*sic*] and Their Collaborators Against the Jews in Yugoslavia. Belgrade, 1954. In English.

Lukacs, John A. The Great Powers and Eastern Europe. Chicago, 1953.

Macartney, C. A. October Fifteenth: A History of Modern Hungary, 1928–1945. Edinburgh, 1957. 2 vols.

——, and A. W. Palmer. Independent Eastern Europe. London, 1962.

——. National States and National Minorities. London, 1934.

——. Problems of the Danube Basin. Cambridge, Eng., 1942.

Macartney, Maxwell H. H., and Paul Cremona. Italy: Foreign and Colonial Policy 1914–1937. London, 1938.

McDermott, Mercia. A History of Bulgaria, 1393–1885. London, 1962.

Machray, Robert. The Struggle for the Danube and the Little Entente, 1929–1938. London, 1938.

Mackenzie, Compton. Wind of Freedom: The History of the Invasion of Greece by the Axis Powers, 1940–1941. London, 1943.

Maclean, Fitzroy. Eastern Approaches. London, 1949.

McNeill, William Hardy. Greek Dilemma: War and Aftermath. Philadelphia, 1947.

——. Survey of International Affairs: America, Britain, and Russia: Their Cooperation and Conflict, 1941–1948. Oxford, 1953.

Makedonija v Narodnooslobodilachkom Ratu i Narodnoj Revoluciji 1941–1944. Belgrade, 1951.

Makedonskiyat vupros: Istoriko-politicheska spravka. Sofia, 1968.

Malinov, Aleksander. Pod znaka na ostrasteni i opasni politicheski borbi. Sofia, 1934.

Manafor, Gruio S. Ustanovyavane na narodnata vlast na 9.IX.1944. Sofia, 1959.

Markert, Werner, ed. Osteuropa Handbuch: Jugoslawien. Cologne, 1954.

Markham, Reuben H. Meet Bulgaria. Sofia, 1931.

Martin, James Calbraithe. The Communist Seizure of Power in Bulgaria. Oberammergau, Germany, 1962.

Martulkov, Alekso. Moeto uchestvo v revolutsionernite borbi na Makedonija. Skopje, 1954.

Massigli, René L. D. La Turquie devant la guerre: Mission à Ankara, 1939–1940. Paris, 1964.

Materiali po istoriya na Bulgarskata komunisticheska partiya, 1925–1962. Sofia, 1965.

Matkovski, Alexandar. "The Destruction of Macedonian Jewry in 1943," *Yad Washem Studies* (Jerusalem), Vol. 3 (1959), pp. 222–58.

———. Tragedijata na Evreite od Makedonija. Skopje, 1962.

Matsulenko, V. A. Razgrom nemetsko-fashistskikh voisk na Balkanskom napravlenii. Moscow, 1957.

Meissner, Otto. Staatssekretär, unter Ebert-Hindenburg-Hitler. Hamburg, 1950.

Mihailov, Ivan. Macedonia; A Switzerland of the Balkans. St. Louis, 1950.

———. Spomeni. Brussels, 1965. 2 vols.

Mihailov, Vasil. Anton Ivanov. Sofia, 1964.

———. Izstradana pobeda: spomeni 1919–1944. Sofia, 1970.

Mihov, General Nikola. Dnevnik [Diary]. Unpublished, but presented as evidence at Mihov's trial before the People's Court and selected entries printed in various Sofia newspapers.

Milovanovich, Nikola. Vojni puch i 27 mart 1941. Belgrade, 1960.

Mitev, Iono. Zapiski po nova i nai-nova politicheska istoriya na Bulgarskiya narod. Sofia, 1947.

Mitev, S., and H. Kovachev. Partizanskata voina. Sofia, 1964.

Mitrev, Dimitar. BKP: Pirinska Makedonija. Skopje, 1960.

———. Pirin Macedonia. Skopje, 1962.

Mojsov, Lazo. Bugarska Radnichka Partija (Komunista) i Makedonsko natsionalno pitanje. Belgrade, 1948. [Macedonian version: Bulgarskata Rabotnichka Partije (Komunisti) i Makedonskoto Natsionalno Prashnje. Skopje, 1948.]

———. Okolu prashanyeto na makedonskoto natsionalno maltsinstvo v Grtsija. Skopje, 1954.

Molho, Rabbi Michael. In Memoriam: Hommage aux victimes juives des Nazis en Grèce. Salonika, 1948.

Momtchiloff, Nikola. Ten Years of Controlled Trade in Southeastern Europe. London, 1944.

Montagu, Ewen. The Man Who Never Was. London, 1953.

Moshanov, Stoicho. Vunshnata politika na demokraticheskata partiya. Sofia, 1946.

Mourin, Maxime. Le Drame des états satellites de l'Axe de 1939 à 1945. Paris, 1957.

Moyzisch, L. C. Operation Cicero. London, n.d.

Muir, Nadejda. Dimitri Stancioff: Patriot and Cosmopolitan, 1864–1940. London, 1957.

Murawski, Erich, ed. Der deutsche Wehrmachtbericht 1939–1945. Boppard am Rhein, 1962.

Mussolini, Benito. Benito Mussolini: Memoirs, 1942–43. London, 1949.

Mylonas, George E. The Balkan States. Washington, D.C., 1947.

Nai-nova politicheska istoriya na Bulgariya. Sofia, 1947.

Natan, Zhak. Byahme v "Enikioi." Sofia, 1967.

———. Stopanska istoriya na Bulgaria. Sofia, 1957.

Natsionalen komitet po balkanistiks. Les Etudes balkaniques et sud-est européennes en Bulgarie: Guide de documentation. Sofia, 1966.

Naumov, Georgi G. Padaneto na Sgovoristkiya rezhim i ustanovyavaneto na narodnoblokovata vlast v Bulgaria prez 1931. Sofia, 1968.

———. Suzdavane na Narodniya blok i idvaneto mu na vlast prez yuni 1931. Sofia, 1967.

Nazi-Soviet Relations 1939–1941. Washington, D.C., 1948.

Nelegalni pozivi na BKP. Sofia, 1954.

Neubacher, Hermann. Sonderauftrag Südost, 1940–45: Bericht eines fliegenden Diplomaten. Göttingen, 1956.

Newman, Bernard. Balkan Background. London, 1961.

Nikolaev, N. P., ed. La Destinée tragique d'un roi: la vie et le règne de Boris III, roi des bulgares. Uppsala, Sweden, 1952.

Ocherki istorii Velikoi otechestvennoi voiny: 1941–1945. Moscow, 1955.

O'Neill, Robert J. The German Army and the Nazi Party. London, 1966.

Oren, Nissan. Bulgarian Communism, 1934–1944. New York, 1971.

———. "The Bulgarian Communist Party 1934–1944." Ph.D. dissertation, Columbia University, 1960.

Ormandzhiev, Ivan P. Federatsiya na balkanskite narodi: idei i prechki. Sofia, 1947.

Otechestvenata voina na Bulgaria, 1944–45. Ed. Lakiki V. Danailov. Sofia, 1961.

Padev, Michael. Dimitrov Wastes No Bullets. London, 1948.

———. Escape from the Balkans. New York, 1943.

Palmer, Stephen E., and Robert R. King. Yugoslav Communism and the Macedonian Question. Hamden, Conn., 1971.

Panaiotov, Ivan. Greeks and Bulgarians: A Historical Outline. Sofia, 1946.

Panchev, Gencho. Nelegalnite pechatnitsi na Partiyata. Sofia, 1965.

———. Vuoruzhenata borba na deveta (Shumenska) Vustanicheska operativna zona. Sofia, 1961.

Pantel, Hans-Henning. Griechenland zwischen Hammer und Amboss. Leipzig, 1942.

Papagos, Alexander. The Battle of Greece, 1940–1941. Athens, 1949.

Papen, Fritz von. Memoirs. London, 1952.

Pastuhov, Ivan. Istoriya na Bulgarskiya narod. Sofia, 1940.

Patmore, Derek. Balkan Correspondent. New York, 1941.

Paunovski, Ivan. Vuzmezdieto. Sofia, 1971.

Pavelich, Ante S. Jugoslavija Trojni Pakt. Buenos Aires, 1956.

Pavlov, Todor. Protiv oburkvaneto na ponyatiyata. Sofia, 1939. Unpaged pamphlet.

———. Za marksicheska istoriya na Bulgaria. Sofia, 1954.

Penchev, Gencho. Nelegalnite pechatnitsi na Partiyta. Sofia, 1965.

———. Pozhari krai ticha: po stupkite na shumensko preslavskiya otryad "Avgust Popov." Sofia, 1969.

Peter II, King of Yugoslavia. A King's Heritage. New York, 1954.

Peterson, Maurice. The Both Sides of the Curtain. London, 1950.

Peti kongres na BKP. Sofia, 1949.

Petkov, Tonio. "Obezvrezhdaneto na nemskofashistkite grupi pri gr. Ihtiman na 5 i 6 septemvri 1944 g.," *Voenno-istoricheski sbornik*, 1964, No. 6.

Petrov, F. N., ed. Balkanskie strany. Moscow, 1946.

Petrova, Dimitrina V. Bulgarskiyat zemedelski naroden suyuz i Narodniyat front, 1934–1939. Sofia, 1969.

———. BZNS v kraya na burzhoaznoto gospodstvo v Bulgaria 1939–1944. Sofia, 1970.

Petrova, Slavka. Borbata na BRP za ustanovyavane narodnodemokraticheskata vlast, mai-septemvri 1944. Sofia, 1964.

———. Devetoseptemvriiska hronika, iyun-septemvri 1944. Sofia, 1969.

———. "Neuspehut na monarhofashistite da likvidirat narodnoosvoboditelnata vustanicheska armiya prez avgust 1944 g.," *Istoricheski pregled*, 1960, No. 5.

Playfair, Major General I. S. O. The Mediterranean and the Middle East. Vols. I and II. London, 1954.

Popovici, Andrei. The Political Status of Bessarabia. Washington, D.C., 1931.

Poptsvyatkov, Gencho. General Vladimir Zaimov: Biograficheski ocherk. Sofia, 1958.

Pospelov, P. N., et al. Istoriya Velikoi otechestvennoi voiny Sovetskovo soyuza, 1941–1945. Moscow, 1960. 6 vols.

Pozolotin, M. Borba Bolgarskovo naroda za svobodu i nezavisimost' v period Vtoroi mirovoi voiny. Moscow, 1954.

Predsmurtni zaveti: Sbornik ot predsmurtni pisma i posledni slova na geroi zaginali v borbata protiv fashizma, 1923–1944. Sofia, 1965.

Prinosut na bulgarskiya narod za razgroma na fashistka Germaniya. Sofia, 1964.

Pundeff, Marin V. Bulgaria: Bibliographic Guide. Washington, D.C., 1965.

————. "Bulgaria's Place in Axis Policy, 1936–1944." Unpublished Ph.D. dissertation, University of Southern California, 1958.

Rabotata ma BKP v armiyata 1941–1944. Sofia, 1959.

Rabotnichesko delo: Izbrani statii i materiali, 1927–1944. Sofia, 1954.

Rabotnichesko delo: 25 godini, 1927–1952. Sofia, 1952.

Radev, Radi. 917 dni smurten: spomeni. Sofia, 1965.

Radomirski, Slavcho. Prez ogun i kurshumi. Sofia, 1962.

Radulov, Dimitur. "Koga i kak zapochna vustanieto na 9 septemvri," *Voenno-istoricheski sbornik,* 1964, No. 4.

Raikov, Apostol, ed. 30 godini bulgarsko administrativno pravosudie 1913–1943. Sofia, 1943.

Reile, Oscar. Geheime Ostfront: Die Deutsche Abwehr im Osten, 1921–1945. Munich, 1963.

Reitlinger, Gerald. The Final Solution: The Attempt to Exterminate the Jews of Europe, 1939–1945. London, 1953.

Rendel, Sir George. The Sword and the Olive: Recollections of Diplomacy and the Foreign Service, 1913–1954. London, 1957.

Ribbentrop, Joachim von. Zwischen London und Moskau. Leoni am Starnbergersee, Germany, 1953.

Rintlen, E. von. Mussolini als Bundesgenosse: Erinnerungen des deutschen Militärsattachés in Rom, 1936–1943. Tübingen, Germany, 1951.

Ristelhueber, René. A History of the Balkan Peoples. Trans. Sherman D. Spector. New York, 1971.

Ristich, Dragisha N. Yugoslavia's Revolution of 1941. Scranton, Penn., 1966.

Roberts, Henry L. Rumania: Political Problems of an Agrarian State. New Haven, Conn., 1951.

Rogger, Hans, and Eugen Weber, eds. The European Right: A Historical Profile. Berkeley, Calif., 1966.

Roosevelt, Elliot. As He Saw It. New York, 1946.

Rossi, A. [pseud. Angelo Tasca]. The Russo-German Alliance: August 1939–June 1941. London, 1950.

Rothschild, Joseph. The Communist Party of Bulgaria: Origins and Developments, 1883–1936. New York, 1959.

Roucek, Joseph S. Slavonic Encyclopedia. New York, 1949.

Royal Institute of International Affairs. Southeastern Europe: A Political and Economic Study. London, 1939.

Runciman, Steven. A History of the First Bulgarian Empire. London, 1930.

St. John, Robert. The Silent People Speak. Garden City, N.Y., 1948.

Samuilov, I. Leon Tadzher. Sofia, 1956.

Sanders, Irwin T. Balkan Village. Lexington, Ky., 1943.

Sarafis, Stefanos. ELAS, 1941–1945: Politikes kai logotehnikes ekdhoseis. N.p., 1959.

Schellenberg, Walter. Memoiren. Lengerich, Germany, 1956.

Schmidt, Paul. Hitler's Interpreter. London, 1951.

Schmidt-Richberg, Erich. Der Endkampf auf dem Balkan. Heidelberg, 1955.

Schneefus, Walter. Donauraüme und Donaureiche. Vienna, 1942.

Schramm, Percy Ernst. Geschichte des zweiten Weltkrieges. Würzburg, 1960.

Schramm von Thadden, Ehrengard. Griechenland und die Grossmächte im zweiten Weltkrieg. Wiesbaden, 1955.

Selby, Walford. Diplomatic Twilight, 1930–1940. London, 1953.

Semmler, Rudolf. Goebbels—The Man Next to Hitler. London, 1947.

Serkedzhiev, Georgi. S purvite antonivanovtsi. Sofia, 1964.

Seton-Watson, Hugh. Eastern Europe Between the Wars. London, 1945.

———. The East European Revolution. London, 1950.

———. Nationalism and Communism. New York, 1964.

Seton-Watson, R. W. A History of the Roumanians. Cambridge, Eng., 1934.

———. The Rise of Nationality in the Balkans. London, 1917.

Sforza, Carlo. Fifty Years of War and Diplomacy in the Balkans. New York, 1940.

Sherwood, Robert E. Roosevelt and Hopkins. New York, 1948.

Shlijepchevich, Djoko M. The Macedonian Question: The Struggle for South Serbia. Chicago, 1956.

Shoup, Paul. Communism and the Yugoslav National Question. New York, 1968.

Shterev, Pantelei. Obshti borbi na bulgarskiya i grutskiya narod sreshtu hitlerofashistkata okupatsiya. Sofia, 1966.

Simeonov, Stefan. Put prez voinata: spomeni na pomoshtnik komandira ot 44-ti Tuidzhanski polk za Otechestvenata voina 1944–1945. Sofia, 1971.

Simeonov, Tsvetan, et al. Burkashkata partizanska cheta: sbornik materiali. Pleven, 1969.

Simoni, Leonardo [pseud. M. Lanza]. Berlino, Ambasciata d'Italia. Rome, 1946.

Skerlev, Stratiya. Dr. G. M. Dimitrov: Lichnost, delo i idei. Munich, 1970.

Skorzeny, Otto. Skorzeny's Secret Memoirs. New York, 1950.

Slessor, Sir John. The Central Blue: Recollections and Reflections. London, 1958.

Smirnova, N. D. Balkanskaya politika fashistkoi Italii, 1936–1941. Moscow, 1969.

Sohl, Klaus. "Die Kriegsvorbereitungen des deutschen Imperialismus in Bulgarien am Vorabend des zweiten Weltkrieges," *Jahrbuch für Geschichte der UdSSR und der Volksdemokratischen Länder Europas*, 3: 91–119. East Berlin, 1959.

Spector, Sherman D. Rumania at the Paris Peace Conference: A Study of The Diplomacy of Ioan I. C. Bratianu. New York, 1962.

Stalin, Joseph. War Speeches. London, 1946.

Statisticheski godishnik na Tsarstvo Bulgaria. Sofia, 1940–1946.

Stavrianos, Leften Stavros. Balkan Federation: A History of the Movement Towards Balkan Unity in Modern Times. Hamden, Conn., 1964 (originally published 1942 by Smith College).

———. The Balkans Since 1453. New York, 1958.

Stefanov, G. "Bulgarie: La politique extérieure," Revue d'Histoire de la Deuxième Guerre Mondiale (Paris), 72 (Oct. 1968).

———. Mezhdunarodni otnosheniya i vunshna politika Bulgaria. Sofia, 1965.

Stefanov, Georgi. "Vunshnata politika na Bulgaria ot nachalnoto na Vtorata svetovna voina do prisuedinyavaneto kum Tristraniya pakt 1939–1941," *Godishnik na Sofiiskiya Universitet, Yuridicheski fakultet*. Sofia, 1958, vol. 49, pp. 403–62.

Stefanov, Tsvetan. Komunisticheskiyat i antifashistkiyat pechat prez vremeto na fashistkata diktatura v Bulgaria. Sofia, 1960.

Stephanove, Constantine. The Bulgarians and Anglo-Saxondom. Berne, 1919.

Steven, Stewart. Operation Splinter Factor. Philadelphia, Penn., 1974.

Stoimenov, Stoyan. "Antifashistkata demonstratsiya v Sofia na 3 mart 1943 g.," *Istoricheski pregled*, 1961, No. 6.

———, and Georgi Georgiev. Predsmurtni zaveti. Sofia, 1965.

Stoinov, Boris. "Boinite grupi—edna ot formite na vuoruzhenata borba," *Istoricheski pregled*, 1959, No. 4.

———. Boinite grupi, 1941–1944. Sofia, 1969.

———. "Kum vuprosa za organizatsiya . . . na boinite grupi," *Voennoistoricheski sbornik*, 1964, No. 4.

———. Nespokoen til. Sofia, 1964.

Stoinov, Ivan. Politicheskata rabota v partizanskite otryadi, 1941–1944. Sofia, 1969.

Stojadinovich, Milan M. Ni rat ni pakt: Jugoslavija izmedju dva rata. Buenos Aires, 1963.

Strakhovsky, Leonid S. Handbook of Slavic Studies. Cambridge, Mass., 1949.

Stratev, Emil. Germaniya i nezavisimost'ta na Bulgariya. Sofia, 1941.

Strugar, Vlado. Rat i revolutsija naroda Jugoslavije, 1941–1945. Belgrade, 1962.

The Struggle of the Bulgarian People Against Fascism. Sofia, 1946.

Studnitz, Hans-Georg von. While Berlin Burns. London, 1964.

Sweet-Escott, Bickham. Baker Street Irregular. London, 1965.

———. Greece: A Political and Economic Survey. London, 1954.

Swire, Joseph. Bulgarian Conspiracy. London, 1939.

Les Systèmes d'occupation en Yougoslavie, 1941–1945. Belgrade, 1963.

Telpuchowski, Boris S. Die Sowjetische Geschichte des Grossen Vaterländischen Krieges, 1941–1945. Edited and critically analyzed by Andreas Hillgruber and Hans-Adolf Jacobson. Frankfurt am Main, 1961.

Terpeshev, Dobri. Spomeni ot zatvora. Sofia, 1955.

Terzich, Velimir. Jugoslavija u Aprilskom ratu 1941. Titograd, 1963.

Terzioski, Rastko. "Nekoi aspekti na denatsionalizatorskata i asimilatorskata politika na fashistichka Bugarija vo okupirana Makedonija, 1941–1944," *Glasnik* (Skopje), 1968.

Terzioski, Ratislav. "Bugarskata pravoslavna tsrkva vo okupirana Makedonija," *Glasnik* (Skopje), 1965.

Thaden, Edward C. Russia and the Balkan Alliance of 1912. University Park, Penn., 1965.

Thompson, William Frank. There Is a Spirit in Europe. Collected by T. J. and E. P. Thompson. London, 1947.

Thrax, Peter. The Bulgars: Self-styled Prussians of the Balkans. New York, 1944.

Tiltman, H. Hessell. Peasant Europe. London, 1936.

Tippelskirch, Kurt von. Geschichte des zweiten Weltkrieges. Bonn, 1951.

Tishev, Dimiter. Edinodeistvieto mezhdu komunisti i zemedeltsi v borbata protiv fashizma. Sofia, 1967.

Tito, Josip Broz. Borba za oslobodjenje Jugoslavije, 1941–1944. Belgrade, 1945.

———. Govori i chlantsi. Zagreb, 1949. 12 vols.

Todorov, Kosta. Balkan Firebrand: The Autobiography of a Rebel Soldier and Statesman. Chicago, 1943.

———. Politichka istorija savremene Bugarske. Belgrade, 1938.

Toma, Peter A. The Changing Face of Communism in Eastern Europe. Phoenix, Ariz., 1970.

Tomashich, Dinko A. Personality and Culture in East European Politics. New York, 1948.

Toscano, Mario. Designs in Diplomacy. Baltimore, Md., 1970.

―――. The Origins of the Pact of Steel. Baltimore, Md., 1968.

Toynbee, Arnold J., ed. Documents on International Affairs: March-September 1939. London, 1951.

―――. Survey of International Affairs: The Eve of the War, 1939. Oxford, 1958.

―――. Survey of International Affairs: Hitler's Europe. Oxford, 1954.

―――. Survey of International Affairs: The Initial Triumph of the Axis. Oxford, 1958.

―――. Survey of International Affairs: The Realignment of Europe. Oxford, 1955.

―――. Survey of International Affairs: 1938. Vol. I. Oxford, 1941.

Trago, Fabijan, ed. Chetrdeset prva. Belgrade, 1961.

Transki, Slavcho. Iz taktikata na partizanskata borba v Bulgaria. Sofia, 1969.

―――. Neotdavna. Sofia, 1965.

―――. Partizanski spomeni. Sofia, 1955.

Trevor-Roper, H. R., ed. Hitler's Table Talk: 1941–1944. London, 1953. [German version: Hitlers Tischgespräche. Bonn, 1951.]

―――. Hitler's War Directives 1939–1945. London, 1964.

The Trial of Nikola D. Petkov Before the Sofia Regional Court: Record of Judicial Proceedings, 5–18 August 1947. Sofia, 1947.

The Trial of Traicho Kostov and His Group. Sofia, 1949. English translation of Sudebnyi protsess Traicho Kostova i evo gruppy, 7–14 December 1949 [in Russian]. Sofia, 1949.

Triska, Jan F., and David D. Finley. Soviet Foreign Policy. New York, 1968.

Tsanev, Peter. Purvomaiskite chestvuvaniya u nas 1893–1944. Sofia, 1956.

Tsion, Rabbi Daniel. Pet godini pod fashistski gnet. Sofia, 1945.

Union of Soviet Socialist Republics. People's Commissariat of Foreign Affairs. Suvetsko-bulgarskite otnosheniya: dokumenti. Moscow, 1944 [in Bulgarian].

United States. Department of the Army. German Anti-Guerrilla Operations in the Balkans, 1941–1944. Pamphlet No. 20–264, August 1954.

―――, ―――. The German Campaign in the Balkans (Spring 1941). Pamphlet No. 20–24, November 1953.

―――. Department of State. National Archives.

———, ———. Bulletin, 1940–1945.

———, ———. Foreign Relations of the United States: Diplomatic Papers 1940–1941; and The Conferences at Cairo and Tehran.

———, ———. Macedonian Nationalism and the Communist Party of Yugoslavia. October 1954.

———. War Department. General Staff. Order of Battle and Handbook of the Bulgarian Armed Forces, December 1943. 1944.

Valev, L. B. Iz istorii Otechestvennovo fronta Bolgarii. Moscow, 1950.

Van Creveld, Martin L. Hitler's Strategy 1940–1941: The Balkan Clue. Cambridge, Eng., 1973.

Vasilev, Orlen. Vuoruzhenata suprotiva sreshtu fashizma v Bulgaria, 1923–1944. Sofia, 1946.

V boi s fashizma—dokumenti, statii, i spomeni iz borbata na Sofiiskite trudeshti se. Sofia, 1959.

Vidinski, Kiril. Podvodnicharite. Sofia, 1963.

Villari, Luigi. Italian Foreign Policy Under Mussolini. New York, 1956.

Vinarov, Ivan. Boitsi na tihiya front: Spomeni na razuznavacha. Sofia, 1969.

Vlahov, Dimitar I. Iz istorije Makedonskot naroda. Belgrade, 1950.

Vneshnyaya politika Sovetskoyo Soyuza v period Otechestvennoi voiny. Moscow, 1944, 1946. 2 vols.

Vneshnyaya politika SSSR 1935–1941: Sbornik dokumentov. Moscow, 1946.

Vojin, Popovich. "Bugarska vojska u okupiranoj Srbiji 1941–1944," *Vojnoistorijski glasnik*. Belgrade, 1952.

Volkov, Vladimir K. Germano-Yugoslavskie otnosheniya i razval Maloi Antanty, 1933–1938. Moscow, 1966.

Vorob'ev, F. D., and V. Kravtsov. Pobedy Sovetskikh vooruzhennykh sil v Velikoi otechestvennoi voine, 1941–1945. Moscow, 1954.

Vporni, D. Spomena kniga na Tretata Makedonska udarna brigada. Skopje, 1957.

Vrachev, Ivan. "Vuoruzhenata borba na bulgarskiya narod ...," *Voenno-istoricheski sbornik*, 1964, No. 5.

Vranchev, Peter. Spomeni. Sofia, 1968.

Vucinich, Wayne S., ed. Contemporary Yugoslavia. Berkeley, Calif., 1969.

Vukmanovich, Svetozar [pseud. Tempo]. Revolutsija koja teche: Memoari. Belgrade, 1971. 2 vols.

Vuoruzhenata borba na Bulgarskiya narod protiv fashizma, 1941–1944: Dokumenti. Sofia, 1962.

Waldeck, Rosie G. Athene Palace. New York, 1942.

Warriner, Doreen, ed. Contrasts in Emerging Societies. London, 1965.

Weidemann, Alfred. Junges Europa. Stuttgart, 1939?
Weisband, Edward. Turkish Foreign Policy, 1943–1945: Small State Diplomacy and Great Power Politics. Princeton, N.J., 1973.
Weizsäcker, Ernst von. Erinnerungen. Munich, 1950.
Werth, Alexander. Russia at War: 1941–1945. London, 1964.
Weygand, Maxime. Mémoires. Paris, 1950. [English version: Recalled to Service. New York, 1952.]
Wilkinson, Henry Robert. Maps and Politics: A Review of Ethnographic Cartography of Macedonia. Liverpool, 1951.
Wir kämpften auf dem Balkan: VIII Fliegerkorps. Dresden, 1942.
Wiskemann, Elizabeth. The Rome-Berlin Axis. London, 1966.
Wolff, Robert Lee. The Balkans in Our Time. Cambridge, Mass., 1956.
Wolfgramm, Eberhard. "Bemerkungen zur bulgarischen Partisanenbewegung," *Jahrbuch für Geschichte der UdSSR*, 8: 505–21. East Berlin, 1964.
Woodhouse, Christopher M. Apple of Discord: A Survey of Recent Greek Politics in Their International Setting. London, 1948.
Woodward, Llewellyn. British Foreign Policy in the Second World War. London, 1962.
Xydis, S. G. Economics and Finances of Greece Under Axis Occupation, 1941–1942. Pittsburgh, Penn., 1943.
Yaz'kava, A. A. Rumynya nakanune Vtoroi mirovoi voiny, 1934–1939. Moscow, 1963.
Yugoslavia. Vojno-istorijski Institut Jugoslovenske Armije. Zbornik dokumenata i podataka o narodnooslobodilachkom ratu Jugoslovenskih naroda. Belgrade, 1954.
———, ———. Hronologija oslobodilachke borbe naroda Jugoslavije, 1941–1945. Belgrade, 1964.
Yust, Walter. Ten Eventful Years. New York, 1947.
Zagoroff, S. D., et al. The Agricultural Economy of the Danubian Countries, 1935–45. Stanford, Calif., 1955.
Zarkov, V. Zapiski na politzatvornika. Sofia, 1959.
Zbornik na dokumenti ASNOM, 1944–1946. Skopje, 1964.
Zhebokritskii, V. A. Bolgaria v period Balkanskikh voin. Kiev, 1961.
Zografski, Dancho. Egejska Makedonija vo nashata natsionalna istorija. Skopje, 1951.
Zotiades, George B. The Macedonian Controversy. Salonika, 1954.
Zotos, Stephanos. Greece: The Struggle for Freedom. New York, 1967.
Zurlov, Ivan. Zapiski na politkomisarya yuni 1941-sept. 1944. Sofia, 1969.
26 godini ot geroichnite srazheniya na treta cheta ot otryad "Hristo Kurpachev," 30.XI.43 i 12.III.44. Troyan, Bulgaria, 1969.

Index

❧

"Adana lists," 109

Aegean Macedonia, 122, 125–30

Aegean Thrace, 99, 122n, 128, 200. *See also* Belomorie

Africa, North, 108, 115, 232

Agence Anatolia, 72

Agrarian Party, 3–5, 153n, 154, 172; Pladne faction, 4, 39, 47, 160f, 194n, 218; Vrabcha faction, 4, 160, 195, 206, 217f; and Fatherland Front, 160f, 163, 163n–64n, 194n; and Bagryanov government, 175–76, 195; and Muraviev government, 205f

air force, Bulgarian, 165–66

Albania, 42n, 82f, 129, 141, 158; Communist partisans in, 133

Aleppo, Syria, 109

Alexander, King (of Yugoslavia), 8

Alexander II (of Russia), 2, 28n

Ali, Rashid, 67

Allies, Western: and Boris, 1, 136–37, 148; and outbreak of war, 13–14, 17–18, 21–22; bombing of Bulgaria by, 52–53, 106, 109, 165–69, 173, 214, 232–33; threats of invasion by, 87–89, 115–17, 135–37; peace negotiations with, 110–15, 169–73, 186f, 189–90; and Aegean campaign, 155–59; and Bagryanov government, 178–82, 186–90, 193, 251; and Muraviev government, 208; Yalta

conference, 219. *See also* Great Britain; France; United States

"All Measures" law, 97, 101

American College, Sofia, 180

Amery, Julian, 42

Andreev, Dimiter, 93, 97

Ankara, 186f, 189, 251

Anti-Comintern Exhibition, 86

Anti-Comintern Pact (1938), 32

anti-Semitism, 22, 93–99. *See also* Jews

Antonescu, Ion, 116–17, 188, 227

Arabs, 67, 104

Arditti, Benjamin, 102

Arendt, Hannah, 105, 241

Armenia, 78

armistice, 169–73, 186f, 189–90

army, Bulgarian, 72–73, 170–71, 217–18; conspiracy in, 79; "political purity of," 120; and partisan movement, 132, 203; and Bagryanov government, 179, 184f; uprisings of, 212–13; mentioned, 3, 7, 83, 88, 109

Atanasov, Nedelko, 206

Athens, 52

Austria, 6, 24n

Austro-Hungarian Empire, 2, 24n

Axis, 3, 30–39 *passim;* Bulgaria joins, 45–51, 54–55; and Stalingrad, 108; and North Africa, 115; and death of Boris, 135, 147; Bulgarian withdrawal from, 170–71, 173, 181,

185ff, 191; Rumania's defection
from, 188–92. *See also by name of
country*
Azerbaijan, 66

Badoglio, Pietro, 116, 147, 158
Bagryanov, Ivan, 136, 154–55, 172, 229,
250f; his government, 103n, 175–94,
204; and anti-Jewish legislation,
182, 190, 213n; and partisan move-
ment, 195, 200, 202; resignation of,
204, 208f; execution of, 217
Balabanov, Ivan, 50
Balabanov, Nikola, 170–71, 173, 181,
208
Balan, A., 202n
Balan, Stanislav, 98, 143
Balchik, 30
Balilla, 82
Balkan Entente, 8–9, 14, 24, 43, 53f
Balkans, 89, 116, 185, 191; and out-
break of war, 13–14, 16; and
Dobruja crisis, 27; competition for,
32–44; Allied policy toward, 156,
169–70, 173; and Aegean campaign,
156–59; and partisan movements,
202–3. *See also by name of country*
Balkan Wars, 2, 25, 122
Baltic states, 37, 227
Barbarossa, Operation, 59–66 *passim*,
160
Barker, Elizabeth, 134
Baruh, Yako, 101
Baur, Hans, 142–43, 246
BBC, 139
Beckerle, Heinz-Adolf, 64, 80, 84,
89, 113; and youth organizations, 74,
82; and Jews, 98–105 *passim*; and
death of Boris, 136, 139, 144ff; and
the Regency, 154f; and Bagryanov
government, 177, 191; mentioned,
107, 117
Bela Kun campaign of 1919, 28n
Belev, Alexander, 98–102, 239
Belgium, 22, 235; government-in-
exile, 48
Belgrade, 47, 52

Belomorie, 99, 122n, 128f, 200
Belomorska Trakiya, 122n. *See also*
Belomorie
Berker, Ali, 43
Berlin, Congress of (1878), 2, 191n
Berliner Tageblatt, 140
Bessarabia, 15, 24, 25, 27f, 226
bezpartien rezhim, 91
Biryuzov, Sergi, 209, 218
Bismarck, Otto von, 2
BKP, 6, 62–63, 145, 166n, 218–20; as
Bulgarian Workers' Party, 4, 16n;
and Soviet Union, 4, 15, 20, 30, 47,
62; coup of 1944, 5, 17n, 19, 212–17;
after Nazi-Soviet Pact, 16–19;
Rabotnichesko delo of, 16–18; and
competition for Balkans, 34–35, 39–
41; Central Committee of, 40; and
Operation Marita, 53; and Barbarossa, 59–60; Central Military Commission of, 63, 195f; RMS, 63n, 199;
and Zaimov, 79; and Jews, 102;
and Lukov's assassination, 117–21;
and Macedonia, 123, 130–34; on
Boris, 135; and Fatherland Front,
159–63, 194n, 216, 250; and Allied
bombing, 167–68; and Bagryanov
government, 176–77, 184, 192–93,
250; partisan activity of, 195–203;
and Muraviev government, 206f,
210–13
Black, Floyd, 180
Bogdanov, Peter, 131
bombings, Allied, *see under* Allies,
Western
Bonn government, 105
Boris III, Tsar, 1–9 *passim*, 64, 71–92
passim, 107–20 *passim*, 230, 236;
and Hitler, 1, 73, 75–77, 85, 90, 110,
116, 130, 137–46 *passim*; and outbreak of war, 13–21 *passim*; and
Dobruja crisis, 27–28, 30; on
neutrality, 32–33; and competition
for Balkans, 35–43 *passim*, 48f,
228–29; and Operation Marita, 53,
55; and Barbarossa, 60f; and Pearl
Harbor, 68ff; and Jews, 96–106

passim, 240; death of, 106, 135–48, 159, 162, 246; and Macedonia, 126, 130; and Kiril, 153–54; and Fatherland Front, 161; and Allied bombings, 166, 169, 173; and partisans, 197, 201

Boshkov, Lyuben, 190

Bozhilov, Dobri, 155, 158–59, 167f, 173f; and Kioseivanov, 176n; and Bagryanov government, 184; executed, 217; mentioned, 165, 177, 180

Bozhinov, Voin, 203n

Bozhurishte airfield, 19

Brannik, 38, 68–69, 82

Bretholz, Wolfgang, 140, 250–51

BRP, 4, 16n. *See also* BKP

Bucharest, 188f, 194

Bucharest, Treaty of, 24n, 25

Budapest, 28n

Bukovina, 24, 28

Bulgaranov, Boyan, 131, 133

Bulgaria: pre–World War II, 1–9, 25, 55, 60n, 81n, 119, 122, 125, 135, 177–78, 185; irredentism of, 1, 8f, 13, 15, 32, 60, 113; politics in, 3–6, 16–19, 34–41 *passim*, 151–53, 159–64, 174–76, 192–95, 204–18 *passim*; economy of, 7, 19, 174, 179; neutrality of, 17, 21–23, 32–33, 38f, 186–94 *passim*, 204, 208; joins Axis, 45–51, 54–55; war declared with Great Britain, 68f, 71, 165; war declared with U.S., 68–71, 81, 165; religion, 77, 96, 125, 127; language, 77, 124f; USSR declared war on, 210; declared war on Germany, 215

Bulgarian Orthodox Church, 96, 125

Bulgarian-Turkish friendship treaty (1925), 44

Bulgarian-Turkish Pact (1941), 44, 49, 66

Bulgarian Workers' Party (BRP), 4, 16n. *See also* BKP

Bulgarian-Yugoslav friendship pact (1937), 8, 14, 132

Bulgars, 77

Burgas, 87, 179, 194n, 199, 204, 215

Burov, Atanas, 39, 153n, 161, 206

Byala Palanka, 209

Cairo, 162, 190, 204, 208

Calinescu, Armand, 17

Carol, King (of Rumania), 29

Casablanca conference, 111

Castelrosso, 157

Caucasus, 87

Chapuisat, Dr., 105

Chesmedzhiev, Grigor, 160f, 194, 218

Chiang Kai-shek, 42n

Chicago *Daily Mail*, 47

Choristi, 127

chrome, 27, 77, 183

Churchill, Winston, 14, 31n, 43; and Chiang Kai-shek, 42n; on Yugoslavia, 50–51; and "Adana lists," 109; at Casablanca, 111; and Aegean campaign, 156–57; and Bagryanov government, 183–84

Ciano, Galeazzo, 27, 50, 226f

Clodius, German emissary for economic affairs, 129

Comintern, 86, 131

Commissariat for Jewish Affairs, 98f, 102

Communist Party in Albania, 133

Communist Party in Bulgaria, *see* BKP

Communist Party in Greece, 133, 244

Communist Party in Macedonia, 123, 130–31, 133

Communist Party in USSR, 4, 16, 86, 131. *See also* USSR

Communist Party in Yugoslavia, 123, 130–34

concentration camps, 70, 103f, 145; in Bulgaria, 63, 106, 176, 193, 196f

Constantinople, 60n

Constitution of Bulgaria, 45, 91, 94, 151–52, 205

Cos, 157

Council of Ministers, 97f, 101

coups: of 1923, 5, 161, 216n; of 1934,

5, 79, 117–18, 161, 216n; of 1944, 5,
    17n, 19, 212–17
Craiova agreement, 29–32
Crimean War, 24n
Croatia, 8, 54, 126. *See also* Yugoslavia
Csaky, Hungarian foreign minister, 25

Dannecker, Theodore, 100–101, 104
Danube international commission, 32
Daskalov, Teodor, 49–50, 72–73, 79
Davidescu, Rumanian Ambassador in
    Moscow, 24
Davies, Mostyn, 200
Davis, Norman, 47
death camps, *see* concentration camps
Dedeagach, 84, 104, 212
democratic parties, 3–6, 18, 204ff, 218;
    on neutrality, 38f, 225; attitude
    toward Boris, 147; and Regency,
    151ff; and Fatherland Front, 159–
    64 *passim*; and Bagryanov govern-
    ment, 174, 176, 184, 193–94. *See also*
    individual parties by name
Democratic Party, 4f, 19n, 153n, 161,
    207
Dikov, Diko, 203n
Dimitrov, Georgi, 176–77, 219–20
Dimitrov, Georgi M. ("Gemeto"), 4,
    47, 218
Dimitrov, Ilcho, 255
Dimov, Vergil, 153n, 206–7
Dobruja, 23–31, 69, 227; Southern, 1,
    3, 25, 28–30, 114, 124, 174, 180, 218;
    Northern, 25, 30
Dochev, Ivan, 217
Doctors' Union, 96
Dodecanese Islands, 156
Doenitz, Admiral, 115
Doiran, Lake, 88
Donovan, William J., 42–43, 230
Doxato, 127
Draganov, Purvan, 15, 25, 28n, 33,
    204; and Operation Barbarossa, 61,
    113; and Bagryanov government,
    175, 179, 184–87, 189
Drama (Greece), 127–28

Dramaliev, Kiril, 160f, 163n
Dulles, Allen, 111, 113
Dumanov, Peter, 30

EAM/ELAS guerrillas, 244
Earle, U.S. Minister to Bulgaria, 68,
    104, 109, 112, 227; on German
    troops in Bulgaria, 43, 231; and
    Operation Marita, 52, 54–55; and
    Barbarossa, 59, 63
Eden, Anthony, 172
Edirne (Adrianople), 2, 67, 78
Eichmann, Adolf, 100
Eisenhower, Dwight D., 166
elections: of 1938, 6; of 1939–40, 19–
    21; of 1945, 219f
England, 7, 22. *See also* Great Britain
Evdokiya (sister of Tsar Boris), 71,
    137, 153
Exarch Stefan, 96, 98, 104

Fabricius, Wilhelm, 29
fascism in Bulgaria, 4, 17f, 20, 21n,
    73–74, 92f, 118. *See also* nationalist
    parties; Tsankov, Alexander
fascism in Germany, *see* Nazis
Fascist Party in Italy, 6, 18, 116
Fatherland Front (*Otechestven
    Front*), 153n, 159–64, 172, 217ff;
    Directorate of, 161; and Bagryanov
    government, 174, 176–77, 192–94,
    250; National Committee of, 194n,
    215; and Muraviev government,
    205–7, 212, 214f, 216
Ferdinand, Tsar, 2–3, 16, 71, 85, 153
Filov, Bogdan, 7, 64, 79–92 *passim*,
    113–19 *passim*; and outbreak of war,
    21f; and competition for Balkans,
    34–35, 37ff, 42; as head of Pen Club,
    38, 94; and Tripartite Pact, 45–46,
    48, 50; and Operation Marita, 54;
    and Barbarossa, 59, 61; and Pearl
    Harbor, 68; on Bulgarian army, 72;
    and Lukov, 73; and Jews, 100, 102–
    3; on Stalingrad, 107f; and Mace-
    donia, 124; and death of Boris, 136,

138–41, 148, 246; Regency and, 151–54; and Aegean campaign, 157–58, 248; and Allied bombings, 167–69; peace negotiations and, 171–73; and Bagryanov government, 175, 177, 179f, 180, 185, 193f; and partisans, 199, 201; and Muraviev, 210, 215; execution of, 217

Finland, 171; "Winter War," 16

Fosteridhis, Andonios ("Andon Tsaous"), 244

France, 3, 6, 8, 29, 184; trade with, 7; and outbreak of war, 13, 18, 22–23; and Tripartite Pact, 33; Vichy government of, 67, 99

Gabrovsky, Peter, 21, 73, 79, 86, 136; and Jews, 97f, 101–2; and Regency, 154f; execution of, 217

Gafencu, Grigore, 29

Genov, Georgi, 248

George VI (of Great Britain), 13, 41

Georgiev, Kimon, 5, 20, 117, 219; and the Regency, 152, 153n; and Father-land Front, 160f, 194n, 216; and armistice, 172

Germany, 1f, 6–7, 9, 80, 107–17 *passim*, 235, 237, 248; Nazi-Soviet Pact, 9, 16–18, 24n, 160; and outbreak of war, 14–18, 21–22; and Dobruja crisis, 25–32 *passim*; competition for Balkans, 32, 36–44, 229; and Tripartite Pact, 32, 46, 48, 50, 228; troops in Bulgaria, 36–37, 46, 88, 229; Operation Marita and, 52–55; and Barbarossa, 59–62; and Soviet-Bulgarian relations, 64–66, 71–73; and Turkey, 66f, 77–78, 183; and Pearl Harbor, 68f; and nationalist opposition, 73–75, 89; and Italian-Bulgarian relations, 82ff, 87; Jews and, 93, 95–99, 103–6; Masons and, 94; and occupation of Macedonia, 122–23, 126, 128–30, 255; death of Boris and, 136, 141, 143–46; and Regency, 152, 154; in Aegean cam-

paign, 156–59; and Salò republic, 158; and Allied bombings, 166f, 169; and Bulgarian peace negotia-tions, 169–73; Bagryanov govern-ment and, 174–88 *passim*; and Rumania's defection, 189–91, 221; and partisan movement, 199–200, 202f; and Muraviev, 204, 208–10, 211, 213–15, 255; Bulgaria declared war on, 215, 255. *See also* Hitler, Adolf; Nazis

Gestapo, 22, 190

Gichev, Dimiter, 5, 18, 153n, 160–64; and Bagryanov government, 192, 195; and Muraviev government, 204–6, 216; imprisonment of, 217f

Gigurtu, Ion, 29

Giraud, General, 115

Girginov, Alexander, 207

Goebbels, Joseph, 76, 144, 155

Golyamo Shivachevo, 199

Göring, Hermann, 75, 145

Great Britain, 1–3, 6ff, 108–18 *passim*, 153, 208, 211; and outbreak of war, 13–14, 18, 22; and Dobruja crisis, 30–31; and competition for Balkans, 36, 41–43; SOE, 42, 48, 200; severed relations with Bulgaria, 47–49; intervention in Greece, 49, 52, 229, 232; bombed Sofia, 52–53; and Suez Canal, 67; Bulgaria declared war on, 68f, 71, 165; and Turkey, 109, 183, 185; and Boris, 148; in Aegean campaign, 156–59; and Bagryanov government, 180–88 *passim*; and Congress of Berlin, 191n; aid to partisans, 200–201

Great National Assembly, 151, 153, 205

Greece, 2f, 7f, 72, 114–16; in Balkan Entente, 8–9, 14, 43, 53f; and com-petition for Balkans, 33, 35–37, 43; Italian invasion of, 35–36, 43; British intervention in, 49, 52, 229, 232; and Macedonia, 122, 125–30, 134, 244; and partisan movement, 133,

198, 203, 244; Communist Party of, 133, 244; and Bagryanov government, 180f, 183–84, 190, 191; mentioned, 50, 88, 104, 165
Greenwich, British consular official, 47
"Grigorov," *see* Kostov, Traicho
Gruev, Pavel, 140–41, 242
Guderian, General, 185

Halifax, Lord, 14, 43
Harriman, William Averell, 191
Harrington, John, 200
Hart, B. H. Liddell, 231–32
Hassell, Ulrich von, 47, 50, 61, 73
Heiber, Helmut, 155, 248
Hilberg, Raul, 95, 99
Himmler, Heinrich, 145
Hitler, Adolf, 55, 59f, 64f, 66f, 113; and Boris, 1, 73, 75–77, 85, 90, 110, 116, 130, 137–46 *passim*; and Dobruja crisis, 29f; and competition for Balkans, 32–33, 35f; on Tripartite Pact, 45–46; and Yugoslavia, 49ff; *Mein Kampf*, 59; and Jews, 99; and Macedonia, 128, 130; and Regency, 157, 172; and Bozhilov, 158–59. *See also* Germany; Nazis
Hitler Jugend, 38, 82
Hoffmann, Otto, 105
Holland, government-in-exile, 48
"Hristo Botev" radio station, 120, 160, 176, 206
Hristov, Docho, 97, 155, 217
Hull, Cordell, 69, 111
Hungary, 7, 44, 139; and Transylvania, 25, 27, 29, 60n, 227; and Bela Kun campaign, 28n; Churchill on, 31n; war with U.S., 68, 81; and Jewish question, 99, 106; and Salò republic, 158

Ihtiman, 209
IMRO, 8, 82, 125–26, 175, 191
inflation, 174, 179
Inönü, Ismet, 109
Insurrection Operation Zones (VOZ), 199, 203n

Internal Macedonian Revolutionary Organization, *see* IMRO
International Red Cross, 105
Ioanna, Queen, 137n, 139–48 *passim*, 220, 246
Iraq, 67
Iron Guard, 17, 29, 94
irredentism, Bulgarian, 1, 8f, 13, 15, 32, 60, 113
Israel, 102
Istanbul, 48, 60n, 159, 170ff, 181, 188
Italy, 6f, 32, 111, 226; Mussolini government of, 7, 22, 35ff, 82ff, 116; and outbreak of war, 18, 22, 27, 29f; Fascist Party in, 18, 116; invasion of Greece by, 35–36, 43; and Pearl Harbor, 68; territorial disputes with Bulgaria, 81–84; and Jews, 116; Badoglio government of, 116, 147f, 158; and Macedonia, 126, 128–29
Ivanov, Anton, 197
Izvestiya, 30, 46–47

Japan, 32, 68–70, 84, 111, 172
Jesserina area (of Macedonia), 82
Jews, 93–94, 99–105, 118, 239f; sparing of, 22, 105–6; legislation against, 38, 94–99, 182, 190, 213
Jodl, General Alfred, 36, 186
Jungenfeldt, von, Colonel, 185

Kaimaxillar, Mt., 244
Kaltenbrunner, SS-General, 158
Karakashev, Vladimir, 39
Kavalla, 84, 127
Kazasov, Dimo, 95f, 138–39, 161, 192
Kerr, Sir Archibald Clark, 211
Kharkov, 135
Kichevo, 133
Killinger, Manfred von, 72
Kioseivanov, Georgi, 5–6, 111, 113, 118, 136; and outbreak of war, 14, 18, 20–21, 224; on Jewish question, 94; and Regency, 152, 154; and Malinov case, 176n; and Muraviev government, 204f

Kioseivanov, Peter, 200
Kiril, Prince, 141f, 151–54, 193, 217, 247
Kirov, Sava, 155, 157f
Kiselov, Georgi, 172–73, 188
Kleist, von, German field marshal, 107, 241
Kliment of Ohrid, 129n
Knatchbull-Hugessen, Sir Hughe, 22, 187
Kolarov, Vasil, 214–15, 219f
Kolishevski, Lazar, 131–32
Kostov, Deni, 95n
Kostov, Doncho, 176
Kostov, Traicho ("Grigorov"), 130, 195, 197, 201–2, 219
Kosturkov, Stoyan, 161, 217
Kozhuharov, Todor, 20, 94n, 227
Krapchev, Danial, 53–54
Kumanovo, 132
Kushev, Dimiter, 80
Kutsarov, Colonel, 193
Kuyumdzhiisky, Angel, 110, 241–42
Kyustendil, 63, 101–5

language, Bulgarian, 77, 124f
Lavrishchev (Soviet Minister), 85, 168
Law for the Defense of the Nation, 95–97
League of Nations, 8
League of Reserve Officers, 39, 175
Legionnaires, 4, 17f, 73–74, 90, 92f, 118, 217
Lerinsko, 133
Lewis, G. L., 236
Luftwaffe, 52, 167, 189
Lukacs, John A., 175, 232–33
Lukash, General, 213
Lukov, Hristo, 4, 60, 73–75, 89f, 92, 94n; assassination of, 117–18, 119n, 198
Lulchev, adviser to Tsar, 103

Macedonia, 49ff, 209–11; Bulgarian occupation of, 1, 3, 122–34, 243; Yugoslav, 3, 8, 123–25, 130, 203; IMRO, 8, 82, 125–26, 175, 191; and

Operation Marita, 53–55; Jews in, 99f, 103; Aegean, 122, 125–30; Communist Party in, 123, 130–31, 133; Pirin, 125, 131, 134; minerals in, 129; partisan movement in, 132–33, 244; and Bagryanov government, 174, 180, 182, 186, 191; mentioned, 62, 152, 168, 255
Macedonian Bank, 233
Macmillan, Harold, 42n
Macpherson, Ian, 200
Mafalda, Princess, 145
Magistrati, Count, 37–38
Maisky, Ivan, 41
Malinov, Alexander, 176
Manstein, von, German officer, 135
Marasesti, 29
Marie Louise of Parma, 82n
Marinov, Ivan, 207, 210, 213–14, 216
Marita, Operation, 43, 49, 52–55, 59, 78, 122
Masons, 38, 94
May Day demonstrations, 18, 120
Mein Kampf, 59
Menemenchoglu, Numan, 53
Michael, King (of Rumania), 188–89
Mihailov, Ivan, 126, 191
Mihov, Nikola, 116, 169, 171f, 199, 210; as Regent, 66, 152–54; as minister of war, 79f; and Boris, 88, 137f, 141, 143, 148; meeting with Hitler, 107ff; and Bagryanov government, 178, 193; execution of, 217
Milanovich, Yugoslav Ambassador, 49–50
Milev, M. H., 111, 170, 184
Military League, 5. *See also* League of Reserve Officers
military service, *see* army, Bulgarian
Minkov, Nikola, 61, 183–84
Mir, 38, 53, 73, 172, 229
Mirkovich, Bora, 50
Mitakov, Krum, 97
Mohrmann (German official), 90
Molotov, Vyacheslav, 24, 33f, 46, 65, 191, 210f
Momchilov, Nikola, 14, 41, 48, 113

Montenegro, 2
Morrell, air attaché in Ankara, 109
Moshanov, Stoicho, 19, 20, 186–90, 204, 208
Muraviev, Konstantin, 5, 153n, 217; his government, 204–17, 255
Musala, Mount, 137f, 140, 147
Mushanov, Nikola, 18ff, 55, 95, 136; and the Regency, 152f; Fatherland Front and, 161f, 164; and Bagryanov government, 186, 192; and Muraviev government, 204ff
Mussolini, Benito, 7, 22, 35ff, 82ff, 116; his Salò republic, 158

Naples, 116
Narodnik Party, 161
Narodno Subranie, 6, 172, 217, 220, 226; and outbreak of war, 19ff, 30; and competition for Balkans, 38f, 41; and Tripartite Pact, 45; and Barbarossa, 61; and Pearl Harbor, 68; legislation against Jews, 95–97, 103; and partisan movement, 120, 201; formation of Regency and, 152f; and Bagryanov government, 176, 186; dissolving of, 190, 207
National Assembly, *see* Narodno Subranie
nationalist parties, 3–6, 17, 73–74, 89–90, 117, 248. *See also* Legionnaires; Ratnitsi; Zveno
Nazis, 1, 6f, 18, 20, 105; and Jews, 93, 95–99, 103–6, 236. *See also* Germany; Hitler
Nazi-Soviet Pact of 1939, 9, 16–18, 24n, 160
Neikov, Dimiter, 218
Neubacher, Hermann, 29, 33, 134
Neues Wiener Tageblatt, 177
Neuilly, 39
Neuilly, Treaty of, 3, 25
neutrality: Bulgarian policy of, 17, 21–23, 204, 208; competition for Balkans and, 32–33, 38f; Bagryanov government and, 186, 189f, 192, 194
New York Times, 139

Nikolaev, N. P., 38
Nikolaev, Nikolai, 38, 61
Nish, 214n
Normandy invasion, 156, 170, 184, 201
North Africa, *see* Africa, North
Norway, 18, 22

Obbov, Alexander, 218
Office of Strategic Services (OSS), 170, 230
Oggi, 246
Ohrid, shrine of, 129
oil, 27; in Rumania, 14, 29, 32, 87, 106, 165; in Caucasus, 87
Operation Barbarossa, 59–66 *passim*, 160
"Operation Bogdan," 202
"Operation Hundessohn," 191
Operation Marita, 43, 49, 52–55, 59, 78, 122
Operation Mincemeat, 115
Oren, Nissan, 202n
Orthodox churches, 96, 125
OSS, 170, 230
Otechestven Front, see Fatherland Front
Otets Paisii ("Father Paisi") society, 4, 248
"Overlord," *see* Normandy invasion

Palestine, 22, 104
Panev, Asen, 30
Panitza, L. B., 101
Panslavism, 46f
Pantev, Colonel, 89, 118–19, 198
Papagal, 21
Papen, Fritz von, 14, 64, 66f, 78, 139, 144
Paris, 8
partisan movement: 1941 failure of, 62–63, 195–97; Gichev on, 163; and Bagryanov government, 174, 192; 1943 revival of, 121, 199–203, 212–13, 253; British assistance to, 200–201; structure of, 198–99, 202–3
Partov, Justice Minister, 98
Pashov, Ivan, 162–63, 194

Pastuhov, Hristu, 18, 136, 153n, 161, 206, 218
Paul, Prince (of Yugoslavia), 49f
Pavelich, Ante, 126
Pavlov, Boris, 210
Pavlov, Todor, 17, 130
peace negotiations, 110–15, 169–73, 186f, 189–90
Pearl Harbor, 67–70
peasants, 3, 62, 82
Pelin, Elin, 96
Peloponnesus, 115f
Pen Club, 38, 94
People's Courts, 141, 210n, 217, 242
Pernik, 213
Peshev, Dimiter, 92, 101–3, 186
Pétain, Henri Philippe, 226
Peter, King (of Yugoslavia), 50
Petkov, Nikola, 4, 153n, 160ff, 163n, 194, 218f
Petrov, Ivan V., 45, 97
Pirin (Bulgarian) Macedonia, 125, 131, 134
Pladne faction of Agrarian Party, 4, 39, 47, 160f, 194n, 218
Pleven, 213
Ploesti, 165–66
Plovdiv, 18, 101, 169, 198, 213
Poland, 17; government-in-exile, 48
police, 53, 63, 117, 120–21, 201
political parties, 3–6; and *bezpartien rezhim*, 91; and Macedonia, 122; abolishment of, 213, 229. *See also by name*
Popov, Ivan, 21, 33, 79, 115, 172; and Tripartite Pact, 49–50; and U.S., 68f; and Jews, 239
Popov, Lazar, 186, 201
Pravda, 46
Prilep, 132
Pulev, Lyuben, 112

Rabotnicheski mladezhki suyuz (RMS), 63n, 199
Rabotnichesko delo, 16–18
Radical Party, 4, 161, 217
Radio Berlin, 47

Radio Moscow, 47
Radio Sofia, 250, 255
Radoinov, Tsvyatko, 197
Rastenburg conference, 137, 140–41
Ratnitsi, 4, 17f, 21n, 92f, 118
Red army, 169, 174, 182, 204, 208–16 *passim*
Red Cross, 104f
Regency, 66, 205; formation of, 151–55; and Hitler, 157, 172; and Bagryanov government, 177, 193, 254; and Muraviev government, 205f, 210; after 1944 coup, 220. *See also* Filov, Bogdan; Kiril, Prince; Mihov, Nikola
Reitlinger, Gerald, 105
religion, 77, 96, 125, 127
Rendel, Sir George, 13, 48, 113f, 135, 224, 236; and death of Boris, 135, 142f
resistance, *see* partisan movement
Rhodes, 157
Rhodope Mountains, 199
Ribbentrop, Joachim von, 45, 51, 116f, 154; and Soviet-Bulgarian relations, 41, 46, 64, 73; and nationalist opposition, 74, 89; on deportation of Jews, 100, 103; at funeral of Boris, 145; mentioned, 37, 55
Richthofen, Herbert von, 15, 27, 64
Riddle, Donald, 200
right-wing organizations, 4–5, 17. *See also* nationalist parties
RMS, 63n, 199
Rome, 116
Rommel, Erwin, 115
Roosevelt, Franklin D., 42, 54, 69, 81, 156; and Casablanca conference, 111
Rotary Club, 38, 94
Rukovoden Tsentur, 161. *See also* Fatherland Front
Rumania, 2f, 7, 96, 115–17; and Balkan Entente, 8–9, 14, 24, 43, 53f; oil fields in, 14, 29, 32, 87, 106, 165; and Bessarabia, 15, 24–25, 27f; Iron Guard in, 17, 29, 94; and Tran-

sylvania, 25, 29, 60n, 227; and Craiova agreement, 29–30; war with U.S., 68, 81; and Jewish question, 94, 99, 104; and Bagryanov government, 178f, 184; defection from Axis, 188–91; mentioned, 13, 44
Ruse, 84, 196
Russia, Tsarist, 2, 6–7, 24f. *See also* USSR

Saavov, Dimiter, 250
Sajitz, Dr., 137f
Salò republic, 158
Salonika, 49, 50, 54
Salonika, Treaty of, 14
Samos, 157
San Stefano, Treaty of, 2, 119, 191n
Sardinia, 115
Saxe-Coburg dynasty, 114, 220
Schaufelberger, Constant, 139, 246
Schellenberg, head of Section VI of the SD, 75, 145
Schmidt, Dr. (Hitler's interpreter), 90
Schönebeck, General, 75, 145
Schulenburg, German ambassador in Moscow, 24
SD, 75, 136, 145
secret organizations, 38, 94, 96
Serbia, 2f, 88, 158, 169, 191; and Tripartite Pact, 50; and Macedonia, 125, 130; Bulgarian troops in, 132, 172, 182, 190, 207. *See also* Yugoslavia
Sevov, Yordan, 68, 82, 108n, 110, 112, 171; and Lukov, 118; executed, 217; and Bagryanov government, 250–51
"Sharlo," *see* Shatarov, Metodi
Shatarov, Metodi ("Sharlo"), 130–31
Shishkov, Peter, 153
Shishmanov, Dimiter, 157, 172–73
Shumen, 215
Sicherheitsdienst (SD), 75, 136, 145
Sicily, 115f
Silistra, 30, 213
Sima, Horia, 29
Simeon, Prince (later Tsar), 144, 151, 246

Simovich, Dushan, 50f
Skopie, 53f, 101, 103, 123f, 157
Skorzeny, Otto, 158
Slavs, 46f, 77, 97, 129. *See also by name of country*
Slessor, Sir John, 170
Sliven, 18
Slovo, 61
Sobolev, Arkadi A., 34–35, 40
Social Democratic Party, 4, 136, 153n, 160f, 194n, 206, 218
Sofia, 47–48, 119, 212f; American college at, 8; and outbreak of war, 18, 22; May Day demonstrations in, 18, 120; Allied bombing of, 52–53, 106, 166–68, 232–33; Soviet legation in, 65, 73; Jews in, 95, 101, 104; and partisan movement, 196ff; mentioned, 46, 54, 190, 233
Sofia Military Academy, 216
Sofia University, 7, 129n
Sonderpolitik, 145f
South East Europe Confederation, 114
Southern Dobruja, 1, 3, 25, 28–30, 114, 124, 218; and Bagryanov government, 174, 180. *See also* Dobruja
Soviet Union, *see* USSR
Spain, 99
Spanish Civil War, 18, 86
Special Operations Executive (SOE), 42, 48, 200
Sredna Gora, 202
SS, 145f
Stainov, Petko, 20, 30, 38, 91, 153n, 205f; on anti-Jewish legislation, 95; and Macedonia, 124; and Bagryanov, 193
Stalin, Joseph, 30, 106, 109, 159
Stalingrad, 61, 87f, 107–8, 119, 197, 245
Stalisky, Alexander, 175
Stamboliisky, Alexander, 3, 6, 8, 205; and IMRO, 125; coup against, 161, 163, 175
Stambolov, Stefan, 21n
Stamenov, Bulgarian ambassador in Moscow, 34
Stanchov, Ivan, 180, 190

Stanishev, Alexander, 175, 193
Steengracht, Baron, 144, 154
Stettinius, Edward, 191–92
Stoyanov, General, 213
strikes, 18–19, 212–13
Suez Canal, 67
Sweet-Escott, Bickham, 48
Swiss Red Cross, 104
Switzerland, 111, 113
Syria, 67, 109

Tadzher, Leon, 196
Taranto, 36
TASS, 40
Tehran conference, 162
Telpuchowski, Boris S., 254
"Tempo," *see* Vukmanovich, Svetozar
terrorism, 8, 82, 119, 198
Thompson, Frank, 200
Thrace, 34f, 72; Aegean, 99, 122n,
    128, 200; Jews in, 100, 103; and
    Bagryanov government, 180, 184,
    186; mentioned, 2, 120, 168, 215
Times, London, 34
Tito, Marshal, 131, 133–34, 168f
tobacco workers, 18, 27
Todorov, Kosta, 4
Tolbukhin, General, 214, 216
Traikov, Kosta, 218
Transylvania, 25, 27, 29, 60n, 227
Trichkov, Vlado, 200
Trifonov, General, 213
Tripartite Pact, 32–38 *passim*, 59, 68f,
    113, 186–87; Bulgaria's signing of,
    45–46, 175; Yugoslavia and, 49–51,
    232
Tsankov, Alexander, 3–5, 217; as
    Mason, 38, 94n; and Boris, 60, 73–
    74, 90; and Jews, 95, 102–3; and
    Regency, 152ff; and Bagryanov
    government, 186, 191; mentioned,
    20, 30, 175, 206
"Tsaous, Andon," *see* Fosteridhis,
    Andonios
Tsar and the General, The (film), 79n
TsVK, 195f
Turkey, 77–78, 87, 108–11, 170–72;

Bulgarian liberation from, 2, 119;
    and Balkan Entente, 8–9, 14, 24,
    43, 53f; and Bessarabia, 24n; and
    competition for Balkans, 34, 37, 41,
    43–44; pact with Bulgaria, 43–44,
    49, 66; neutrality of, 44, 66–67, 159;
    and Operation Marita, 53; "Adana
    lists," 109; and Lukov's assassina-
    tion, 118; Allied policy toward, 156;
    and Bagryanov government, 179,
    183, 185–89; property tax in, 236;
    mentioned, 60n, 72f, 96, 141, 168
Turnovo region, 199

Union of Bulgarian Lawyers, 96
Union of Exporters, 233
Union of Soviet Socialist Republics,
    see USSR
Union of Writers, 96
Union of Young Workers (RMS),
    63n, 199
unions, 82. *See also by name*
United Nations, 180f
United States of America, 1, 6, 8, 111–
    14, 170–71, 173; Donovan's visit
    to Bulgaria, 42–43, 230; and Turkey,
    44, 109, 183; and Operation Marita,
    54; Pearl Harbor, 67–70; war with
    Bulgaria, 68–71, 81, 165; OSS, 170,
    230; and Bagryanov government,
    181, 183f, 187–88, 191
USSR, 5f, 46–47, 85–87, 168, 204;
    Communist Party in, 4, 16, 86, 131;
    and Boris, 9; Nazi-Soviet Pact, 9,
    15–18, 24n, 160; and outbreak of
    war, 15–19, 21, 24–25, 27–28, 30;
    and competition for Balkans, 32–41
    passim; and Baltic states, 37, 227;
    and Operation Barbarossa, 59–62,
    77; Stalingrad, 61, 87f, 107–8, 119,
    197, 245; legation in Bulgaria, 64–
    73 *passim*, 84; and Fatherland
    Front, 160, 162; Red army, 169, 174,
    182, 204, 208–16 *passim*; and
    Bagryanov government, 176–94
    passim; and Turkey, 183, 185; and
    Rumania, 188–89; and partisan

movement, 196, 202; and Muraviev
government, 205–16 *passim*, 255;
declaration of war on Bulgaria,
210–12, 255; mentioned, 105, 159,
218f, 235
Uzunov, Doncho, 98

Vardar (Yugoslav) Macedonia, 3,
8, 123–25, 130, 203
Varna, 84, 86, 179, 204, 215; Soviet
consulate in, 65, 182; Jews in, 101;
and partisan movement, 202; strikes
in, 213
Vasilev, Slaveiko, 103, 171–72, 175–76,
201
Vazov, Ivan, 153
Velchev, Damian, 5, 103n, 117, 161,
216n, 219
Veliko Narodno Subranie, 151, 153,
205
Versailles, Treaty of, 7
Vichy France, 67, 99
Victor Emmanuel III (of Italy), 7,
82n, 135, 137, 144, 220
Vienna settlements, 32, 83, 237
Volchev, representative of *Welt-
Presse*, 74–75
VOZ, 199, 203n
Vrabcha faction of Agrarian Party,
4, 160, 195, 206, 217f
Vranchev, Peter, 163
Vranya, 168
Vukmanovich, Svetozar ("Tempo"),
133

Waffen-SS, 89
Wagner, Colonel, 232
war crimes, 217
Warlimont, General, 167
Weichs, von, Field Marshal, 185
Welles, Sumner, 54
Welt-Presse, 74
White Russian immigrants, 64

Woermann, Ernst, 15, 25, 28n
World War I, 25, 55, 81n, 122, 125,
135, 177–78, 185

Yakovlev, Soviet chargé d'affaires,
211, 214
Yalta, Allied conference at, 219
Yanakiev, Kulcho, 119
Yanev, Sotir, 41, 61–62, 86;
assassination of, 118, 119n, 198
Yankova, Violeta, 198, 253
Yaranov, Professor, 54
Yeni Sabah, 44
youth organizations, 74, 90; Brannik,
38, 68–69, 82; German, 38, 82; RMS,
63n, 199; Italian, 82
Yugoslavia, 7, 13, 16, 29, 114, 218;
Serbia, 2f, 50, 88, 125, 130, 132, 158,
169, 172, 182, 190f, 207; and Macedonia, 3, 8, 122–25, 128, 130, 203;
Croatia, 8, 54, 126; and Balkan
Entente, 8–9, 14, 24, 43, 53f; friendship pact with Bulgaria, 8, 14, 152;
and Tripartite Pact, 49–51, 232;
and Operation Marita, 52ff; Communist Party in, 123, 130–34; and
Bagryanov government, 180f, 183–
84, 190; partisan warfare in, 198,
201, 203
Yugov, Anton, 131, 219

Zagorov, Slavcho, 79, 94, 148
Zagreb, 126
Zahariev, Nikola, 136
Zaimov, Vladimir, 79–80, 117f, 197
Zhekov, Nikola, 22, 226
Zheleskov, Colonel, 190, 204
Zhivkov, Todor, 212
Zietzler, Colonel, 37
Zlatev, Pencho, 152
Zora, 54, 128
Zveno, 5, 172, 193, 206, 218–19; and
Fatherland Front, 153n, 160, 162f